The Legend of Zelda
and Philosophy

Popular Culture and Philosophy®
Series Editor: George A. Reisch

Popular Culture and Philosophy®

The Legend of Zelda and Philosophy

I Link Therefore I Am

Edited by

LUKE CUDDY

OPEN COURT
Chicago and La Salle, Illinois

Volume 36 in the series, Popular Culture and Philosophy®,
edited by George A. Reisch

**To order books from Open Court, call toll-free 1-800-815-2280, or visit our
website at www.opencourtbooks.com.**

Open Court Publishing Company is a division of Carus Publishing Company.

First printing 2008
Second printing 2009

Printed and bound in the United States of America.

Library of Congress Cataloging-in-Publication Data

The Legend of Zelda and philosophy : I link therefore I am / edited by Luke Cuddy
     p. cm.—(Popular culture and philosophy ; v. 36)
   Includes bibliographical references and index.
   Summary: "Chapters address philosophical aspects of the video game The
Legend of Zelda and video game culture in general"—Provided by publisher.
    ISBN 978-0-8126-9654-7 (trade paper : alk. paper)
    1. Legend of Zelda (Game) 2. Video games—Philosophy. I. Cuddy, Luke, 1980-
GV1469.35.L43L45 2009
793.93'2—dc22

                                                   2008038443

This one goes out to the Livermore and Chico gamers, and the Cuddys east and west, all of whom made this book possible through their direct, and in some cases indirect, support. Oh yeah, and Shigeru Miyamoto— can't forget about him.

Contents

Acknowledgments

First, of course, I owe the authors a debt of gratitude for support-ing this project from the beginning. A work like this doesn't get off the ground without capable and willing writers. If it wasn't for George Reisch, this book—at least in its current form—wouldn't exist, so my debt to him and the other folks at Open Court is immeasurable, including Eric Reitz and David Ramsay Steele. I'm also thankful for the support of the philosophy department at San Diego State University. In particular, Steve Barbone provided very valuable comments, criticisms, and advice from day one. I'm grate-ful, too, to Robert Arp for his advice early on and to Richard Greene for his advice in the later stages.

Setting Up the Game

LUKE CUDDY

*A waterfall cascades down a rocky mountain range in the opening screen for the original Zelda (*The Legend of Zelda, *Nintendo, 1986).*

The criticisms leveled at videogames are familiar to us all, whether we're criticizing them ourselves or defending our favorite titles against the Luddites. Images of pubescent kids with *Super Mario Brothers* shirts fiercely wielding Nintendo controllers abound. At one point it might have been appropriate to call videogames a social outcast, analogous to the proverbial high school loner quietly consuming the thin ham slices in his lunchable, watching the popular kids enviously from afar.

And yet, despite being cast aside by some, videogames have settled into their own cultural niche—a niche that, since its inception some three decades past, has leaked through and corroded pop culture like a divine solvent, inciting the admiration and devotion of a generation. This profound cultural movement has resulted in subcultures of die-hard, ultra-devoted fans of specific games.

One of the most popular and pervasive subcultural divisions is the one owing its allegiance to the *Legend of Zelda* franchise and its creator, Shigeru Miyamoto. Beginning with the original *Legend of Zelda* game on the Nintendo Entertainment System (NES) and continuing through to the current *Phantom Hourglass* on the Nintendo DS (see below), the tale of Link is familiar to any gamer: the little elf-looking kid (or adult, depending on the game) named "Link" is on a quest to rescue Princess Zelda and reunite the once-united Triforce to save the land of Hyrule. Along the way he encounters the likes of Oktoroks, Gohmas, Ganondorfs, and weird old men who charge him for door repair. Of course, that the storyline, enemies, characters, and even music change slightly with each game is part of the fun. In case your studiously-arranged *Zelda* collection isn't at hand, here is a list of the games of the franchise in chronological order based on release date, complete with the console they were released on:

- *The Legend of Zelda* (1986)—Nintendo Entertainment System

- *The Adventure of Link* (1987)—Nintendo Entertainment System

- *A Link to the Past* (1991)—Super Nintendo Entertainment System

- *Link's Awakening* (1993)—Game Boy

- *Ocarina of Time* (1998)—Nintendo 64

- *Majora's Mask* (2000)—Nintendo 64

- *Oracle of Seasons* (2001)—Game Boy Color

- *Oracle of Ages* (2001)—Game Boy Color

- *Four Swords* (2002)—Game Boy Advance

- *The Wind Waker* (2002)—Gamecube

- *Four Swords Adventures* (2004)—Gamecube

- *The Minish Cap* (2004)—Game Boy Advance

- *Twilight Princess* (2006)—Nintendo Wii

- *The Phantom Hourglass* (2007)—Nintendo Developer's System (or Dual Screen)[1]

Zelda Culture

The release of the movie *Grandma's Boy* gave gamers a reason to be proud. *Grandma's Boy* does for gamers what *Half Baked* does for stoners—both films legitimize the plight of a group often perceived as dead weight on society. Not only does *Grandma's Boy* give a behind-the-scenes look at what goes into making a videogame, but it accurately portrays gamer archetypes, from the pot-smoking cool guy who gets the girl to the arrogant super-nerd who proudly proclaims, "I did beat *The Legend of Zelda* before I could walk."

The *Zelda* franchise itself has become a cultural wellspring—forget about just videogames. *Zelda* is not big but *huge*. From spin-off cartoons in the 1980s to present day comedic skits on YouTube, the franchise is prolific. *Zelda* has spread through the videogame world like De Niro through the film world. Calling yourself a gamer entails at least a knowledge *of Zelda*. There are websites devoted to *Zelda* and nothing but (if you don't believe me, google *Zelda*). Many of these sites have sections for timeline theories, not to mention item listings, walkthroughs, forums, ringtones, game art, and more. There are *Zelda* comic books. And the *Zelda* music—that memorable little tune beginning as computer-generated notes on the NES has been reproduced and rearranged by guitarists, pianists, and orchestras. Need to know anything about the *Zelda* franchise, anything at all? Just look it up on zeldawiki.org—an online *Zelda* encyclopedia.

There's a program called "ZeldaClassic"—a tribute to the original *Zelda* which allows users to create their own *Zelda* games. Think about that for a second: *Zelda* is so well respected by the gaming community that a program was created allowing the layman fan to make games *like* it. If that doesn't cement *Zelda*'s status as one of the greatest game franchises of all time, I don't know what does.

---

[1] I acknowledge the existence of other *Zelda* games—like the ones for the CDi (not developed by Nintendo)—but I think it would be safe to say that the list above covers the games of primary importance to the franchise.

But beyond all that the original gold-plated Nintendo cartridge has sentimental value for many of us. It marked the beginning of a saga, or maybe our childhood. While your love for *Zelda* may not have landed you a date for the prom—depending, I suppose, on whom you wanted to take to the prom—it gave you a chance to guide Link through the fantastic world of Hyrule. That the gamer can *guide* Link is one of the reasons why *Zelda* is so ripe for philosophical speculation. A moviegoer cannot guide Luke Skywalker; she can only sit back and hope Luke doesn't give in to Vader and hate and the Darkside. Despite having some fixed elements, a *Zelda* game is not entirely out of the gamer's control; the gamer plays the game as Link and is not a passive observer.

A Philosophy Book about a Videogame!

While social theorists, critical theorists, and others have been writing about videogames for over a decade, the vast majority of philosophers have yet to jump aboard. If nothing else, philosophers should contribute to the conversation lest non-philosophers do their philosophy for them. It also seems significant that videogames are in some sense a crowning achievement of computer science, artificial intelligence, and general game design (there were games before videogames, for those of you who've forgotten). And the best games combine elements of cinema, literature, music, and more.

Are videogames as significant a cultural phenomenon as Shakespeare plays or Mozart symphonies? Can certain games unveil truths about the human condition with the level of profundity found in, say, a *Hamlet* soliloquy? Maybe so, maybe not—the fact is we don't know yet, just as no one knew about Shakespeare when the Globe Theatre first opened it's doors. Videogames are an emerging cultural form and, while some would like to lump them together into one indication of declining values (as shows like *The Simpsons* were once lumped), I am more optimistic. One of the beautiful things about being a philosopher (or more generally, a thinker) is that you look to the future with wonder and anticipation. What *does* the future hold? We are surrounded by gamers, and their number is only increasing. Will this change the way we think about the world? Can studying games teach us something about who we are? Or is it naïve to think so?

Whatever the case, those of us who've played videogames, and that includes the writers in this book, find value in at least some videogames. That is, enough value to tackle the following questions concerning the epic *Zelda* franchise. What *is* the nature of the gamer's connection to Link? Does Link have a will, or do we project ours onto him? How does the gamer experience the game? Do the rules of logic apply in the gameworld? How is space created and distributed in Hyrule? How does time function and how does its functioning effect the gamer? Is *Zelda* art? Can Hyrule be seen as an ideal society? What about the Triforce? Is there anything symbolic about courage, wisdom, and power? Why do we want to win and defeat Ganon? Can the game be enjoyable without winning? Why do fans create timeline theories in such detail? Can these theories adhere to scientific standards? How is death treated in Hyrule? How do repetitive tasks performed in the game differ from repetitive tasks in everyday life? Does *Zelda* perpetuate a stereotype of female inferiority?

That there are differences of opinion and interpretation from one chapter to another should not be surprising. This book doesn't support one point of view over the other any more than philosophy does. Philosophers have been in disagreement since the Greeks and this book doesn't propose to break that tradition. Furthermore, *Zelda* does not itself state a philosophical position. *Zelda* does not do philosophy. But it does bring some very interesting philosophical questions to the table, inciting the thinkers in this volume to adopt their own positions.

Philosophy, *Zelda*, and the AHA! Feeling

However, *Zelda* does do something for you that you may not consciously recognize. Many of you, I'm sure, know that feeling of finally understanding something, of struggling and struggling and struggling with—in the case of philosophers—Kant, or Heidegger, or Wittgenstein to no avail until, lo and behold, everything becomes clear. It's like a puzzle has settled into place in your brain, and you can just sit back and admire the beauty of it, and you know the struggle was worth it. These moments of clarity are sometimes referred to as the AHA! feeling by philosophers.

The ancient master, Plato, had a bit to say about this feeling (although he didn't specifically call it that). In his dialogue *The Meno*, a discussion between Socrates and a Slave Boy reveals the nature of the AHA! At a certain point, Socrates has just, through questioning, got the boy to reveal his knowledge of a two foot by

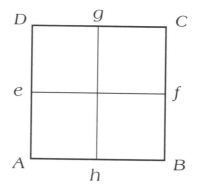

two foot square with two lines drawn horizontally and vertically though the middle (figure below).

The boy knows it's a square, has sides of two feet, and has an area of four feet. Socrates keeps questioning. He asks the boy "Now could one draw another figure double the size of this, but similar, that is, with all its sides equal like this one?"[2] Here the boy answers incorrectly about the area of the double-sized figure: he answers eight instead of sixteen.

After going through some Socrates-style teaching, the boy realizes that the area of a figure double the size of a two foot square will be sixteen. As the dialogue goes:

SOCRATES: How big is it then, won't it be four times as big?
BOY: Of course.
SOCRATES: And is four times the same as twice?
BOY: Of course not.
SOCRATES: So doubling the sides has given us not a double but a fourfold figure?
BOY: True.
SOCRATES: And four times four are sixteen, are they not?
BOY: Yes.

What's important here is that the boy's attitude went from thinking he knew, *to actually knowing*. And his answers—like "of course," "true," and "yes"—are indicative of that fact. This is the AHA! feel-

---

[2] Plato, "The Meno" in Baird and Kaufmann, *Ancient Philosophy* (New Jersey: Prentice Hall, 2003), p. 167.

ing. That point when you finally see why something is the case, when something finally clicks.

It isn't hard to make a parallel to *Zelda*. In most of the games of the *Zelda* franchise the gamer has to struggle through dungeons, solve difficult puzzles, and defeat tough enemies. Toward the end of such endeavors he often encounters a secret room with a special item like the ladder, the raft, or the silver arrow. As Link holds the item above his head and those four familiar gradually rising notes ring out (duh, duh, duh, duh!) it can be seen as the gamer being rewarded for his struggle. And the gamer feels a sense of gratification, a sense of achievement—a feeling not far off from Plato's AHA!

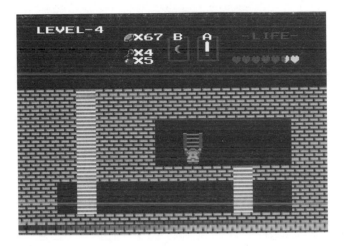

Link comes across the ladder in an item room in Level 4 (The Legend of Zelda, *Nintendo, 1986).*

When Link holds the ladder above his head it is especially significant since a ladder symbolizes a climbing to the next level, a moving beyond. As the AHA! feeling leaves the philosopher ready to do more philosophy, to make more discoveries leading to new AHA! feelings, so acquiring the ladder leaves the gamer ready to do more puzzle solving and game exploration. Both philosopher and gamer can file their new knowledge (or item) away for use in future endeavors.

Having read this far, you are now prepared to put down the Wii-mote and embark on an intellectual battle with Plato, Aristotle, and Socrates . . . Am I right? Then again, if you'd rather power up the old NES, pop in that gold cartridge, and beat the original *Legend of Zelda* for the twenty-seventh time, I wouldn't blame you at all. I can only hope that you put down the controller and take a glance at this book before entering the labyrinthine Level 9. Perhaps some philosophical insights about life's meaning will establish the requisite patience to navigate room after incredibly difficult room en route to the Red Ring.[3]

---

[3] All screenshots were captured by the authors of the chapters in which they appear. Part opening images were captured and rendered by the editor.

Level 1

Emotion, Experience, and Thought

1

Why Do We Care Whether Link Saves the Princess?

JONATHAN FROME

When you're playing *The Legend of Zelda: Wind Waker*, it's easy to understand why you feel a swell of pride when you defeat the final boss, Ganondorf. It's taken you many hours of gameplay to get to this point, and to beat him requires considerable skill. You can't mindlessly mash buttons and rely on easy combos. You've got to master the parry attack and use your shield to deflect Light Arrows.

After Ganondorf goes down, as you watch the final cut-scenes, you might reflect on your first combat lesson with Orca, who explains to Link how to manage a sword (and at the same time explains to you how to use the controller to fight enemies). Back then, you couldn't deal with a group of Green Chu-Chu's, but now, you're an expert at combat. You have achieved something and have every right to be happy with your performance.

You might also have some strong feelings about the game itself, outside of your performance in it. A lot of people criticized this game for its cel-animation style graphics, but maybe you like them. In their own way, they're simple yet appealing. The anime design of the characters isn't realistic, but it lets their expressions come across more easily. When Tetra shoots Link out of a cannon into the Forsaken Fortress, the graphic style makes it easy to appreciate his absurd expression of frightened surprise. On the other hand, the game has faults as well. The sailing is, frankly, kind of boring. At first, it's cool to sail through the waves and hunt for buried treasure chests. As the game progresses, the minutes between islands start to feel like hours. These sorts of design decisions made by the game's creators frequently cause emotions such as disdain or admiration.

But there's one area in which your feelings about *Wind Waker* are a little harder to explain. In some ways, you respond to the game as if it were real. You care about Link and Zelda as *people*. You care about their story and the challenges they face. You want them to succeed. Yes, part of the reason you maneuver Link all over Hyrule is because you want to overcome the challenges the game puts your way, but that can't explain why it's sad when Link leaves his grandma on Outset Island to search for his sister Aryll, or why you feel slightly touched when Aryll gives Link her telescope on his birthday. Later in the game, there is a plot twist regarding Tetra that is quite surprising. You're not surprised because the new information changes your strategy; you are surprised that Tetra is not really who you thought she was. It's character development that surprises you, not gameplay.

You may feel scared by some of the game's monsters. On Dragon Roost Island, you face the large, flame-spewing scorpion Gohma. When you first walk into the final cavern, there is a cutscene in which you see Gohma slowly rise to his full height, towering over Link, and you think, "This is not good." Your eyes widen and your heart rate increases just a little bit as you look at this threatening monster.

You also have some more subtle emotions during the game. There's a small sense of majesty when you conduct the Wind's Requiem and you see the wind suddenly change direction and blow past Link with great force. The majesty isn't because the change allows you to more efficiently sail to the next island, it's because the animation and music in that small cut-scene captures a sense of wonder and awe at the power of nature.

It makes sense that we're happy when we win the game or feel admiration for the game design. The game is a real game. The graphics are real graphics. But there is not a real hero named Link or a real princess named Zelda. Gohma is not actually dangerous and there is no actual majestic wind blowing over Hyrule. We rarely think about this disconnect because we're so used to enjoying fictional entertainment. We care about characters; that's just a component of our interaction with media. Yet, there is something deeply strange about this. Why do we care about people who don't exist? We are used to being scared by enemies in videogames. The sight of a Gold Elite in *Halo* can make you jump back in fear. Why? You know it can't really hurt you.

Do You Really Believe that Zelda Kills Ganondorf?

Theories about why we respond to fictional characters usually start with some common-sense notions about emotional responses to real events. Consider a potentially intense emotional event in real life. Imagine that you're at a videogame convention and you've bought a raffle ticket. The grand prize is a fifty-thousand-dollar dream home theater with all the latest videogame consoles, a huge television, top-of-the-line stereo equipment, and dozens of games. You're listening to the winning numbers being announced. Number after number matches, and when the final number, fifteen, matches the last number on your ticket—you've won the grand prize. You are thrilled. You can't believe your good luck. You start imagining how you'll fit this equipment into your apartment. As the numbers are repeated, you suddenly realize that what you heard as "fifteen" was actually "fifty." You have won nothing. Your overwhelming positive feelings are quickly replaced with a strong sense of disappointment. Scenarios like this suggest that our emotions are based on our beliefs about the world. You were thrilled when you believed that you had won the grand prize, but when you came to believe that you had lost, your positive emotions disappeared.

The notion that belief is essential to emotion underlies what is sometimes called the paradox of fiction: we care about characters that we don't believe in. When you play *Wind Waker*, you feel sympathy for some of the non-player characters, such as the Deku Tree. If you find the story compelling, you are very happy to see Link finally plunge his sword into Ganondorf's head, and at the end of the game you feel a mix of sadness and satisfaction when Link leaves Outcast Island (for good?) and sails off with Tetra's pirate ship.

But you don't believe that there is or was a Deku Tree, you don't believe that a boy named Link leaves a real place called Outcast Island, and you don't believe that the game is an account of actual events. Given that this is all made up, why should you respond emotionally to it? When you stop believing that you won a raffle, your happiness disappears. Why don't your emotions disappear when you realize that you don't believe in the characters of *Wind Waker*?

But It All Seems So Real . . .

Several philosophical theories have been developed to explain this apparent paradox. A common view is that when we watch fictional stories we perform a mental activity we call "the willing suspension of disbelief," a phrase first used in 1817 by the poet Samuel Taylor Coleridge.[1] According to this theory, we have emotional responses to *Wind Waker* because we temporarily believe in its reality. Once we suspend our disbelief, we forget that the Boko Baba we are looking at is not a real carnivorous plant. This view is sometimes called the *illusion theory* because it suggests that we are under the illusion that what we are seeing is real.

There's a clear problem with this position, however—we don't act as if we think the events we are watching are really happening in front of us. When we throw a Bomb Plant to blow up a boulder on Dragon Roost Island, we don't move the GameCube off the top of our TV so that it doesn't get knocked to the floor. When we see Aryll taken away by a huge bird, we don't call the police and report a kidnapping. We never really suspend our disbelief; we always have some disbelief in the events on the screen or else we would respond to them as we respond to real events.

Defenders of the illusion theory may say that suspending our disbelief doesn't mean that we think the game events are real; it means only that we suspend *any* belief about the game's level of reality. We neither believe in them nor disbelieve in them. This response attempts to ward off the objection that we do not act as if we believe the film is real. This response isn't compelling, however. Since emotions seem to rely on beliefs, why would someone who does not *literally* believe that the events of *Wind Waker* are real have an emotional response to the events and the characters in the game?

Think about Link's Grandmother

Noël Carroll suggests that the illusion theory is based on the false premise that we need to believe in the existence of something in order to respond to it emotionally. He argues that emotions can, in fact, be generated by thoughts alone, and he proposes what he

---

[1] Samuel Taylor Coleridge, "Biographia Literaria," *Selected Poetry and Prose of Coleridge* (New York: Random House, 1951).

calls the *thought theory*.[2] He gives the example of standing on the edge of a dangerous precipice. We are in no real danger of falling off the edge; our feet are planted safely, there is no wind, and we have no intention of jumping. But if we vividly imagine going over the edge, plummeting, and hitting the ground, we can be genuinely scared. We're scared, not by a belief that we are in a dangerous situation, but by the mere thought of something bad happening. Carroll also notes that when something bothers us emotionally, we often try not to think about it or to deflect our attention from it to lessen our emotions.

According to the thought theory, we're sad when Link leaves his grandmother on Outcast Island because the *idea* of a young boy leaving his grandmother to engage in a dangerous and possibly deadly mission is sad. We are happy when we rescue Makar and return him to Forest Haven, because the *thought* of returning a lost Korok to his family is pleasing.

But these explanations may strike some as empty. When we vividly visualize being killed, emotion is created because we are consciously constructing a vivid image in our minds. Without that type of visualization, we don't have a strong emotional response to the scenario. But if our thoughts only cause emotional response when we visualize them, then this doesn't explain your response to *Wind Waker*, because you don't visualize the world of the game while you play. You don't have to—you see it onscreen. In fact, it's very hard to play a videogame and simultaneously visualize something else. Also, some events that spur emotions, such as a monster suddenly popping up in front of you, happen too quickly to form conscious thoughts. The thought theory doesn't explain why actually seeing these fictional images without consciously reflecting on the game's situations can create emotion.

Let's Pretend We Want to Kill Ganondorf

A third theory that attempts to dissolve the paradox of fiction is the *pretend theory*, which has been championed by the philosopher Kendall Walton.[3] Walton's theory is a general theory of how we interact with artworks, but it is as applicable to videogames as to

---

[2] Noël Carroll, *The Philosophy of Horror* (New York: Routledge, 1990).

[3] Kendall Walton, *Mimesis as Make-Believe* (Harvard University Press, 1990).

paintings or films. The pretend theory is an approach that is more plausible than it may first appear and is a primary framework through which philosophers discuss works of art. Walton argues that interacting with representational art is analogous to playing children's games of make-believe. He says that in games of make-believe, children use props to imagine fictional scenarios. For example, Tom and Jane might play a game of make-believe in which they pretend to be Link and Tetra. Tom grabs a yardstick and swings it as if it were a sword. Jane grabs a cardboard tube and looks through it as if it were a telescope. The yardstick and the tube are props they use to play the game of pretend. On Walton's account, Tom and Jane's actions authorize them to imagine certain events in their game. Jane might hand the tube to Tom, point to a house, and say "we're approaching Windfall Island!" Her actions suggest to Tom that he is supposed to pretend that the house is a place called Windfall Island.

Walton claims that the process of using props in pretend play is analogous to the process of engaging with artworks. In fact, Walton thinks that the analogy is so strong that we should actually think of engagement with representational fictions as a form of pretend play. When we play a videogame, the images and sounds of the game are props like the yardstick and tube in the children's game. The game player is authorized by these images and sounds to imagine features of the fictional world of the game in the same way children might use props to imagine certain features of the fictional world of their pretend play.

When you play *Wind Waker* and see the image of The King of Red Lions talking to Link, you're authorized to pretend that a magical talking boat really exists. These images authorize you to pretend that this boat exists in the same way that Jane's actions authorize Tom to pretend that they're approaching Windfall Island. Or imagine that you walk into a room where your friend is playing *Wind Waker* and you see Link sailing in the ocean. You say, "Oh, you finally figured out how to get the sail." You don't believe that you are looking at an actual sail; you understand that what you are seeing is a flicker of light on a screen. Nonetheless, you refer to it as a sail. According to the pretend theory, your comment indicates that you are pretending that what you see is a sail, even though you know it isn't.

Walton uses this theory to explain how artworks generate emotional responses. Walton describes Charles, who watches a horror movie about a deadly slime.[4] During the film, when the slime approaches the camera, Charles screams. Later, Charles claims that he was terrified of the slime. Walton states that Charles cannot really be afraid of the slime because Charles knows the slime cannot really hurt him. Rather, Walton claims, Charles *imagines* that he is afraid of the slime. Charles plays a game of make-believe in which he imagines that the slime exists, that it is coming towards him, that he is in grave danger, and that he is afraid of the slime. Part of this game of pretend is for Charles to act as scared as he would if he were actually in danger, but Walton does not think that Charles's emotion is limited to actions—Charles *feels* scared as well. Charles's response, which Walton calls "make-believe fear" or "quasi-fear," feels the same as regular fear. It is make-believe not because it is devoid of real feeling but because it is based on Charles *imagining* he is in danger rather than *believing* he is in danger. Walton, recognizing that film viewers often feel things that they may not choose to feel, describes make-believe emotions as involuntary. You pretend to have the emotions whether you want to or not.

Walton's theory provides an internally consistent explanation for the paradox of fiction. We're happy when Link defeats Ganondorf not because we actually believe that he has saved Hyrule, but because we're pretending. Just as we use the patterns of light on the screen to imagine that there is a hero named Link and that he defeats a villain named Ganondorf, we use these images to pretend that we are happy about these events. This response feels like a real emotion but is not because it is caused by a fictional situation. Or so goes the theory.

Problems with Pretending

Unfortunately, the pretend theory is not a good solution to the paradox of fiction. Noël Carroll criticizes the theory by arguing that if Charles is merely pretending to be scared of the slime, then he should be able to start and stop pretending at will, because pretending is a voluntary activity. Indeed, an essential part of the idea of pretending is that the person pretending is consciously choosing to treat one thing as another. When Tom pretends that a yardstick is a sword, he does this by choice. The notion that Charles is

---

[4] "Fearing Fictions," *Journal of Philosophy* 75:1 (1978).

involuntarily pretending seems to stretch the meaning of pretending past its limits. Walton must agree that Charles's pretending to be scared is involuntary because most readers and viewers do not voluntarily pretend to have emotions when reading books, watching films, or playing videogames. This issue highlights a significant difference between children's games of make-believe and playing videogames. Walton says that when you see Link using the sail, you pretend that the image you see is a sail. Yet it is almost impossible *not* to see that image as a sail. You can't just "stop pretending" and decide to see the image as a bundle of individual pixels. In contrast, Tom and Jane can stop pretending to be Link and Tetra at any time. They can just stop pretending that the yardstick is a sword and the cardboard tube is a telescope.

Tom and Jane also have a lot more freedom in their pretend play than you have in playing a videogame. They decide how to use the props in their fictional world. Tom can pretend the yardstick is a sword or a lantern or a pogo stick. Any of these choices work in the context of his pretend world. When playing a videogame, however, you don't have that degree of freedom. It's true that videogames are much more interactive than traditional media like films or books. You can choose how to move your character and, in some videogames, what your character looks like. But your choices are somewhat constrained. If you walked in on your friend playing *Wind Waker* and said, "Hey, you found the giant lollipop," they would think you were nuts.

Also, when they are playing make-believe, children can use the same prop very differently. Jane might pretend that her cardboard tube is a telescope, but another kid can take it and pretend that it's a megaphone. In videogames, players can't do this. When you press the B button, Link swings his sword. Everyone who plays the game would say the same. You're not really free to pretend that pressing the B button makes Link stand on his head. Why do videogame players all pretend the exact same thing when kids with cardboard tubes don't? For many reasons, pretend doesn't seem to be the right approach.

Why Are We Scared of Gohma?

None of these three theories can satisfactorily answer the questions posed at the beginning of this chapter. Earlier, I asked why our eyes widen and our heart beats faster when we see the fire-breathing scorpion Gohma rise above us. We don't run away from the screen, so the illusion theory must be wrong in saying that we temporarily think Gohma is really dangerous. We are more scared of actual monsters than the thought of monsters, so the thought theory can't explain the whole story. And if our fear involuntarily causes our heart to race, that emotion hardly seems like "pretending."

The main problem with these three theories is that they implicitly characterize the mind as monolithic and discuss only the conscious mind in their explanations. Under the guise of concepts such as imagination and thought, these theorists gloss over the variety of mental activity and the numerous unconscious processes that are part of our emotional responses to artworks.

The illusion theory says that since we react emotionally to artworks, as we watch them we must think they are real. The assumption is that our conscious judgments about an artwork must fully accord with all aspects of our emotional response. The pretend theory says that we know that the artworks are not real, so our emotional responses to them must be pretend. Again, the premise is that emotional responses are based on beliefs and must be consistent with conscious judgments. The thought theory says that we emotionally respond to both artworks and reality because both generate evocative thoughts or ideas. Although this is true, the theory gives no account of why we respond differently to artworks and reality, and it does not discuss the role of unconscious mental activity. The theory avoids the question of why our responses to artworks are partially but not fully like those to real life.

A Multi-Level Mind

The concept that the mind is not monolithic but has potentially competing aspects goes back at least to Plato, who offered a model of the mind in *The Republic*. Plato notes that people can be thirsty yet not drink, and some can be happy in their suffering. Plato also describes Leontius, who was simultaneously repulsed by rotting corpses and yet wanted to look at them.[5] Plato concludes that the mind (or, as he called it, the soul) must have separate components that are motivated by different goals.

---

[5] Plato, *The Collected Dialogues of Plato* (Princeton University Press, 1961), lines 439b–e.

Cognitive science, which construes the brain as an information-processing device, developed the idea that the mind has multiple systems, in part through the notion of mental modules as described by Jerry Fodor in *The Modularity of Mind*.[6] Fodor suggests that our minds include a number of relatively separate information-processing modules which process information without feedback from higher-level mental processes. An optical illusion can illustrate this concept:

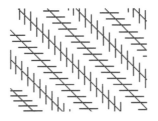

In this figure, the diagonal lines are parallel even though they don't *look* parallel. If we use a ruler, we can convince ourselves that they are parallel, but even if we know that they are, it's impossible for us to see them as such. Although our conscious judgments tell us that the lines are parallel, our visual systems perceive them otherwise. This example shows how two mental systems can come to contrary conclusions about the same object.

The notion that the mind has multiple levels helps us explain our emotional responses to videogames and other artworks. Torben Grodal has suggested that there are important connections between psychology and art which can help us understand what happens when we watch representational art.[7] According to Grodal, when we perceive something in the world, we make an evaluation, perhaps non-consciously, about whether we are perceiving something directly or are perceiving a representation of that thing. We can distinguish between looking at a real boat, a reflection of a boat, a painting of a boat, or a boat on a television screen.

Determining whether something is real or a representation is what Grodal calls a *global appraisal*. Global appraisals are contrasted with *local appraisals*, which are lower-level unconscious judgments such as whether something is blue or green or whether

---

[6] Jerry Fodor, *The Modularity of Mind* (MIT Press, 1983).
[7] Torben Grodal, *Moving Pictures* (Oxford University Press, 1997).

something is moving or still. Local appraisals are inputs to global appraisals but more limited in the types of information they evaluate. The distinction between global and local appraisals is not black-and-white; these categories describe a spectrum of mental activity. However, they are useful for understanding why we respond to artworks as we do.

When we evaluate whether something is real or a representation, we're making a global appraisal based on a wide variety of information, including information initially processed by local appraisals. We might call the final judgment a determination of the object's *reality-status*. When we see a GameCube controller, we process a lot of information about it at a local level. What color is it? Is it three-dimensional? Is it moving? How does it feel if we touch it? We make a judgment about its reality-status: it is a real GameCube controller. When we see The King of Red Lions onscreen when we play *Wind Waker*, we also process a lot of information about it at a local level. What shape is it? Does it cast a shadow? If I move my head to the side, can I see more of it? We can also bring in other types of general knowledge. Can boats talk? Can boats move themselves? We make a judgment that The King of Red Lions is not real. We're looking at a representation of a boat, not an actual boat.

Since reality-status is a global appraisal, it makes no sense to ask whether objects are locally appraised as real or not. In terms of local appraisal, there is simply no evaluation of reality. Consider the local process of detecting motion. The motion, at a local level, is not seen as real or unreal. The system that detects motion does not see a real thing moving or an image moving or a fictional object moving—it simply sees motion.

Evaluating *Zelda*

This same process applies to artworks. When we look at the fire-breathing scorpion Gohma, we note (perhaps unconsciously) that he appears to be two-dimensional, that he emits light rather than simply reflecting it, and that he moves in a strangely repetitive manner. These local appraisals feed into a global appraisal that Gohma is not a real monster but just a representation of one, and that we are not in danger. However, our various appraisals are not necessarily unified. When Gohma breathes fire towards us, we might reflexively lean backwards. On one level of our minds, we see fire coming towards us, and we move to avoid it. But we don't run out of the room, because at a higher global level, we realize that we are not in any real danger.

Why are we sad when Link leaves his grandmother, or touched when Aryll gives Link her telescope? Because we have these feelings in real life when witnessing similar scenes. Although at one level we understand that we are just watching computer-generated images, parts of our minds still process these human interactions as if we were watching real people.

This understanding of our emotional response explains something that was not addressed by the thought theory offered earlier. Why does the thought of winning the grand prize at a videogame convention not excite us as much as actually winning? Because the thought of winning may activate some local appraisals that lead to happy feelings, but actually winning activates many more appraisals, both local and global, and the feelings are thus much more intense. The reality-status of an event is an important determinant of how much and what kind of emotion it generates. Similarly, if you were actually faced with a huge, fire-breathing scorpion in real life, you would be much more scared than you are when facing Gohma onscreen.

It's very natural to think that we have full access to our mental activity and to assume that we act according to our beliefs. It's also natural to assume that our emotions are based on what we believe. Unfortunately, none of these assumptions happen to be true.

When we assume that our minds are rational and consistent, the fact that we have emotional responses to videogames forces us into questionable conclusions. If our emotions are based on our beliefs, then we must believe either that fictions are real or that our emotions are not real (they're just pretend). Or, if our emotions are not based on our beliefs, then they are based on thoughts about situations—but then it's not clear why thoughts and reality cause different emotions.

We react to videogames and other art forms[8] in some ways as if they are representations and in some ways as if they were reality. Different parts of our minds react differently to the same stimuli. We know that *Wind Waker* is a game and we're happy when we win. We know that it's been designed, and we admire many of the design decisions. But, although at a high level we know the char-

---

[8] For an assessment of *Zelda* itself as art, see Chapter 12 in this volume.

acters are not real, some unconscious aspects of our minds don't know this, and they react as if it were real. Our non-unified minds cause emotions at multiple levels and can result in strange combinations of feelings and behavior. And as videogame simulations approach reality, we may expect that our emotional responses to them will approach our responses to reality as well.

2
Look Before You Warp

DOUGLAS WILSON

There was always more in the world than men could see, walked they
ever so slowly; they will see it no better for going fast. The really precious things are thought and sight, not pace. It does a bullet no good
to go fast; and a man, if he be truly a man, no harm to go slow; for
his glory is not at all in going, but in being.

— John Ruskin (quoted in Alain de Botton, *The Art of Travel*, p. 218)

Ask any serious hiker: the joy of backpacking lies not in the destination, but rather in the total journey. Romanticized wisdom, perhaps, but wisdom nonetheless. In Yosemite National Park, for
example, the drive to Glacier Point provides some of the most dramatic scenery in the park; but the easy, one-hour drive, as well as
the postcard vistas framed by the Point's pre-constructed viewing
platform, betray a surface-deep tourism that encourages the quick
consumption of space. The tough seven-mile trek up to Cloud's
Rest, by contrast, rewards grit and patience with a more nuanced
understanding of the park, its terrain, its wildlife, and its general
character.

In the multifaceted virtual worlds of videogames, journeys aren't
so straightforward. In many games, the destination becomes the
central goal. Often, the ever-looming challenge to reach the next
level or world plays a key role in a game's entertainment value.

One particularly familiar videogame convention that prioritizes
destination is warping—instantaneous travel between or within virtual environments. According to traditional game design wisdom,
warping keeps players entertained by allowing them to jump to the
next gameplay goal, straight into the action. Yet many videogames

are no longer simple games, but complex three-dimensional virtual worlds. Warping increasingly seems like an anachronistic artifact of the 8-bit age.

The tension between "game" and "virtual world" is particularly evident in Nintendo's *The Legend of Zelda: The Wind Waker. Wind Waker* shows that even though the convenience of instantaneous travel may gratify in the short-term, we lose something valuable in the process. Warping fragments our experience of space, preventing a deeper understanding of the total environment.

Environmental Presence

In making claims about environmental presence (and its degradation), I'm considering a very specific human sensation: the experience of physical place (or in this case, virtually physical place), both perceptual and psychological. Roughly speaking, presence is the feeling of "being there." More specifically, presence can be defined as "a psychological state in which virtual objects are experienced as actual objects in either sensory or nonsensory ways."[1] Environmental presence, then, might be described as the experience of a virtually physical place as an actual physical place.

Not all presence-related phenomena stem directly from the virtual environment. Researcher Kwan Min Lee (pp. 44–45) identifies both social presence ("virtual social actors are experienced as actual actors") and self presence ("virtual self/selves are experienced as the actual self"). In practice, the general feeling of presence usually exists as a mix of different types.

Environmental presence, unlike social or self presence, relies on a feeling of transportation into the virtually physical place. Furthermore, environmental presence is not just an illusion, or a failure to consciously notice the virtuality of a place. Sense of place also depends on the active construction of personal linkages to the environment.

From Spaces of Flows, Back to Spaces of Places

To understand the lasting legacy of warping, we must start with Nintendo's classic *Super Mario Bros. Super Mario Bros.* wasn't the

---

[1] Kwan Min Lee "Presence, Explicated," *Communication Theory* 14 (2004), p. 27.

first videogame to allow instantaneous travel, but it certainly popularized the practice. A huge commercial success and burgeoning cultural phenomenon, *Super Mario Bros.* single-handedly altered the landscape of videogame design. Mario, the player avatar, travels between levels by jumping into special green pipes. Certain pipes, hidden in hard-to-find areas called "warp zones," let players skip forward through the game, multiple levels at a time. A powerful and oft-discussed secret, the warp zone cemented its place in videogame lore.

Mario uncovers one of several secret warp zones. This specific warp zone allows players to skip directly to Worlds 2, 3, or 4 (Super Mario Brothers, Nintendo).

The lure of warping as shortcut was an inevitable product of the game's linearly forward trajectory. Separated by end-of-level celebrations, the environments of *Super Mario Bros.* function as obstacle courses. The game offers little encouragement to wander around and enjoy the worlds themselves.

Quite the opposite, players are pressured to complete each level within a certain time limit. Mario isn't even allowed to run backwards past the left edge of the screen, which means players are prevented from retracing their steps. This linearity also manifests itself in the way players progress from level to level, as Mario can't return to previously beaten worlds. The notion that players might even want to revisit completed levels seems somewhat absurd: the point of *Super Mario Bros.* is to survive, conquer the coming challenges, and move on. In short, the goal of level completion is prioritized over everything else.

It's an oversimplification to claim that games like *Super Mario Bros.* are entirely about destination. The fact that *Super Mario Bros.* remains so enjoyable to play and replay proves that the "journey" is indeed enjoyable in its own right. But a journey through *Super Mario Bros.* occurs in a type of space very different than the physically contiguous, self-contained places in which we live. A game like *Tetris*, for instance, exists in a space that is almost purely kinetic. Borrowing terminology from Manuel Castells, we can think of such a space as a "space of flows"—one in which places are dominated by the movement between and within those places. In other words, the space of *Tetris* is more a process than it is a place.

No videogame—not even one as abstract as *Tetris*—can completely escape the "space of places." As Castells writes, "Places do not disappear, but their logic and their meaning become absorbed in the network."[2] *Super Mario Bros.*, for example, does indeed consist of (virtually) contiguous levels that are navigated much like traditional places. But those levels exist solely to be completed, or even skipped; they aren't valued in and of themselves.

In designing any videogame world, there always exists a tension between spaces of places and spaces of flows. When warping became convention back in the 8-bit age, this tension was easily ignored. As close offshoots of the coin-op arcade tradition, videogames like *Super Mario Bros.* were games first and virtual places second. But as videogame worlds become richer and more complex—as they become virtual places to be enjoyed on their own terms—this tension becomes increasingly problematic.

The Legend of Zelda: Wind Waker serves as an instructive example of the tension between spaces of places and spaces of flows. Like *Super Mario Bros.*, *Wind Waker* is a game that can be completed; among the set of concrete gameplay goals, players must conquer a series of dungeons. As a game, *Wind Waker* clearly emphasizes movement through the game world. But as an expansive, three-dimensional world brought to life by a diversity of possible audiovisual interactions, *Wind Waker* seems to champion environmental presence.

---

[2] Manuel Castells, *The Rise of the Network Society* (Malden: Blackwell, 1996), p. 412.

Wind Waker is by no means the only videogame to feature expressive, open-ended virtual places. However, its vast oceanic world does stand out from the crowd in its audacious starkness. Because the virtual ocean dwarfs the world's tiny islands, players spend significant amounts of time sailing on open waters. Sailing between distant islands—a largely uneventful voyage—can take more than ten minutes. During these trips, it's precisely the virtual world that steals the spotlight: when gameplay mechanics are de-emphasized, we can't help but pay attention to the motion of the waves, the artfully rendered cloud patterns, the stylized wisps of wind, and the slowly changing positions of sun, moon, and stars. At night, even the background music fades away, leaving only a quiet soundscape of wind and waves.

Link rides across the sea at sunrise (The Legend of Zelda: Wind Waker, *Nintendo*).

The designers themselves seem to acknowledge that the game operates at a slower pace. One character, clearly poking fun at an outdated, action-centered view of videogames, exclaims, "You're the adventure guy, sailing from island to island. Action! Excitement! Right?" Another character, speaking to the core *Wind Waker* experience, advises us, "Why, just walking around and having a look at things is quite fun! *That's* the mark of a great town!"

Wind Waker is a space in which idle experimentation and unstructured play—whether flying around in seagull mode, discovering picturesque little islands, hang-gliding from rooftop to rooftop, or sailing about just for the simple thrill of it—become experiences enjoyable on their own terms. Furthermore, the pre-specified gameplay goals are curiously easy, perhaps intentionally so. *Wind Waker* wants players to wrestle with its enemies, environments, and puzzles, but it also tries to make those challenges somewhat painless. *Wind Waker* sometimes feels less like a game and more like a virtual world in which quests and gameplay challenges exist as an afterthought—that is, until Link learns the Ballad of Gales.

Warping as Annihilation of Space and Time

After completing the first third of *Wind Waker*, players learn the Ballad of Gales, a magic song that allows Link to teleport across the ocean. For players who find the sailing repetitive, the Ballad of Gales comes as a welcome new ability. Still, the Ballad signifies a shift to a virtual existence dominated by gameplay objectives. The experience of instantaneous travel warrants closer examination.

The specific practice of warping may be unique to digital media, but its effects are hardly unfamiliar. The experience of mass transportation—subway, train, and airplane—recalls a similar devaluation of place. In particular, the advent of railway travel in the early nineteenth century provides apt precedent for thinking about warping.

Historian Wolfgang Schivelbusch argues that, for travelers of the time, the railroad heralded an annihilation of space and time. Because the railroad "knows only points of departure and destination,"[3] railway passengers—like *Wind Waker* players who use the Ballad of Gales—can't accurately be called travelers, but rather "human parcels . . . untouched by the space traversed" (p. 39). The easy, comfortable, and cheap accessibility of expedient travel robs destinations of their previous value as remote and out-of-the-way places. Analogous to a work of art, the unique, inimitable experience of a place is also the condition of its genuineness. In the words of Castells, places lost in a network of destinations tend towards "architecture whose forms are so neutral, so pure, so diaphanous, that they do not pretend to say anything"

---

[3] Wolfgang Schivelbusch, *The Railway Journey: The Industrialization of Time and Space in the Nineteenth Century* (University of California Press, 1986), p. 38.

(p. 420). The meaning of a place—and therefore environmental presence within that place—is inescapably diminished in a space of flows.

Simply put, convenience is a poor substitute for continuity of space. As Marcel Proust so eloquently observed:

> The special attraction of the journey lies not in our being able to alight at places on the way and to stop altogether as soon as we grow tired, but in its making the difference between departure and arrival not as imperceptible but as intense as possible, so that we are conscious of it in its totality, intact, as it existed in our mind when imagination bore us from the place in which we were living right to the very heart of a place we longed to see, in a single sweep which seemed miraculous to us not so much because it covered a certain distance as because it united two distinct individualities of the world. (Quoted in *The Railway Journey*, pp. 39–40)

By emphasizing destination over the places in between, warping encourages a "quick visit, move-on-to-the-next-place" mentality that frames space as disposable. Steven Johnson therefore underestimates videogame worlds when he writes, "But most of the time, when you're hooked on a game, what draws you in is an elemental form of desire: the desire to see the next thing."[4] The somewhat fleeting reward of seeing the next place pales in comparison to uncovering more facets of an already familiar environment. In short, instantaneous travel facilitates a kind of escapist virtual tourism that is pleasant, but ultimately shallow.

But if players care about environmental presence, can't they simply choose not to use the Ballad of Gales? Not quite; the very existence of such a choice colors the experience of space. Distance traveled will always be viewed in context of the distance that *could* have been traveled. By encouraging players to warp between islands, the game designers effectively imply that the places between islands are ancillary to the next dungeon, the next challenge, the next objective. Because most other items and abilities are necessary for progressing through the game, the Ballad of Gales carries a certain weight of inevitably ("if I have this ability, I should probably use it"). Contrary to traditional game design principles

---

[4] *Everything Bad Is Good for You: How Today's Popular Culture Is Actually Making Us Smarter* (New York: Riverhead, 2005), p. 37.

that tout player choice, the very possibility of instantaneous travel degrades environmental presence.

Warping and Abstract Map Space

The process of using the Ballad of Gales is itself a telling example of the tension between environmental presence and instantaneous travel. After playing the Ballad on Link's magical baton (. . . don't ask), we are taken to a view of the World Map. Using the map, we are able to select from a number of predetermined locations—represented as grid squares—scattered around the world. With a simple press of a button, we are then transported directly to a new place.

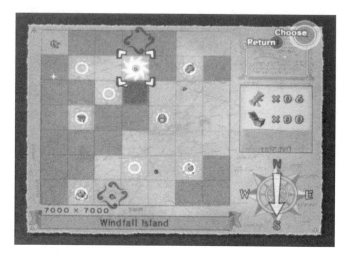

*A map-based interface is used to select one of the preset warping destinations (*The Legend of Zelda: Wind Waker, Nintendo).

It's no coincidence that the warping ability is performed through a map-based interface. Instantaneous travel is by its very nature reliant on a map-like conception of space; in teleporting to a distant place, we're forced to consider a space outside of and above our immediate surroundings. Borrowing from Michel de Certeau, we can understand the juxtaposition of 2D map and 3D space as the opposition between "panoptic" (overhead) and "everyday" (in-the-thick-of-it) experiences of place. The panoptic experience—as exemplified by looking out over a city from atop a skyscraper—

simplifies space with a certain super-rational legibility: "One's body is no longer clasped by the streets that turn and return it according to an anonymous law."[5] Its panoramic view abstracts away space into a kind of grid, allowing us to read it from above, looking down like a god. In making the complexity of the surrounding environment "readable," the panoptic view works against the protean character of everyday spatial experience.

The 3D view provides the more natural perspective (or at least some approximation) of everyday life. We look out into—and not onto—the surrounding environment. We become embodied in the virtual world as inhabitants ourselves: "Escaping the imaginary totalizations produced by the eye, the everyday has a certain strangeness that does not surface." And it's precisely this unreadable "strangeness" that generates what de Certeau calls "the poetic experience of space." Because we can never immediately parse the total 3D environment in one glance, surrounding space maintains an air of mystery. To look above, we must actively gaze upwards; to look around a corner, we must physically move to another location. The process of discovery—and the accompanying sense of place—is inextricably woven into the very fabric of three-dimensional existence.

In practice, though, the distinction between panoptic and everyday experiences of space isn't so clear-cut. Even in "reading" the city from thousands of feet above, we fill the space below with our own perceptions and memories. Revisiting our railway example, it can be counter-argued that the panoramic views afforded by train travel allow for a more holistic appreciation of space, potentially heightening sense of place. Schivelbusch, for instance, describes the emergence of a modern consciousness that perceives not "a picturesque landscape destroyed by the railroad," but rather "an intrinsically monotonous landscape brought into an aesthetically pleasing perspective" (*The Railway Journey*, p. 60). Some of the most memorable highlights of *Wind Waker* are precisely those activities that create panoramic views: hang-gliding over Outset Island, riding the Windfall Island Ferris Wheel, or flying around in seagull mode.

---

[5] Michel de Certeau, *The Practice of Everyday Life* (University of California Press, 1984), p. 92.

A hang-gliding trip opens up dramatic views of Outset Island
(The Legend of Zelda: Wind Waker, *Nintendo*).

The problem, however, is that the panorama tends to domi-
nate the places it encompasses. By transforming place into
image, the panorama endows environmental presence with a
kind of postcard-ready clarity. Panoramic views may confer an
exhilarating sense of the landscape, but reducing sense of place
to distant glimpses sacrifices spaces of places for spaces of flows.
Strong sense of place requires that panoptic experience be carefully balanced with everyday physical—or virtually physical—
experience.

Warping, however, offers no semblance of such a balance.
Modern transportation, at the very least, moves through the space
it annihilates. The discontinuity of warping, by comparison, nulli-
fies even panoramic experience. The spaces between are no longer
merely degraded—they're altogether ignored. In terms of environmental presence, even panoramic experience is preferable to the
pure mathematical logic of the map grid.

Game versus Place

Despite my emphasis on environmental presence, there is of course
nothing "wrong" with action-oriented game design. After all,
videogames are by definition *games*; at least on some level, they
rely on structured gameplay objectives. We should also acknowledge that there's no one correct approach to game design.

Videogames encompass a diversity of styles and genres, and environmental presence is only one of many possible experiences afforded by the medium.

In some virtual worlds, place-centered design might even detract from the game experience. Most massively multiplayer online games (MMOs), for example, provide easy ways to teleport or expediently travel across their huge three-dimensional worlds. Though newer MMOs boast artfully rendered environments, these places often feel empty—and not just due to an absence of other players. In these worlds, place functions primarily as a vessel for activities such as battles, social interaction, architectural creation, and identity exploration. The lasting appeal of MMOs like *World of Warcraft* and *Second Life* clearly lies in *social* and *self* presence, rather than environmental presence.

Criticisms aside, warping may ultimately serve as a reasonable compromise between competing design demands. *Wind Waker* in particular seems full of such compromises. The game's designers might argue that the Ballad of Gales is only earned after players have had ample time to "soak in" the virtual world. Also, players can only teleport to a pre-selected list of places; they must still sail short distances to their exact destination. By guiding the pace of the game, the Ballad of Gales attempts to balance the open-ended virtual world with goal-oriented dungeon crawling.

These points in mind, I only mean to call attention to the fact that goal-oriented gameplay and environmental presence exist in unavoidable tension. In moderation, sense of purpose can make a place come alive. But when we focus on moves, strategy, puzzles, and other performance-oriented tasks, we're left with little cognitive room to appreciate the surrounding environment. Any ability—especially an ability as powerful as warping—comes with consequences. So any game designer who aims to create memorable places enjoyable in and of themselves must take this tension into account.

Nor are my concerns simply academic. As Castells warns, the unchecked dominance of spaces of flows—which produces segmented places that are increasingly unrelated to each other—fragments culture and meaning. In a similar spirit, Henry Jenkins suggests that open-ended virtual places provide an important substitute for the backyards, neighborhood forests, and fields that are disappearing in the face of urbanization:

Videogames constitute virtual playing spaces which allow home-bound children like my son to extend their reach, to explore, manipulate, and interact with a more diverse range of imaginary places that constitute the often drab, predictable, and overly-familiar spaces of their everyday lives.[6]

The rewards of open-ended digital places aren't limited to just children. As Kevin Lynch argues, all urban citizens are in need of environmental stability: "The city environment is itself changing rapidly . . . These changes are often disturbing to the citizen emotionally, and tend to disorganize his perceptual image."[7] It doesn't seem far-fetched to believe that environmental presence in virtual space might act as one source of psychologically stabilizing spatial organization.

Virtual worlds that nurture environmental presence offer more than just escapist pleasure or action-based thrills. They give us a way to make sense of ourselves. As de Certeau observes, our experiences of places draw from and feed back into our own personal narratives. "Places are fragmentary and inward-turning histories, pasts that others are not allowed to read, accumulated times that can be unfolded but like stories held in reserve" (*Practice*, p. 108). For me, hazy memories of my own childhood seaside adventures lent *Wind Waker* a certain emotional resonance. In turn, these virtual adventures would later color my experience of the ocean in the material world. The game fostered a dialogue between my virtual and real lives, to the enrichment of both.

As commodity, *Wind Waker* is certainly wise to adopt design principles that optimize entertainment value. But if we fathom videogames as virtual worlds—as an emerging art form in an increasingly placeless world—*Wind Waker* and its Ballad of Gales leave us only to imagine the depth of experience that might be gained from a more uncompromising vision of digital place. Until then, you can find me in the High Sierras, somewhere on my way to Cloud's Rest.

---

[6] "Complete Freedom of Movement: Videogames as Gendered Play Spaces," in *Barbie to Mortal Kombat: Gender and Computer Games* (MIT Press, 1998), p. 263.

[7] *The Image of the City* (MIT Press, 1960), pp. 111–12.

3

Legend and Logic: Critical Thinking in the Gaming and Real Worlds

ROBERT ARP and DENNIS MILARKER

All gamers are geeks. This is how Rob Arp used to stereotype people who spent so much of their time on computer games trying to conquer make-believe worlds, steal all of the king's treasure and marry the queen, or kick some alien's ass over on Planet X. He drew the conclusion that "all gamers are geeks" because so many gamers he knew were, in fact, geeks.

But a moment's reflection tells us that Rob isn't justified in drawing this conclusion; just because Rob knew a *few* gaming geeks doesn't mean that they're *all* geeks. It's probably the case that gamers run the gamut from being stoners, studs, and street cleaners to grandparents, grape harvesters, and grain elevator operators. In other words, there are a lot of gamers who definitely aren't geeks.

Stereotypes like this can be morally and logically harmful. The moral harm occurs when we assume that "if one or a few are like this or that, then they must *all* be like this or that." Shigeru Miyamoto is the Japanese designer of *Zelda*, as well as other Nintendo successes like *Donkey Kong* and *Mario Brothers*. A Caucasian American might think that, because of his Japanese heritage, Shigeru must take pictures wherever he goes as a tourist, or he wants to take an American's job away, or he wants to convert everyone to Shintoism. "After all," thinks the American, "Shigeru is Japanese, and they're all like that . . ." Consider all of the racism, sexism, ageism, and every other negative "ism" that results from people inappropriately jumping to conclusions like these.

The logical harm of stereotypes occurs because the conclusion drawn isn't supported by the reasons given for that conclusion. The conclusion that "they're all like that" or "they all must have that same feature, quality, or characteristic" doesn't follow from and can't be fully supported by reasons having to do with one or a few instances being "like that" or having the certain feature, quality, or characteristic. You've probably met your share of Japanese folks who take pictures as tourists, but you couldn't ever legitimately draw the conclusion that *all* Japanese folks take pictures as tourists. Likewise, not *all* gamers are geeks. Stereotyping is bad *and* it's bad reasoning.

Fallacious reasoning, like stereotyping, is way too common in the real and gaming worlds. Racists think that just because they have had a bad experience with a person of a particular race, creed, or color, then "they must all be like that." A novice *Zelda* gamer thinks that an item picked up in a dungeon *necessarily* will be used to slay that dungeon's boss. Instead of seeking to become an authority in a particular matter ourselves, we too often blindly accept what someone tells us as "The Gospel Truth" because we perceive them to be an authority concerning that particular matter. Think of all of the gamers who spend hours or days in line to get the next big gaming console—because some big-wig on *Gamespot* said it was "totally awesome"—who wind up disappointed with that console. On reflection, we see we're not justified in concluding either that "they're all like that," an item picked up in a dungeon necessarily will be used to slay that dungeon's boss, or it's true just because the big-wig on *Gamespot* said so. In these cases, the conclusions that we draw don't follow from the reasons that are given as supposed support.

As we've seen already, people don't always abide by the principles of logic—Rob Arp included! The way people reason has consequences not only for our gaming decisions but also, more importantly, for how we live our lives in the real world. Good and bad reasoning affect the beliefs we are willing to die for, the policies we adhere to, the laws we make, and the general way in which we live our lives.

Some have argued that videogame violence is directly responsible for cases of violent crimes committed by kids in the real world. As a result, these same people want to see laws enacted that limit the production and sale of, or ban altogether, "rated M for Mature" kinds of violent videogames. Now, there probably are individual cases where a violent game has been partially—note *partially*—influential in causing some kid to be violent in the real world. But, can we draw the general conclusion that violent videogames, even if viewed by kids, are bad for *all* kids, from evidence that supports the fact that they're bad for *some* kids? Further, should we ban the production of these games altogether, even if kids play them, especially since they are so popular for adults? Maybe adults shouldn't be playing them either?[1] Hmmm.

Adventures in Argumentation

An argument is made up of two or more statements, one of which is the *conclusion*. The conclusion is the statement in the argument that is supposed to be justified by, warranted by, supported by, shown to be the case by, demonstrated by, or proved to be the case by the premise or premises. A *premise* is a statement in the argument that is supposed to justify, warrant, support, show, demonstrate, or prove the conclusion.

The basic goal of an argument is to convince or persuade others of the truth of one's concluding statement. So, if Link were to lay out an argument, presumably he'd want others to be convinced or persuaded of the conclusion he arrived at and believes to be true, and he would use another statement, or other statements, as supposed support for the truth of his conclusion.

Rob's fallacious argument from the beginning of this chapter can be laid out, simply, like this: "Because every gamer I have ever met has been a geek (the argument's premise), therefore all gamers are geeks (the argument's conclusion)." There's at least one premise and only one conclusion in a fully complete argument, but they usually have two or more premises. So for example, a typical *Zelda* gamer reasons like this:

Premise 1: If I want to reach the chest on the ledge, I'll need the *Clawshot*.

Premise 2: If I want to find the *Clawshot*, I need to search for it in dungeons.

---

[1] For discussions of violence in relation to videogames, movies, television, and the like in the media, see: Henry Jenkins, "The War Between Effects and Meanings" in *Fans, Bloggers, and Gamers* (New York University Press, 2006); Dave Grossman and Gloria Degaetano, *Stop Teaching Our Kids to Kill: A Call to Action Against TV, Movie, and Videogame Violence* (Crown, 1999); Steven Kirsh, *Children, Adolescents, and Media Violence: A Critical Look at the Research* (Sage, 2006).

Conclusion: Therefore, if I want reach the chest on the ledge, I need to search for the *Clawshot* in dungeons.

And so, the gamer enters a dungeon in the hope of locating the *Clawshot* and reaching the chest on the ledge.

The premises and conclusions in an argument are also statements. A *statement* is a claim, assertion, proposition, judgment, declarative sentence, or part of a declarative sentence—resulting from a belief or opinion—that communicates that something is or is not the case concerning the world, self, states of affairs, or some aspect of reality. Statements are either true or false. Our beliefs and opinions are made known through statements, either in spoken or written form. For example, the statements "This chapter was typed on a computer" and "Din is a goddess" are true, whereas the statements "Rob and Dennis were president and vice-president of the United States in 2000" and "the sun revolves around Venus" are false.

Statements are shown to be true or false as a result of *evidence*, which can take the forms of either direct or indirect observation, the testimony of others, explanations, appeal to definitions, appeal to well-established theories, appeal to appropriate authority, and good arguments, to name just a few. So, that this chapter was typed on a computer is shown to be true by observation, that Din is a goddess is true by definition of "Din," (as defined in *Zelda* universe mythology) that we were president and vice-president of the US is false because of the testimony of others and authorities, and that the sun revolves around Venus is false because of observation as well as the well-established heliocentric theory.

As critically thinking adults we must defend our beliefs. And we must give a reason (the premise of our argument) for why we hold to a particular belief (the conclusion of our argument). So, for example, there is a debate among *Zelda* gamers about the exact chronology of events as they happen to Link and others. Let's say you believe that the storyline in the original *The Legend of Zelda* represents the earliest adventure for Link and want to convince others that your belief is true. You might put forward an argument that looks like this:

Premise 1: Because *The Legend of Zelda* came out in 1986;

Premise 2: And, because all the other *Zelda* games came out after this original one (1987–2007);

Premise 3: And, because 1986 is earlier than 1987–2007;

Conclusion: Hence, *The Legend of Zelda* represents the earliest adventure for Link.

Check out a few things about this argument. First, it has been placed into *standard form*, which means putting the premises of the argument first, the conclusion last, and clearly dividing the premise(s) and conclusion with a horizontal line. Restating arguments in standard form is handy because it aids in making the logical form and parts of the argument transparent. Also, standard form makes the argument easier to evaluate in terms of whether all the premises are true as well as whether the conclusion follows from the premises (which we'll get into later).

Second, notice the word *because* before the premises and the word *hence* before the conclusion. *Because* is an example of a premise-indicating word, along with words like *since, as, for,* and *for the reason that,* among others. *Hence* is an example of a conclusion-indicating word, along with words like *therefore, thus, so, this shows us that, we can conclude that,* and *we can infer/deduce/reason that,* among others. These words are an important first-step in identifying an argument because they usually let us know that premises and a conclusion are coming in an argument. In fact, what was just said in this last sentence can be taken as a simple argument: *because* these words usually let us know that premises and a conclusion are coming in an argument (premise), *therefore* these words are an important first-step in identifying an argument (conclusion). Often times, it's difficult to tell if someone is putting forward an argument when they're speaking or writing, so you can be on the lookout for these indicating words to see if there's an argument in front of you or not.

More Hy-Rules of Reasoning

There are two basic types of arguments, *deductive* and *inductive*. With deductive arguments, the speaker intends the conclusion to follow from the premise(s) with certainty so that, if all of the premises are true, then the conclusion must be true without any doubt whatsoever. Also, the conclusion of a deductive argument is already found in the premise(s) in a way that there is absolutely no other conclusion that could be inferred from the premise(s). To say that a conclusion *follows* from a premise means that we are justified in having reasoned appropriately from one statement (the premise) to another statement (the conclusion).

Recently, while he was in a gaming shop, Rob overheard two boys (no more than ten years old) talking about their desire for the new Nintendo Wii system. One of the boys put forward a deductive argument that went something like this:

Premise 1: If we both do our chores, then we'll get $20.00 (total) from our parents;

Premise 2: And if we get $20.00, then we'll be able to buy a (new) Nintendo Wii console;

Conclusion: So, if we both do our chores, then we'll be able to buy a Nintendo Wii console.

Provided that the two premises are true, we can see that the conclusion absolutely must be true. We can also see that there's no other conclusion that could possible follow from the premises—from looking at the premises alone you can recognize the conclusion before even seeing it. The previous argument about *The Legend of Zelda* representing the earliest adventure for Link is also a deductive argument. Just like with the Nintendo Wii argument, if all the premises are true then the conclusion has to be true, there isn't any other conclusion that could possibly be drawn from the premises, and you can figure out what the conclusion is without even seeing it.

Unlike deductive arguments, with inductive arguments the speaker intends the conclusion to follow from the premises with a degree of likelihood or probability only so that, if all of the premises are true, then the conclusion likely or probably is true. But it's still possible that the conclusion is false. The night before Nintendo Wii came out, several hard-core gaming geeks camped out at the local Best Buy in the hope of getting their hands on a console. These geeks might have reasoned like this:

Premise 1: In the past, when I camped out at a store for the Gamecube, I was able to get one,

Premise 2: And because this camping adventure is similar to the last one,

Conclusion: Therefore, it is likely that I'll get a Nintendo Wii.

We can see that, provided the premises are true, the conclusion is probably or likely true, but not definitely true. It makes sense to conclude that you'll get the Nintendo Wii, given your past experience with the Gamecube. But the truth concerning your success in getting the Gamecube in the past does not guarantee that, with absolute certainty or without a doubt, you *will* get the Wii. It's still possible that Best Buy had a shipping problem or, say, some scumbag tramples over you when the doors open and gets *your* Wii, so the conclusion is merely probable or likely. In fact, many of those happy campers (pun intended) did get their consoles, but they need not necessarily have gotten them.

Consider the kind of reasoning someone may have utilized just before *Zelda II: The Adventure of Link* came out in 1988. Because of the wild success of the original *Zelda*, and because of the general rule, "If it ain't broke, don't fix it," someone might have concluded that *The Adventure of Link* would be like the first one in that Link would collect rupees and the view of the game would be a top-down perspective. But no one would bet their life on this conclusion and, in fact, it turned out to be false. Surprisingly—and to the dismay of many *Zelda* fans—in *The Adventure of Link* there aren't any rupees to collect and the view of the game is actually a side-scrolling perspective. This is an example of inductive reasoning where it seemed as if the conclusion was going to be true, but turned out to be false in the end.

Even Ganon Needs to Put Forward Good Arguments

The goal for any rational creature—Ganon or gaming geek—isn't simply to form arguments. We need to form *good arguments*, and we need to evaluate the arguments of others. In both the deductive and inductive realms, there are good and bad arguments. In either realm, a good argument has to meet two conditions: the conclusion must logically follow from the premises, and all of the premises must be true. If either one of these conditions (or both) is missing, then the argument is bad and should be rejected.

In the deductive realm, the term *valid argument* is reserved for an argument where a conclusion does, in fact, follow from premises (and *invalid argument* if the conclusion does not follow). When an argument is valid and all the premises are true, the argument is a good, *sound argument.* The conclusion, then, is without a doubt, absolutely, positively true. In the inductive realm, the term *strong argument* is reserved for an argument where a conclusion likely will follow from premises (and *weak argument* if the conclusion likely does not follow). When an argument is strong and all the premises are true, the argument is a good, *cogent argument.* The conclusion most likely or probably is true. Absolute truth and probable truth are good things, so sound arguments and cogent arguments are, by definition, good arguments in the deductive and inductive realms, respectively.

Thus, as critically thinking creatures, we must always go through the two-step procedure of checking our own arguments—and the arguments of others—to see if: (1) the conclusion follows from the premises (Is the argument deductively valid or inductively strong?); and (2) all of the premises are true (Have you provided evidence to show the premises to be true?). If the argument fails to meet either (1) or (2) or both, then we should reject it, thereby rejecting the person's conclusion as either absolutely false or probably false.

For example, the ten year-old's argument for doing chores in order to buy a Nintendo Wii console is a bad one because Premise 2 is false, given the information. It's not true that if they have $20.00, then they'll be able to buy a *new* Nintendo Wii console, because new Wiis are more expensive than that. In the case of this particular deductive argument, the conclusion "If we both do our chores, then we'll be able to buy a Nintendo Wii console" is false and unsupported by one of the reasons given (again, Premise 2 is false).

On the other hand, the camping out in front of Best Buy argument probably is a good one. It's usually true that when geeks camp out at stores for Gamecubes and other consoles, they're often able to get them. And given this fact, plus the fact that the one geek got his own Gamecube in the past, he had a strong case for drawing the conclusion that he would get the Wii.

Farore, Four Swords, and Fallacies

Checking to see if conclusions follow from premises and if premises are true can be very difficult. In the gaming and real worlds, there are times when characters and people try to convince us of the truth of their statements in order to deceive us, sell us something, beckon us into their lair, get us to vote for them, become part of their group, or share their ideology. Further, characters and people try to convince us that a conclusion follows from a premise or premises when, in fact, it does not, kind of like what Rob has done with his "all gamers are geeks" bit of bad reasoning (rest assured, he doesn't think this way anymore).

A fallacy occurs when we incorrectly or inappropriately draw a conclusion from a reason or reasons that don't support the conclusion. In fact, fallacies are so frequent and common that logicians have names for different types of fallacies.

A common fallacy is *hasty generalization.* In a hasty generalization, a person incorrectly draws a conclusion about characteristics of a *whole group* based upon premises concerning characteristics of a *small sample of* the group. When we conclude, "They're all like that" in talking about anything—gamers, goddesses, liberals, philosophers, cars—based upon a small sample of the group we're talking about, we commit a hasty generalization. There's usually no way *definitely* to conclude something about the characteristics of an entire group since we have no knowledge of the entire group. It may be that the next member of the group we encounter turns out to have different characteristics from members of the group we know thus far. Any form of stereotyping and prejudice, by definition, involves a hasty generalization. Consider the way Rob hastily generalized that all gamers are geeks . . . Tsk, tsk.

Another fallacy that people commit regularly is an *argument from inappropriate authority.* This fallacy occurs when we incorrectly draw a conclusion from premises based upon an illegitimate, non-credible, non-qualified, or inappropriate authority figure. We have to be careful about which "authority" we trust. It would seem that, for example, people who give advice about *Zelda* gaming strategies at the LegendofZelda.com or Zelda Universe websites likely would be more trustworthy than, say, Joe Schmo at Wikipedia or Gary Gamer in his latest blog entry. The best way to avoid this fallacy altogether is to become an authority concerning some matter yourself by getting all of the relevant facts, understanding the issues, doing research, checking and double-checking your sources, dialoguing with people, having your ideas challenged, defending your position, being open to revising your position, and the like. So, if you want to avoid fallacious reasoning concerning the Zelda series, then you should become an expert on it. But since we can't become authorities on everything, we need to rely upon others. Just be careful that "the others" you rely upon are credible.

A *false dilemma* is the fallacy of concluding something based upon premises that include only *two* options, when, in fact, there are three or more options. Rob actually fell victim to this kind of bad reasoning when he was trying to play Space Invaders on his original Atari system "back in the day" (yep, he's a bit of an old bastard). The game would not start, the screen was fuzzy, and Rob reasoned like this:

Premise 1: The problem with the game not starting is either that the cartridge is not pushed in all the way (first option) or the Atari system is not plugged into the TV (second option).

Premise 2: I checked and the Atari system is plugged into the TV.

Conclusion: Therefore, the cartridge is not pushed in all the way.

So, guess what Rob did next? He tried to push the cartridge in all the way. Guess what happened then? Nothing. Still a fuzzy screen. Why? Because Rob committed the false dilemma fallacy. He incorrectly thought there were only two options (cartridge not pushed in or system not plugged in) when, in fact, there was a *third* option that he had not considered, namely that the TV was on Channel 4 when it should have been on Channel 3! So, he fallaciously drew the conclusion that the cartridge was not pushed in all the way—and that this mishap is what accounted for the fuzzy screen—when, in fact, there was a third option he had not considered. This is another Pitfall you should avoid whether it's Burger Time, or you're on an Asteroid, or you're chasing a Centipede, or you're in the Pole Position, or you're Mr. Do himself. (See, gamers aren't the only geeks.)

Another fallacy to avoid is *equivocation*. Equivocation occurs when someone draws an inappropriate conclusion where the meaning of one of the words (or set of words) has shifted in the move from premise to premise, or from premise to conclusion. In other words, someone changes the meaning of a word (thus, equivocates) at some point in the argument. For example:

Premise 1: The war in Iraq is no news,

Premise 2: And no news is good news,

Conclusion: Therefore, the war in Iraq is good news.

In this argument, an equivocation occurs with "no news;" in Premise 1 no news means "known by all or most," while in Premise 2 no news means "nothing bad is happening." So, making the argument transparent, we actually see this:

Premise 1: The war in Iraq is known by all or most,

Premise 2: And, nothing bad is happening is good news,

Conclusion: Therefore, the war in Iraq is good news.

Now we can all see that the conclusion has absolutely nothing to do with the premises and in no way, shape, or form follows from the premises. In fact, we can also ask, "What the heck do the premises have to do with one another?!?"

Notice that in the argument about Link's earliest adventure a few pages ago, we also equivocated by shifting from talking about the *order in which the games were commercially released (came out) on Planet Earth* to talking about *the order in which Link's adventures occurred in the Zelda universe*. However, the Planet-Earth release-order of the games doesn't necessarily relate to the chronological ordering of adventures in the *Zelda* universe. Because the argument contains an equivocation, it isn't deductively valid, and we aren't entitled to the conclusion even if (and even though) the premises are true. And, in fact, our conclusion isn't just unsupported: it's plainly false! In November of 1998, *Nintendo Power* published an interview with Shigeru Miyamoto in which he identified *Ocarina of Time* as the earliest story in the *Zelda* timeline. Of course, several *Zelda* games have been produced since this interview, and it might be outdated information, but it's sufficient to establish that our conclusion above (that the original *The Legend of Zelda* is the first adventure) is false. (Incidentally, note that we've just made an argumentative appeal to authority, but it's a good one: Shigeru Miyamoto is the creator of the fictional *Zelda* universe, and presumably we couldn't hope for a better authority regarding it.)

Another common fallacy is *ad hominem*. In this fallacy, one inappropriately concludes that a person's statements or arguments are not worth listening to or their conclusion is false because of premises that deal with an attack on the actions, personality, or ideology of the person putting forward the statement or argument. *Ad hominem* is Latin for *to the man*. In other words, instead of focusing on the person's issue, statements, or argument, one attacks the person. This strategy is used when we try to discredit a person's argument by discrediting the person. But notice, the person and the person's arguments are two distinct things—to attack one isn't necessarily to attack another.

If Gamer Gary claims that playing games for so many hours in a day is addictive and wants to tell you why it is so, *and* he has a joystick in his hand when he is telling you this, you cannot conclude automatically that what he has to say is worthless or false. You could accuse Gary of being a hypocrite, but you cannot conclude that what he is saying is worthless or false without first hearing his argument!

The *slippery slope* is another fallacy often utilized regularly by people in their bad thinking. This fallacy happens when one inappropriately concludes that a chain of events, ideas, or beliefs will follow from some initial event, idea, or belief and, thus, we should reject the initial event, idea, or belief. It is as if there is an unavoidable "slippery" slope that you're on, and there is no way to avoid sliding down it. Consider this all-too-real-sounding made-up slippery slope: "If we allow games like *Doom, Grand Theft Auto*, or *Hitman* to be mass produced, then they'll corrupt my kid, then they'll corrupt your kid, then they'll corrupt all of our kids, then games like these will crop up all over the world, then more and more kids will be corrupted, then all of the gaming world will be corrupted, then the corrupt gaming producers will corrupt other areas of our life, etc., etc., etc. So, we must not allow *Doom, Grand Theft Auto*, or *Hitman* to be mass produced; otherwise, it will lead to all of these other corruptions!!!" We can see the slippery slope here. It doesn't follow that corrupt gaming producers will corrupt other areas of our life. All of a sudden we're at the bottom of the slope! What in Nayru's name just happened!

End Game

There are many other fallacies (unfortunately), and the reader can find them analyzed in many simple books about logic.[2] Occasionally, even the sharpest people forget to check if all of our premises are true, or believe that a conclusion follows from premises when it doesn't.

As you read the chapters in this book, be mindful of statements, arguments, deductive arguments versus inductive arguments, good versus bad arguments, evidence, and fallacies that are spoken about by the authors. We hope that the authors have avoided fallacies and bad arguments in putting forward their own positions, but watch out! With this *Legend* logic lesson in mind, you can be the judge of that.

Level 2

Dodongo and Death

4

Link's Search for Meaning

TONI FELLELA

If man, as the existentialist conceives him, is indefinable, it is because at first he is nothing. Only afterward will he be something, and he himself will have made what he will be.

—Jean-Paul Sartre, *Essays in Existentialism*

Time passes, people move. Like a river's flow, it never ends. A childish mind will turn to noble ambition. Young love will become deep affection. The clear water's surface reflects growth. Now listen to the Serenade of water to reflect upon yourself.

—Sheik, *Ocarina of Time*

I have a confession to make. I don't finish what I start. Specifically, the *Zelda* games I start. I get right to the end, to the final fight with Ganon, and I just give up—but I don't like to say give up; I prefer to say stop or pause. It's less like a taking a breather after strenuous game-playing pause and more like a permanent pause. At that point I'm just not as invested. I know it's going to be over. The game will end and, yeah, maybe I'll get a nice Zelda and Link reuniting movie but after that nothing, game over, the rupees stop here.

As I write I have two *Zelda* games on the brink of completion, *Ocarina of Time* and *Twilight Princess*. What gives the game its thrill for me is not some end-game payload of killing the big bad guy; it's the super-involved and detailed process that took me there. I derive a sort of existential joy from collecting the heart pieces, getting letters, giving letters . . . finding free lantern oil!

Existentialism seems a fitting philosophy to consider alongside
the *Zelda* games because both are largely preoccupied with the
meaning—or meaninglessness—of the repetitive and mundane
tasks of everyday living. Unfortunately, both videogames and existentialism have suffered from a bad reputation. Both are often
viewed negatively by the uninformed, considered to be realms in
which disaffected teenagers escape reality in order to celebrate
their apathy with conviction. The occasional study reported in the
sidebar of *Newsweek* applauding the hand-eye coordination that
comes from video gaming does little to allay the popular image of
the loner teen with a bad case of Nintendo thumb[1] and a copy of
Albert Camus's *The Stranger* shoved in the back pocket of his old
black jeans.

Though I admit that the picture of a self-absorbed, moody teen
does look very much like the one in my eighth-grade yearbook
(accompanied by the quote "That which doesn't kill me makes me
stronger"), many years later, as a slightly less apathetic adult, I still
really enjoy both Nietzsche and Nintendo.

Jean-Paul Sartre tells us that man creates his own meaning.
What interests me in life and in game playing is that process of
becoming, that process of self-definition and meaning-creation. I
relate to the Link character who's met with challenges he's initially
unequipped to handle, and though this may be just a part of some
usually suppressed shopping instinct, I love making Link go off on
his collections, getting the blue swimming coat, the red fireproof
coat, the bottles . . . Every item I collect brings me one step closer
to realizing that hero role that, in my eyes, is the true goal of the
game. For me, it's all about finally having the multitude of skills and
equipment necessary to be the hero of Hyrule, to realize the maturity that is dramatized so well in *Ocarina of Time* and in Sheik's
words in the epigram to this chapter.

"Time passes, people move . . ." Sheik's advice to Link that he
needs to engage in self-reflection demonstrates a keen understanding of the fluidity and instability in life, in which a person (or a
Hylian, if that is in fact what Link is) can feel lost and alone. The
existential purpose of this game is to take Link out of any initial or
nagging sense of isolation and into a life that is intrinsically mean-

---

[1] For those who don't know this is when a callous develops after many hours
of intense game play.

ingful (in the sense of his own development into a hero) and also extrinsically meaningful (in the sense of his importance to the world around him). I may even go so far as to call killing Ganon and ending it all an afterthought. Some may say this is simply the rationale of someone who doesn't have the skills for the big battle; I'd say this is just my existential approach to *Zelda.*

Finding the Triforce in a Hostile Universe

A defining phrase of existentialism is from Jean-Paul Sartre's *Nausea*:[2] "Existence precedes essence." Basically, this means that a person's life does not have a specific fated meaning at birth. Each person has the freedom and responsibility to create their own life's meaning. Any notion of an all powerful, all controlling God pretty much gets abandoned here (which may be why so many authority-challenging teenagers take to it).

Part of the reason for existentialism's questioning of the power of God is in its historical context. Although evidence of existentialism, in some form or another, has been traced as far back as the ancient Greeks, existentialism's heyday is considered to be the post–World War II period. In a world that had to come to grips with great evil, the concept of god was under serious re-evaluation. If God was supposed to care for everything and everyone how could such a heinous tragedy as the Holocaust have occurred?[3] The answer for many was an uneasy one that fluctuated between questioning the very existence of God or at least the reach of God.

For some the answer was simply "God is dead." This famous phrase can be found in its appropriate context in Friedrich Nietzsche's *The Gay Science*, written in 1887, which though predating World War II remained topical for many because of its grappling with questions of God and morality. But this proclamation that "God is dead" was more than just a crazy, cocky philosopher verbally murdering God; this was a plea, a shocking attempt to voice a call to action for human beings to claim responsibility for their actions. In context, the phrase is elaborated upon, "God is dead. God remains dead. And we have killed him. . . . Is not the greatness of this deed too great for us? *Must we ourselves not*

---

[2] With book titles like this, you can see how the existentialists may be viewed as over-dramatic sourpusses.

[3] For a look at God and evil, see Chapter 18 in this volume.

become gods simply to appear worthy of it?"[4] With the freedom from
a pre-determined life comes the responsibility for making that life
a good, exalted, and *meaningful* one.

The Triforce and the harmony that it symbolizes is shattered,
and through Link's actions he must restore that harmony. He must
bring meaning back into the hostile, godless Hyrule. Although existentialism has sometimes been seen as a loner's branch of philosophy, a dark and godless belief system, this is not quite the case.
There's a complex duality at play in the existentialist worldview.
There's a sense of solitude in that every man is responsible for his
own life and making himself into the god he needs to be to live
well, but at the same time there is this solidarity in the shared
human condition. It's notable that Nietzsche uses the first person
plural "we"—we must become gods.

In the *Zelda* games, Link is essentially alone. But there is a connection, a link, if you will, between our hero and the rest of the
game world. He has his helpers in the figures of the old men, old
women, Navi, Twili and others, but more importantly his solitary
actions are shown to have great effects on his entire world. In
Ocarina, we can see Link's heroism unfreeze the waters of Zora's
Domain and rid the verdure of Kokiri forest of man eating plants
and nasty spiders. The harmony his actions restore even create an
aural harmony in a switch of game music from sinister to soothing.
Although physically alone, the life of Link, and the life of a human
in existentialist thought, is anything but entirely isolated and inef-
fectual. The struggle for personal meaning and morality inveitably
benefits the world beyond. By saving the world, Link is existing in
a way that will realize his essence as a hero.

In some ways Link's heroism is absurd. He does not exactly
choose his quest so much as it is thrust upon him. Not only is the
problem of choice at play in *Zelda*, but there is also the overwhelming repetition of the hero's tasks—another labyrinth to map
out, more Dodongos to feed bombs, and with each new game in
the *Zelda* series, yet another world-repairing quest. It almost seems
that the task of the *Zelda* gamer is what we'd call a "Sisyphean"
task. In Greek mythology, Sisyphus was a man condemned by the
gods to push a rock to the top of a mountain, at which point the

---

[4] Friedrich Nietzsche, *The Gay Science* (New York: Vintage, 1974), p. 181 (my
italics).

rock would fall back down for Sisyphus to go after and on and on for eternity.

Albert Camus does an existential reading of this myth that depicts Sisyphus as an "absurd hero," one who is happy even in his punishment.[5] Sisyphus's contentment comes from his self-awareness. Camus writes of Sisyphus's ownership of his task, "His fate belongs to him. His rock is his thing. Likewise, the absurd man, when he contemplates his torment, silences all the idols" (p. 91). By reflecting on his fate the absurd hero in his task becomes somehow more important than the gods that gave it to him. We see a similar shift in emphasis in *Zelda*. Link has to save the world (again and again) because Ganon has put the world in peril (again and again), but Ganon's instigating role barely even matters. It is the hero Link, the little boy trying to save the princess and become a man, that we care about.

Life of Link: Boy Becomes Man

In *Legend of Zelda*, though Link does seem to have a slight degree of pre-determination in his life, the game is centered on his *fulfillment* of his hero role, his god role; it is not something he is born with, or even enters the game with the full capability of performing. The *Legend of Zelda* series is all about growth, with Link moving through stages of development (demonstrated through increased strength, or even, as in *Ocarina*, actual physical growth) as he accomplishes the game's tasks. This echoes the effort towards maturing into a meaningful life that lies at the core of existential philosophy.

Ocarina of Time epitomizes this growth in a way the other games of the series allude to, but never overtly. *Ocarina* opens with a very pronounced "existence preceding essence" moment, with an elaborate drama about Link having finally received a fairy, specifically Navi. Getting a fairy is an early sign of growing up, sort of like Link's first signs of a mustache. Whether Link gets teased or congratulated—and although Navi may be the most insipid *Zelda* character next to Tinkle—the attainment of his fairy is something noticed by all the townspeople as a necessary stage in Link's maturity.

---

[5] Albert Camus, *The Myth of Sisyphus and Other Essays* (Knopf, 1967).

The *Zelda* series generally uses the very opening of the game to highlight Link's unequipped initial state. In the original (and my favorite) *Legend of Zelda*, Link doesn't even start with a sword! Of course, all you have to do as Link is to walk into the first door you see, but that action sets the tone that not only will you have to do standard videogame things like fight bad guys, but you'll also need to obtain the necessary equipment to do so (and there is a lot of it!).

The second *Zelda* game also begins with grabbing a sword that rests right in front of you. *Ocarina* goes into a little more detail with the swordlessness, requiring Link to crawl around and find it. Whatever phallic implications it might have that it is a sword needed for little Link to save the imperiled princess can be left for a Freudian to analyze, but the point remains that the drama of acquiring necessary tools is part of the fun of the *Zelda* games. Moreover, this existential acquisition process is chronologically our first, and perhaps even our primary focus throughout.

Link as Landscaper

Much of the time in a *Zelda* game is spent doing what could easily be called drudge work. In trying to explain what the many, many hours of playing *Zelda* are actually comprised of, I find myself summarizing that for all practical purposes Link is a landscaper who just happens to be met with this task of saving a princess. He may have this rather elevated and daunting end-task, but his day to day life is mostly about cutting down trees, grass, and bushes. That's how he makes money, or rupees, or glittering little gems that sometimes make a triumphant twinkling noise, whatever you want to call it.

Link would never succeed in his goal of saving the beautiful princess Zelda, who I guess is his girlfriend-figure, without the money he makes from his day job as glorified gardener, turning over stones, bombing low walls, even killing spiders for cash. Without this hard-earned loot he couldn't buy the bombs, candles, shields and whatnot integral to the labyrinthine efforts he must endure to see his beloved lady. It's like the too true maxim of the old jazz song, "Can't get no romance without finance."

The princess Zelda is lovely and wonderful, but is she really worth all of this? Is it so important for Link to rescue her that he has to slave away at the hard manual labor of collecting 250 rupees to buy the blue ring, ninety rupees for the big shield, eighty for the arrows . . . it never ends. But, as we all know, this game is about far more than just getting the girl; it's also about saving the world from a dark, plant-killing, rock-hoarding, water-freezing, princess-abducting evil. The game player needs to find the existential meaning; remember that all this drudge work and day-to-day grind of earning money to buy equipment is all an integral part of fighting the good fight against Ganon, against evil, emptiness, and meaninglessness.

The psychological and physical battle against inconceivable evil is part of what caused one man, Viktor Frankl, to incorporate an existential philosophy into his psychiatry. Frankl survived existence in a Nazi concentration camp and his book, *Man's Search for Meaning* (originally titled *From Death Camp to Existentialism*) relates the story of how he was able to cope with the intense suffering he witnessed and experienced. Although not an atheist like many existentialists, Frankl similarly emphasizes the existential need to find meaning in order to live. He repeatedly quotes Nietzsche's words, "He who has a *why* to live can bear with almost any *how*."[6] Although the lives of the people in the camp consisted of the worst kind of senseless monotonous drudge work—work designed to break spirits—Frankl felt that without a purpose or a meaning, despair could kill almost as easily, and perhaps more insidiously, than physical torture.

Frankl spent a lot of time recounting the daily details of the cruel and meaningless lives the camp inmates were forced to lead. They were ordered to spend hours moving heavy stones from one pit to another, only to be ordered to move them all back again later. Frankl learned that a person needed to be reminded of a future goal in order to resist the allure of suicide amidst these conditions of hopelessness. He would talk about life after they were released and the responsibilities awaiting his fellow inmates, reunion with children or completion of a book (as he himself held on to). "A man who becomes conscious of the responsibility he bears toward a human being who affectionately waits for him, or to an unfinished work, will never be able to throw away his life" (p. 80).

Taking these realizations into his post-Holocaust philosophy and practice, Frankl applied what he called "logotherapy" techniques to

---

[6] Viktor E. Frankl, *Man's Search for Meaning* (New York: Clarion, 1962).

all his patients. Logotherapy was a term Frankl coined to impart what he thought was most essential in any therapy session: getting the patient to find an individual meaning for life. The extreme tragic experience Frankl underwent served as a greatly magnified example of a lesser despair he found in many others who hadn't been through the same thing. Everyone, he found, could use a reflection on and reminder of the unique meaning of their lives. Whether it's a valuable friendship or a desire to compose a symphony or even a heroic quest, a meaning can be found in everyone's life. Frankl advises people to not become hopeless over current suffering and great distance from future goals in life. Suffering is a part of life. Further, dissatisfaction is not only inevitable but necessary.

> Mental health is based on a certain degree of tension between what one has already achieved and what one still ought to accomplish, or the gap between what is and what one should become. Such a tension is inherent in the human being and therefore is indispensable to mental well-being. We should not, then, be hesitant about challenging man with a potential meaning for him to fulfill. It is only thus that we evoke his will to meaning from its state of latency." (*Man's Search for Meaning*, pp. 106–07)

Although it may seem crazy to make a connection between a real life tragedy as immense as the Holocaust and the enjoyable entertainment of a fantasy videogame, through its narrative of struggle, growth, and triumph, *Zelda* can still tell us something about how individuals cope when faced with apparently insurmountable obstacles. To return to Camus's Sisyphus, the dedication to the undertaking of the drudge work itself is oddly glorifying. Pushing the rock up the mountain for the millionth time, "Each atom of that stone, each mineral flake of that night-filled mountain in itself forms a world. The struggle itself towards the heights is enough to fill a man's heart. One must imagine Sisyphus happy."

In life, people need unfinished business, they need future goals, they need to waver on the brink of satisfaction. Perhaps that's why Nintendo keeps fashioning newer and more elaborate *Legend of Zelda* quests. Game players don't ever really want it to be over. Maybe that's why I always leave the big battle at a permanent pause. I like having that one thing left to do (also, I hate to admit, the end fights can be almost infuriatingly difficult).

Why I Can Play *Zelda* for Four Hours Straight

I do believe like Frankl that there's an existential purpose in every part of life and that the individual is responsible for discovering what that purpose is, realizing his own personal will to meaning. But, for some reason, this always seems so much easier to understand in the game world than in the real world. When I worked at a laundromat regularly folding sixty pounds of towels and sheets for an upscale spa, it was difficult if not impossible to see how that repetitive and not very gratifying act would result in some worthy end goal (unless you count a minimum wage paycheck, which isn't exactly a big motivation). But still, there is something to it.

Everything we do has some effect on the world around us right? My folding those spa towels probably made someone incredibly happy—maybe the spa customer and my paycheck wasn't totally unappreciated. Jean-Paul Sartre tells us that "in your most insignificant actions, there is an enormous amount of heroism."[7] This is never truer than in the world of *Legend of Zelda*. Every stone wall you bomb, every fairy you catch in a bottle (like a child playing with lightning bugs) is one step closer to saving Hyrule. Nearly every action performed in the game, even if it is really just goofing off and postponing going into the dungeon (like I have a tendency to do), can be said to have a greater value. Heck, even gambling which seems to be a totally useless and degraded pastime has significance in *Zelda*. If you're lucky and you pick your rupee right, you can get that much closer to buying that quiver of arrows and thereby being ready to save the princess.

The side tasks of the game are endlessly enjoyable because they are not only made important by being essential to the ultimate completion of the game, but they are also immediately rewarding. There's a serious existential drive to the game, with the need to face challenges and place importance on growth, development and responsibility, but there is also great levity written into the game that softens the seriousness. The musical chime whenever a rupee is found, the heart pieces that Link triumphantly raises above his head in blissful victory.

Much of existentialism concerns itself with the question of freedom, especially since the concept of an all powerful God is

---

[7] Jean Paul Sartre, *Nausea* (New Directions, 1961), p. 161.

abandoned. Viktor Frankl understands freedom in a nuanced sense: "To be sure, a human being is a finite thing, and his freedom is restricted. It is not freedom from conditions but it is freedom to take a stand toward the conditions" (p. 131). So, as in the *Zelda* games perhaps there is a sense of fixed limitations. These fixed limitations may be where the disconnect is between real life theories of existentialism and the storyline of the *Zelda* games. Link can take a stand towards his conditions but his options are definitely limited. However, I wouldn't say that has to mean that *Zelda* is nothing but an escape from the freedom and subsequent responsibilities of real life.

Although people are free, much more free than characters in a fixed storyline, restrictions exist in everyday life just as they do in *Zelda*. The difference is that these real-life restrictions are more fluid and less transparent than they are in a videogame. Unfortunately, in *Zelda*, you can't just beat the shopkeeper over the head and steal the meaty drumstick you need, but rather than grumble about it you can spend the requisite time slashing trees, burning bushes and collecting enough rupees, content in knowing that this is not only necessary, but somehow meaningful. In real life you could hit the shopkeeper over the head, but the legal restrictions and repercussions may give you pause. Perhaps this game, with its narrative limitations and heroic development process, can actually be used as a tool to reflect on the existentialist concept that freedom is accompanied by responsibility.

Just like in *Zelda*, in life there is quite often a need for going through a long, arduous process and taking the responsibility to endure even the most banal of undertakings. However, any mundane task of daily life that is necessary can be made meaningful. Washing the dishes allows me to have that kick-ass dinner party, teaching another group of disaffected freshmen brings me, maybe, closer to those few students that get it, or at least my paycheck. These are smaller scale of course, but your will to meaning is what you can make it with the conditions available. This is the existential lesson available in the *Zelda* series. If only that triumphant "duh, duh, duh duh!" music would chime every time I took out the trash.

5

The Hero with a Thousand Hearts: Death in *Zelda*

ANNA B. JANSSEN

After over a dozen official titles the *Legend of Zelda* franchise may be considered many things, from childish to iconic, and at times it seems a little bizarre, but rarely is it accused of being macabre. Something is amiss in the gamer psyche if they have never thought of *Zelda* in this way because it undeniably has a preoccupation with death.

You can see this as a comforting fact. The concept of death and mortality has fascinated philosophers and scientists alike for the better part of two millennia. It should be reassuring to know that even in something as light as *The Legend of Zelda*, our individual need to explore death comes through.

The dominant view in the *Zelda* mythos is materialist; all we are is the physical, and thus there is no afterlife. But there's also room to explore the dualist notion of death, which holds that there's some form of immaterial soul beyond physical stuff.

Of course, it's through the endearing Link that the gamer inter acts with the gameworld, the Kingdom of Hyrule. What's surprising is that Link portrays the most traditionally unappealing vision of immortality—that of eternal purgatory.

A Hero in Limbo

The *Zelda* franchise isn't merely preoccupied with death; it shows us the worst case scenario: the meaningless life. As philosopher Georg Hegel believed, man has to realize the idea of death, come to terms with it. By reconciling himself with his own mortality a man enables himself to pass on to a better place after his life is over. In the Hegelian world view Link is in the least desirable position available: realizing death but being perpetually 'reborn' as himself in order to fulfil the players' needs. Imagine for a moment a *Zelda* game in which Link is allowed to die only once; because Link cannot resurrect, his death ends the game. Given this condition, it's unlikely that even the most dedicated player would get far on his path to Hyrule without encountering an impassable evil. Without the possibility of resurrection, the game would be incredibly challenging and utterly pointless.

To some, even the possibility of heavily limited resurrections is pointless. In the early game *Donkey Kong*, for example, the player gets three lives to navigate through repetitive and increasingly difficult terrain. Of course, this feat isn't beyond some, to which the movie *King of Kong* attests.

So what does this say of the real world? If Link were a true human avatar, obeying the laws of our reality within the fantasy world of Hyrule, the gamer would be stuck in a world with no— or very few—second chances. Reality starts to sound like a pretty tragic videogame: no resurrection, no second chance, one life. If you actually had to buy such a game from a store you would likely grow frustrated and toss it aside. This game of "reality" certainly wouldn't be as well loved as your *Zelda* cartridge. And yet, unlike the player of this hypothetical game, we do not fall into a pit of pointlessness when faced with such a stark situation in the real world. Instead, we go to great lengths to preserve our one life, even sometimes at the cost of a potential means of great enjoyment. This doesn't mean that people don't still devote themselves to seeking answers, but many are content just accepting things as they are. So why would such an established and beloved franchise as *Zelda* bastardize the very notion of the meaningless life in the way it does?

This idea has not been overlooked by philosophers. Actually it's been embraced. The reason we're willing to suspend the nature of death in a simple game, and as a result condemn Link to a type of purgatory, is that we are incapable of contemplating the nature of death.

This can be seen as a modern philosophical problem, as it was traditionally tackled only in relation to religion. Even the most liberal philosophers of days past acknowledged the existence of a soul, and usually far more: a God and an afterlife. But the modern philosopher is faced with the concept of nothingness in death. If you reject a God that allows some sort of afterlife, regardless of how appealing or non appealing it may be, and further disregard the concept of a soul, what does that leave? A body lying in the ground. Nothingness . . . the absence of all experience. No wonder people can't comprehend this situation. There is never a point in people's lives at which a comparable scenario occurs, except for the event of dying when it's too late. So how could anyone truly grasp the concept?

The only similar situation in which we "experience" death is in the virtual world. Consider Link when you're not controlling him—not when you pause your game to go to the bathroom, or even to get a drink—but when the game is turned off. Assume Link is a human avatar, and for the sake of argument we ascribe to him human traits, thus allowing us to view our own mortality through him. Is the off game not this absence of experience? Link is "alive" when you are playing the character. When he dies he is "resurrected" and continues in a purgatory-like state, an avatar for the Hegelian concept of the soul. It's only when the game is off that Link acts as an avatar for the experienceless death. He's not "alive" but neither does he experience an absence of life. There is nothingness. You can even go so far as to say his "body" decays if the cartridge is damaged over time or its data is corrupted.

Although most people find it impossible to comprehend existing in a state without experiences, the videogame medium can function as a metaphorical looking glass, albeit a non-intentional simulation of death from the perspective of the game designers. The designers expended no effort to create this period of experiencelessness, but its occurrence is inevitable. Even the hardcore gamer eventually has to power down his console.

So how should the present day philosopher interpret this analysis? It could be said that the act of turning off a *Zelda* game is a perfect metaphor for biological death, considering both situations result in an absence of any experience. Link is not deprived of experience forever, just indefinitely. The player could return to the game at any time, so there is nothing approaching the degree of finality that comes with biological death. Unlike the reality it models, *Zelda* is organized, sensical, and follows a strict formula. The *Zelda* gamer gains something far more valuable than an abstracted view of death; she gains a structured view of the universe.

The Order of the Triforce

The fact that the *Zelda* series has managed to carve out a place in gamers' hearts for so long is in part due to its strong formulaic nature. The only way to get a truly unpredictable experience from a *Zelda* title is to be playing it for the first time . . . or you could try playing it backwards. While certain aspects of a *Zelda* game may vary, enough elements are consistent to provide a familiar environment for the gamer.

Starting a *Zelda* game is a prime example of a successfully applied formula. In each game it's necessary to provide the player with certain tools and skills that will assist her with later challenges. This foundation has to be laid in order to get to the more varied and unpredictable aspects of any *Zelda* title. These elements mirror certain aspects of everyday existence that could be viewed, especially by the school of existential philosophy, as having a distinct order. So it would appear that the formulaic elements of the *Zelda* series parallel aspects of everyday existence in the real world.

But there's one vital difference between the fantasy of a *Zelda* game and real life: the load saved game screen. The save game is a vital requirement of many contemporary videogames that allows the player to suspend his reality and enter the games. But it also provides a level of control that is simply not possible in everyday life. While there are formulaic and repetitive aspects of day-to-day life, they don't necessarily equip you to deal with all, or even most, unexpected occurrences. For example, the fact that you got to Target too late to get one of the first copies of *Twilight Princess* might have caused you to reserve a copy of *Phantom Hourglass* upfront. But how could you have known that your Nintendo DS was going to break the day before the *Phantom Hourglass* shipment was in?

In contrast, most of the skills Link learns throughout a *Zelda* game will play a key role in solving later problems. Even if the player screws up while facing a boss, she can always reload an earlier game, allowing her to test different strategies and control as many aspects of the world as she likes. The few repetitive aspects of the real world seem tame in comparison—in fact reality seems almost chaotic. You can't replay your day so that your DS does *not* break.

But when you play *Twilight Princess,* or *Phantom Hourglass* there's a definite beginning, middle, and end. You are Link, you live in a small village, you begin a heroic (and undeniably fun) quest, you save the princess, everyone is happy, and the cycle goes on. . . .

And that's what's so valuable about this game series. Contemporary philosophers and medical scientists are in agreement on one very simple point: people like patterns. The world may be vast and incompressible, but that doesn't mean people don't like to see patterns and formulas in it. As kids, many of us enjoyed picking out shapes in clouds. The *Zelda* series can be seen as a more complex manifestation of this need.

In fact, *Zelda* is so formulaic it is almost surreal. This fantastical reality is so alien from that of the everyday world, it's surprising gamers find it so easy to get immersed in. The fact that it's easy to fall into Link's imagined reality reinforces the notion that people like to be driven by a single, overarching goal. Not only does it become relaxing, but it is a potential coping mechanism in a cruel and illogical universe.

Surprisingly, however, there is one group of creatures in *The Legend of Zelda* that does obey the rules of death in the real world: the dungeon bosses.

The Humanity of the Bosses

The *Zelda* bosses have a tendency to inspire both love and hate in the player. They often require determination to defeat for the first time—after swearing and angrily throwing down the controllers, of course. The *Zelda* bosses provides a steadily increasing challenge to the player. At times they engender a great deal of anger and frustration, but not because of their persistent desire to eliminate the beloved Link. No. It's something far simpler . . . the bosses inject a touch of reality into Hyrule. Unlike every other character encountered in the game, the bosses are mortal.

As strange as it sounds, every gamer knows this to be true. For all the hours spent defeating one of the big bosses, it has to be conceded that you only encounter them once. Return to the dungeon as many times as pleases you, but you will find that once frightening dungeon room empty. Once you have vanquished the boss and he has no more lives, he's gone forever, making him, arguably, more human than any other entity in the game.

Link's lifespan can be increased by the player almost indefinitely, making the character effectively immortal, and the minor minions always re-spawn. But, like the gamer existing in the real world, a boss has a certain amount of life energy that, once exhausted, is utterly gone.

Vanquishing a boss allows the player to continue on to the next stage of the linear journey. But where does that boss go? Back to the darkness? Does it respawn in a new form as a different boss, obeying the rules of some sort of Hylian reincarnation? Or is it simply buried within the heart container Link receives as his reward?

The quest of every philosopher who wishes to know the meaning to life is first to start questing for the meaning of death—or more accurately, for an understanding of what death is. Because unless you know what happens after, how can you ever determine the point of life? Many biologists will quickly tell you that the purpose of life is simple: to pass on our genetic material. But that answer isn't satisfactory—plus it's boring.

Of course you could devote your life to finding this meaning, and that would probably provide you a clear purpose. But why not instead explore those possibilities in the space of a forty-hour game, whose fictional world encapsulates varied philosophical ideas about death? Where there's even a place for the human plight: in that of the bosses.

The Kingdom Goes On, and On, and On . . .

There is one philosophical school of thought that has no apparent place in the *Legend of Zelda* series, that of dualism. This concept was favoured by the likes of Plato and many of his contemporaries: the notion of the immortal soul trapped in the mortal body. Dualism is one of the earliest answers to the question "What is death?" but it has suffered somewhat of a fall from grace since Nietzsche. During the nineteenth century, Nietzsche's philosophy fuelled a growing skepticism against the traditionally held beliefs in faith and religion. The nihilistic philosophy Nietzsche became particularly known for in his later life was at loggerheads with the notion of an immortal soul. Today the major religions still hold fast to their ideas about death and the afterlife, but the popularity of these notions has never returned to its pre-Nietzschean dominance.

But dualism does have a role in *The Legend of Zelda*. Unlike other concepts that can be seen in each individual *Zelda* game, this one arches over the whole series. For, as is clearly stated in the opening sequence of *Wind Waker*, there is always a Link born to fight the evil Ganon, lending credence to the dualist notion of an immortal soul. The heroic archetype of Link is perpetuated throughout the centuries, in the form of a new boy each generation who has to grow up and vanquish a growing evil. Presumably Princess Zelda is also graced with this same trait, as she is always present for Link to save.

There is something very romantic about one boy every few generations being fated to play the hero of Hyrule. Since it's one of the clear drawing points of the *Zelda* series, it works exceedingly well with this notion of an immortal soul. But this latter notion has garnered harsh criticism, probably more so than any other school of thought on death. It could be a result of its heavy ties to religion, but it does also seem outdated. Further, this viewpoint seems to contradict commonly held scientific views, like the law of the conservation of energy, which says that the energy in each system is conserved. If there is a separate system of immaterial substance (like a soul) affecting the physical, we should see an increase in the energy level of the cosmos, but this increase does not occur. It's a modern luxury that society can rely on an abundance of factual information to support ideas and beliefs, but the idea of an eternal soul can not be supported in any such way.

Contemporary philosopher William Bernard had much to say on the flaws of immortality, and generally seemed to find the concept unappealing. But he did point out one very interesting problem. The appeal of immortality relies partially on the notion that the afterlife is enjoyable. What about in the case of Link who is fated to put himself in serious danger, and have a generally difficult life for a questionable reward? Or Ganon, who is dragged back every generation only to be defeated? Most people would feel little desire to tolerate either of these situations. And yet a repetitive life cycle is Link's fate.

Game Over

There seem to be few more gaping questions of human existence than why are we here, and more importantly, where do we go next? Over several millennia we have yet to come to a religious, scientific, or philosophical answer to this question that suits everyone. Or at least one that seems sensical to everyone. The philosophy of death, as it stands, is still broken into two camps; the dualists and the materialists.

Both philosophical camps have recently acquired a new technological weapon to explore ideas: videogames. If there's one thing the *Zelda* franchise, and to a greater extent all videogames, do demonstrate, it's the strength of this tool for exploring existential questions. *Zelda* is a successful means of exploring the notion of nothingness after death, as well as being a potential means for gaining structure and formula in a chaotic universe. But the saga also can be used to tackle older philosophical notions in regard to the philosophy of death like what it means to have an immortal soul, contrasted with the contemporary criticisms of this theological perspective.

The game's creators tackle such notions subconsciously, or at least as a secondary goal. Creator Shigeru Miyamoto has a very strong personal philosophy, but this cannot be his primary driving force when shaping *The Legend of Zelda*. As an experienced game designer, he knows that there are more important elements that need to be prioritised—intuitive game design and enjoyable play experiences, for example. But whether Miyamoto injected his personal philosophy into *The Legend of Zelda*, or had no interest in doing so at all, the franchise is a useful means of exploring the seemingly unexplorable; what happens after experience ceases.

The *Zelda* saga stirs up the most passionate emotions in gamers, and after such a strong run, it rightly should. *Zelda*'s artistry, music, and consistently engrossing game play make it an essential group of titles for any videogame collection. But the series also makes a fantastic vessel for philosophical inquiry. *Zelda*'s cultural and philosophical impact will likely be remembered long after society's memory of game cartridges has gone a little hazy.

Level 3

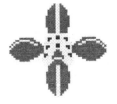

Don't Get Manhandled by Manhandla— or . . . Mind-handled?

6

Slave Morality and Master Swords: Ludus and Paidia in *Zelda*

KRISTINA DRZAIC and PETER RAUCH

Kristina is playing *Ocarina of Time*. Her avatar Link is running through Hyrule field. Suddenly, Link jolts and takes flight through the air. This isn't supposed to happen. She can't land. Peter enters: "Are you winning? Whoa! Awesome! How did you do *that*?" "I'm stuck in the air" exclaims Kristina. The screen goes dark. The game crashes. "Oh no! You're toast!" exclaims Peter, "Let's do it again!"

What happened? Peter and Kristina encountered one of *Ocarina of Time's* glitch secrets. By moving in the exact right way, they initiated a bug that causes Link to fly momentarily, then crashes the game. Following this incident, the two of them practiced flying to see how far they could "break" the game. This did not help them win—crashing the game thwarts winning, apparently—but they were having fun, being naughty. Making Link fly was not about playing to win and saving the land.

Over the years, gamers have come to know our hero Link well. As the protagonist of the *Legend of Zelda* series, Link has saved the Hylians, defeated various evil wizards, and rescued Princess Zelda again and again. Players, of course, have followed right along with him, experiencing every single one of Link's battles and triumphs. Yet how are the experience of Link the Hero and the experience of the player connected? Does the player *lead* Link on these daring adventures? Does the player *become* Link? Or does the player merely *observe* Link? All of these ideas are, from certain perspectives, true. The relationship between Link and the player is a complicated one, due to the inherently dualistic nature of the avatar.

The Avatar: Link Says "..."

Defined colloquially as the person or thing the player controls
("plays as"), the avatar is simultaneously an extension of the player
into the gameworld and a second, fictional character who is *not* the
player, whom I call the protagonist. Link is presented to the players as something of a blank slate, allowing them to imbue Link with
elements of their own personalities. The fact remains that Link is
not the player. Hyrule is a fictional place for the player, while to
Link—a fictional character who *lives* in Hyrule—it's very real
indeed. Link has a childhood the player does not see, and it can be
assumed that, when the player is not around, he even talks.[1] (The
non-player characters of Hyrule do not seem to share Link's pre-
disposition for silence.)

To interpret a *Zelda* game as a work of fiction one must imagine Link as a person, and a person whose goals and motivations
are not necessarily those of the player. One can assume that Link,
the protagonist, has a specific goal in mind: to restore peace and
justice to the persistently threatened Hyrule. This is the goal of the
narrative, or storyline, the goal that is generally espoused earliest
in instruction manuals. It's an admirable goal, requiring great skill,
courage, and personal sacrifice on Link's part. Moreover, Link's
actions in the course of this quest are, by and large, morally unim-
peachable. He kills no human innocents, and (with very rare
exceptions) he does not steal, even when doing so might help him
save Hyrule. Items won from a boss, for instance, are won in a fair
fight rather than through sneaking and trickery. In fact, one might
say Link's greatest sin is breaking an ungodly number of clay pots!
Players of the *Zelda* games intuitively understand why Link is such
a resolute white-hat. He has no choice.

Good by Default

More accurately, *we*, the players, have no choice. The *Zelda* games
offer a fairly linear play experience. Players may go about different
objectives in different orders, but many events must happen in a
certain order, and most of these events are necessary to complete
the game and the accompanying narrative. The selection of things

---

[1] Chapter 5 in this volume interprets the player's absence as an experienceless
state for the inhabitants of Hyrule.

Link can do is quite limited, and players simply aren't allowed to diverge from the narrative very effectively. Players cannot make Link into a brigand or a despot. Aside from a repeating motif involving killer chickens, Link usually can't physically hurt anyone or anything that isn't a direct threat to his safety. Even Link's in-game muteness aids his perfection—because Link doesn't talk, the player can't make him lie!

Link's good deeds may be morally significant in the game's narrative, but a story has been written for Link in which he must perform certain actions, and the player may perform only those actions. This is how a player "wins" by the designed rules of the game. This is not to say that players must follow the path exactly. A look at the Zelda players—the ones gathered in online message boards, the ones writing FAQs, and the ones posting videos of their exploits on YouTube—suggests that some recent *Zelda* games (*Ocarina of Time*, *Majora's Mask*, *Wind Waker*, and *Twilight Princess*) allow two distinct modes of play, with radically different approaches to both story and player freedom.

"Being" Link

Everyone plays a game differently of course. I, for example, like to find every secret and explore every inch of the map (yes, overkill, I know). Others tend to rush through and beat the game in record time, then lord this accomplishment over those who are slower. What this means is that gamers have a diversity of play styles. Every player prioritizes certain weapons, tactics and approaches above others. What is significant, however, is that while the way one plays varies the means of achieving a given goal, these styles of play do not change the goal itself. Players who play the game "start to finish," in a straightforward fashion, are all striving for the same goals: save Zelda, defeat Ganon. They are therefore playing within the sanctioned and expected rules of the game.

This may at first appear to be a depressing thought. You must do what the designers want Link to do. Are you really stuck with the pre-made choices of the gamespace?

In a word, no! A designed play experience like *Zelda* may strive to keep players in line with the rules of the game, but game designers have only so much control over the player. If a player decides to design his own goals within the gamespace, goals outside of the expected game design, then suddenly the mode of play is switched.

The player is in charge, and the game is at the player's mercy. Remember the story about Link flying? Kristina made a switch from following the game narrative to something wholly outside of it: she made Link fly and crashed the game cartridge. This was a goal of her own design and another mode of play. What we can take from this is simply that switching goals changes the rules in which the players operate, both in terms of what actions are desirable and in terms of the player's approach to the game's internal physics.

Think of it this way: if a game designer designs a game goal then you are playing within the moral values of the *Zelda* game-world. However, if you design your own goal you are playing with your own values and thus circumventing the moral tendencies forced upon a player in the "normal" state of the game. Case in point: in *Majora's Mask* one of the goals of the game is to stop the moon from crashing into the land and destroying everything. However, within the game there is a glitch that allows a character to attain the height of power in the game (allowing Link to transform into a Fierce Deity) the day before the moon kills everyone (and a day before one is usually allowed to attain the Fierce Deity form). The glitch allows one to run about the land as a powerful giant figure, killing every monster in sight with a single shot, getting stuck in doorways, and acting like a lumbering troll. The game invariably crashes, but boy, is it fun while it lasts!

What we can take from this is that, by making our own game goals from the discovery of bugs and glitches, we play a game of our own design outside of the identity ascribed to Link the protagonist. While he still cannot be evil—you need a story for that—Link is no longer a moral figure. He has two modes of play.

Modes of Play: Ludus and Paidia

These two modes of play are best thought of as two separate games: the *ludus* game and the *paidia* game. The terms *ludus* and *paidia* are derived from Roger Caillois's examination of play. Callois defined *ludus* as "the taste for gratuitous difficulty" that categorizes the activities generally referred to as games.[2] After all, the rules of a game are ultimately proscriptive: players have a goal, but

---

[2] Roger Caillois, "The Definition of Play: The Classification of Games," in Katie Salen and Eric Zimmerman, eds., *The Game Design Reader* (MIT Press, 2006), p. 141.

the goal only makes sense in context of how they are *not* allowed to achieve it. In golf, players can't just pick up the ball and drop it into the hole, nor can they kick it around. The rules forbid them from doing anything with the ball other than hitting it with a specifically sanctioned instrument called a golf club. The rules of the game are determined primarily in terms of what you *can't* do. *Ludus* stresses order and encourages specific behavior. *Paidia,* conversely, is defined as the "basic freedom . . . central to play in order to simulate distraction and fantasy," and is manifested in unstructured play (p. 141).

The difference is subtle, and open to debate. It's tempting to suggest that the difference lies in the presence or absence of rules, but even the most unstructured play has *some* rules. Gonzalo Frasca, applying Callois's theories to videogames, suggested a more useful defining characteristic: a play activity that can be won or lost falls into the realm of *ludus,* while a game with no such end condition can be thought of as *paidia.*[3] Videogames, in practice, generally vary between *ludus* and *paidia,* both between texts and within them. In the videogame *The Sims,* for example, the player generates a neighborhood of simulated humans complete with homes, material possessions, careers, and emotions. Players manipulate the environment to change aspects of the simulation and strive for player-generated goals such as "own the largest house on the block" or "become the best master thief ever." These types of player-generated goals might seem to exclusively emphasize *paidia* play, since there seems to be no outright goal at all.

Without any explicit way to "win" the game, many (including creator Will Wright) don't consider *The Sims* to be a game at all, but rather a set of tools that can be used to *make* games. Yet, *The Sims* is not without rules. It takes place in a world with generally consistent physics; action "A" performed in context "B" will reliably produce result "C," and these results are generally replicable. There's a loose structure to be found, and in practice most players pursue roughly similar goals: happiness, wealth, professional success, and more. Conversely, highly linear games like Zelda: *Twilight Princess* that would seem to exclusively emphasize *ludus*

---

[3] Gonzalo Frasca, "Videogames of the Oppressed: Videogames as a Means for Critical Thinking and Debate" (Master's thesis, Georgia Institute of Technology, 2001), p. 9.

play inevitably produce in players a desire to exploit open-ended elements of the game (such as side-quests and glitches) for *paidia* play—gamers are not a well-behaved bunch, and many relish going "off the path," away from the goals the designers intended them to follow, whenever possible. While some games might emphasize one mode of play more strongly than the other, *ludus* and *paidia* are both present in any game text. This variance represents the difference between structured problem solving and unstructured play in a fictional world. Put quite simply, if a game seems "trapped" by the constraints of a story, it tends towards *ludus* play, whereas if a game emphasizes free-form gameplay, it tends towards *paidia* play.

Observe, Play As, Play With

From this description *Legend of Zelda* games might seem stuck in a *ludus* loop. Players must save Hyrule, Princess Zelda, and so on. But as we've seen in earlier examples (the flying Link glitch and the Fierce Deity glitch), *paidia* play can be present as well, via player-generated goals. Does this help us answer our questions about the player's relationship to Link? I said earlier that in a sense a player *observes* Link, and *becomes* Link, and *leads* Link. Each of these relationships is defined by the sort of engagement one has as a player.

- **Observation occurs during cut-scenes. When a player loses control of Link, they are observing his choices. Since most of the meaningful narrative events occur during cut-scenes, the process closely resembles film, with the player acting as an audience.**

- **When a player becomes Link, they *play as* Link, and are engaging in the *ludus* game. They are following the designed rules of the game and pursuing the ultimate game goal. The role of the player is that of an actor: some degree of improvisation is allowed, and even encouraged, but ultimately the script must be followed.**

- **When a player leads Link, they *play with* Link, and are engaging in the *paidia* game. They are creating their own game rules and goals and playing outside of the game's story, and outside the moral structure of that story. The role of the player is not to be found in the**

gameworld at all. The player can be described as a director, organizing the world's various actors and props to his liking, or a game designer, defining goals to be met and rules to be observed. The player can even be described as aspiring to godhood, since she is not merely playing with Link, but with every element in the game.

Paidia play generally ignores what the designers "ask" the player to do. Often, *paidia* goals involve doing things the designers did not even intend to be possible. Unsurprisingly, the *paidia* game—which, after all, requires a great deal more time, skill, creativity, and dedication than the *ludus* game—is considered to be a more elite form of play by many gamers. In gaming culture, secrets are equated with mastery: the more (and better) secrets one finds, the better the player. The prevalence of fan-written FAQs for *Zelda* games attest to a hierarchy of fans: those who read FAQs, and those who write them.

Examining play, Johan Huizinga writes of the importance of secrecy:

> The exceptional and special position of play is most tellingly illustrated by the fact that it loves to surround itself with an air of secrecy. Even in early childhood the charm of play is enhanced by making a 'secret' out of it. This is for *us,* not the 'others.' . . . We are different and do things differently.[4]

It would be considered ridiculous for anyone to brag, in an FAQ or online message board, that they had completed the *ludus* game. For these players, the path intended by the designers is merely a starting point, too easy and not secretive enough to generate true esteem among elite players. In this sense, *paidia*-minded players reject the *ludus* game and play games of their own design. Searching for "Zelda" on YouTube produces a number of fan videos of glitches, machinima, and so on. Comments fill the pages, video responses are issued, and most importantly, the videos circulate virally among fans.

These strange and varied accomplishments have no narrative meaning in the gameworld, nor do they have moral meaning: Link cannot be said to be a good person for achieving them. What is

---

[4] Johan Huizinga, *Homo Ludens,* (Boston: Beacon Press, 1971), p. 12.

honored, then, is power itself, the abilities of the player and not the actions of the protagonist. Link is "good" as opposed to "evil"; the player is "good" as opposed to "bad." This dichotomy of *ludus* and *paidia,* protagonist and player, gameworld and "real" world, has a parallel in moral philosophy.

Masters of Paidia, Slaves of Ludus

In *Beyond Good and Evil,* Friedrich Nietzsche writes that there exist two fundamental types of morality: master morality and slave moral-ity.[5] Master morality, being first, is created from the tension between rulers and the ruled. "In the first case, when the ruling group deter-mines what is 'good', the exalted, proud states of the soul are expe-rienced as conferring distinction and determining the order of rank" (p. 394). To be "good" is here understood—as it is in videogame fan cultures—as belonging to an elite group. "It is obvious," writes Nietzsche, "that moral designations were everywhere first applied to *human beings* and only later, derivatively, to actions" (p. 395). This transition is a simple one: a "good action" is whatever a "good per-son" does. Like the *paidia* player, this archetypal "good" man needs no outside authority (or author) to determine the morality of his actions: "The noble type of man experiences *itself* as determining values; it does not need approval; it judges, 'what is harmful to me is harmful in itself'; it knows itself to be that which first accords honor to things; it is *value-creating.*" Slave morality follows from master morality, not in the sense that it directly *adopts* the values created by masters, but attempts to subvert them:

> Suppose the violated, oppressed, suffering, unfree, who are uncertain of themselves and weary, moralize: what will their moral valuations have in common? . . . The slave's eye is not favorable to the virtues of the powerful: he is skeptical and suspicious, *subtly* suspicious, of all the '"good" that is honored there . . . The opposition reaches its climax when, as a logical consequence of slave morality, a touch of disdain is associated with the "good"' of this morality. (*Beyond Good and Evil,* p. 397)

The master's "good" thus becomes the slave's "evil." Indeed, the black-and-white morality exemplified in Link the protagonist is defined in opposition to another: Ganon, a figure of which

---

[5] *Basic Writings of Nietzsche* (Modern Library, 2000).

Nietzsche would likely approve far more readily than Link. When Link is "good," it generally means he's undoing or thwarting the actions of Ganon's "evil." In each *Zelda* game, the evil against which Link fights precedes his involvement: Link does not initiate action of his own accord, but merely reacts to the machinations of Ganon. He does not seek to remake Hyrule according to his will, but to restore equilibrium by opposing and neutralizing the will of Ganon.

At the end of the story, Link is quite different than he was when his journey began. Hyrule itself, however, forever returns to the condition in which it existed before the intervention of Ganon. The inhabitants of Hyrule—the ones who talk, anyway—clearly prefer this pre-lapsarian Hyrule to the one in which Link does battle. However the adventure might change Link, the net result for the Hylians is freedom from fear. According to Nietzsche, fear marks the most concise difference between master and slave morality. The master seeks to inspire fear, while the slave seeks to avoid it. In slave morality, "those qualities are brought out and flooded with light which serve to ease existence for those who suffer: here pity, the complaisant and obliging hand, the warm heart, patience, industry, humility, and friendliness are honored" (p. 397). It would be difficult to describe the moral character of Link more accurately than this. But remember, this is "protagonist" Link. The player is a different matter.

Can We Play Beyond Good and Evil?

No, really, can we? When we explored the play styles of ludus and paidia, we argued that as the player of the game it is possible to play against the grain of the game's story, and therefore the protagonist's morality; this complicates the design of any morally meaningful choice the game might present.

Even when a protagonist's morality is chosen by designers, enterprising players will inevitably find ways to opt out—and this "opting out" might be more important to players than the game the designers *thought* they made. We do not, of course, mean to suggest that the *Legend of Zelda* games validate the theories espoused by Nietzsche; as far as moral philosophy goes, one ought to be skeptical of mad, anti-Semitic Germans. Rather, looking at Nietzsche through the lens of *Zelda,* and vice versa, yields intriguing new perspectives on both.

Whether or not the opposition of good and evil comes from slave morality, in videogames it is irrevocably connected to *ludus*. In the *Zelda* games, the rejection of that *ludus* is neither good nor evil. Some people want to be heroes, some people want to be villains, but some people—many *Zelda* fans among them—just want to be naughty.[6]

---

[6] This work draws from the authors' masters theses: Kristina Drzaic, "Oh No I'm Toast!: Mastering Secrets in Theory and Practice," Massachusetts Institute of Technology, 2007, http://cms.mit.edu/research/theses/KristinaDrzaic2007.pdf; Peter Rauch, "Playing with Good and Evil: Videogames and Moral Philosophy," Massachusetts Institute of Technology, 2007, http://cms.mit.edu/research/theses/PeterRauch2007.pdf.

7

Shape Shifting and Time Traveling: Link's Identity Issues

RACHEL ROBISON

Part of the charm of the *Zelda* series is that there are classic elements of the story that remain the same, but each individual game manages to be unpredictable. Virtually anything is possible; the characters are not bound by the laws of physics and can change from old to young and from one kind of creature to another. In early *Zelda* games, the princess plays a standard damsel in distress role. In later games, her personality is wholly different. Her attitude takes on a feminist kick and she can be found knocking down the baddies right alongside the boy in green. Given the drastic changes the characters undergo within any given game or from one game to another, it's puzzling to see how their identity remains the same over time, but the story tells us that it does.

This is a problem not only for characters in the *Zelda* games, but also for philosophers. Thinkers struggle with the concept of how a person's identity can persist through time and change. For example, humans transition from having tiny bodies and abnormally large heads into creatures that are much larger and better proportioned. Cells die and are regenerated so that the physical substance that constituted the baby is entirely different from the physical substance which constitutes the adult. We gain emotional maturity as we progress as well. This problem is commonly known as the persistence problem. It seems to be an even bigger problem for the *Zelda* characters because they are going through substantially more significant changes. How we can conceive of the *Zelda* characters as the same people throughout time?

This question can be divided into two sets of interesting issues. First, we could consider the *Zelda* characters as fictional entities. If we consider the question from this perspective, identity issues arise such as how the character Link that I move with my controller is the same Link as the one you control with yours. They may proceed through the game in different fashions. My Link, for example, may pummel right through the game while your Link takes its time and completes all the additional puzzles that are not essential to complete the game. It's puzzling to see how we have one, uniform concept of who Link is, given that his characteristics are so different between my game and yours.

This question might be answered by appeals to theories in the philosophy of language. In this chapter, however, I'm going to come at it differently. Given the metaphysical constraints of the *Zeldac* universe, how can the identity of the characters possibly persist through time?

Numerical Identity: *The people believed that the Hero of Time would again come to save them*

Imagine that Link encounters two Boko Babas planted firmly right next to one another. They have no apparent differences. The baddies may be exactly similar, but they are not numerically identical. A thing is numerically identical only to itself. One thing is numerically identical to another if and only if they share all the same properties. The beasties might seem to have all the same properties. They both have long, spiky stems and resemble Venus flytraps. They both leave a cluster of nuts behind for Link to use in his slingshot when they are killed. But they are not identical because each whatever it is called has properties that the other does not. Each Boko Baba has the property of taking up a particular place in space and time.

The concept of numerical identity raises problems for personal identity. A little twist on a classic example will help to illustrate this point. Imagine the following case. Tetra's (aka Zelda's) ship leaves on a voyage from one side of the ocean to another. A little while after setting off, a nail falls out of one of the floorboards on deck and sinks to the bottom of the ocean. Tetra quickly puts one of her fellow pirates on the task of replacing the missing nail. No harm is done, and they continue along on their journey. After they travel for a few more miles, another piece of the ship falls off and sinks to bottom of the ocean. It is replaced and the crew continues their trip. This keeps happening for the duration of the excursion until every part of the ship has sunk the bottom of the ocean and been replaced with a new part.

Now imagine that villainous Ganon is stewing up an evil plot. He determines that in order to carry off his wicked scheme, he needs a ship just like Tetra's. He summons the various pieces of Tetra's ship from the bottom of the ocean and puts them back together to form an entire ship. Link, in his quest to rid the world of evil, must find Tetra's true ship. Which one should he choose? Is the ship that Tetra finishes the voyage with the true ship or is the ship with all the original pieces pulled together from the bottom of the ocean the true ship? It's possible that we don't even need to imagine a case where the ship falls apart. The ship when it travels two miles may fail to be numerically identical to the ship that has only traveled one mile because it no longer occupies the same place in time. On the basis of this we must either conclude that neither of the two ships are the true ship of Tetra or we must pick one and identify the essential characteristic or set of characteristics that makes one of them the same as the ship that it was when it started out.

If we opt for the first solution to the problem, we can't think of characters in the game as the same people over time. If we take the second approach, we must identify the necessary and sufficient conditions required for the essential characteristic or set of characteristics which make it the same. Necessary conditions are conditions which, taken together guarantee that a thing is of a particular kind. For example, if Link's quest is to find the Triforce, the collection of each piece is a necessary condition for the whole Triforce. A sufficient condition is one which, if met, guarantees that a thing is of a particular kind. For example if Link found the whole Triforce already united, this would be sufficient for finding the Triforce.

Physical Continuity Accounts: *What's all the matter? Y'all lookin' to start over again, Link?*

One immediate answer to this kind of question is that it's a person's soul that makes them the same person through time. Because a person's soul is always present, it's the common element that persists. There are philosophical problems with the concept of a soul. But even if this is the right response, it's not clear that it's the right response in the context of the *Zelda* games. We know that ghosts exist in the metaphysics of the games, but there's no consistent view of souls or life after death that would conclusively justify this kind of answer to the problem.[1]

Another solution may be to identify some physical feature of an individual that may persist through time. At first glance, a promising candidate for such a view may be an individual's DNA makeup. This doesn't seem satisfactory however, because on this view, a person's clone would be identical to them even though they may have been born at a different time, in a different place, and have different life experiences. Other physical continuity models identify the relevant physical component to be something like the brain. Both of these models fall short of explaining what is going on in the case of the *Zelda* games. Even bigger problems arise if we apply this type of a view to the *Zelda* games.

In a number of the games, Link performs a spell on another creature so he can move with their body. This may be so he can fly to reach something too high for him to reach otherwise or perform some other sort of task that he was unable to perform in his Hylian body. The spell Link casts makes it the case that his consciousness is somehow projected into the creature he is controlling. He does this on multiple occasions in *Wind Waker*. He's able to control seagulls to see things that are up high or far away. He's also able to control the bodies of temple mages to achieve various ends. If the physical continuity model is applied in this case, we can't make any sense of how it is actually Link controlling the creature. Once Link is disconnected from his physical body, he is no longer Link.

Another problem for the physical continuity view occurs in *Twilight Princess*. Link transforms into a wolf in various scenes throughout the game. Certainly his brain does not transfer over to his new wolf body, so if we accept the physical continuity model, we would have to accept the result that Link is no longer the same person when he is in wolf form.

Psychological Accounts: *The memory of the kingdom vanished, but its legend survived on the wind's breath.*

The first approach to solving this problem is a psychological approach. This kind of theory identifies an aspect of an individual's

---

[1] In Chapter 5 in this volume, Anna Janssen interprets the existence of multiple Links throughout the franchise as possible evidence for a dualistic view of the *Zelda* universe.

psychology as being the essential characteristic which makes a person the same person even through time and change.

One famous advocate of such a view was John Locke (the one in seventeenth-century England, not the one in *Lost*). Locke argued (in his *Essay Concerning Human Understanding*) that the essential psychological characteristic of a person is their memories. Experiences, thoughts, and actions come together in the form of memory and this kind of psychological continuity provides persistence of personal identity through time. So, as Locke sees it, a person at a later time is identical to a person at an earlier time if and only if the person at the later time has all the same memories as the person at the earlier time.

This view is not without its problems. For example, a person at age twenty may have memories from when she was five. The person at age fifty may have memories from when she was twenty. The person at age fifty, however, may not have memories from when she was five. The person at age twenty is the same person as the people at age five and age fifty, but the people at age five and age fifty are not identical to one another. Contemporary followers of Locke's view argue for psychological continuity but add additional conditions that protect the account from this criticism. They argue that a person a later time is identical to a person at an earlier time if psychological states at the later time arise or are caused by psychological states at the earlier time.

This account also faces problems when applied to personal identity in the *Zelda* games. For example, in *Ocarina of Time*, Link transforms back and forth from his ten-year-old self to his adult self. In this case, the response from the advocate of psychological continuity is hard to pin down. Link's adult self does not have psychological continuity with his younger self early in the game because the things he has done as his younger self in some sense hasn't happened yet. In fact, it may be that things he does as his older self actually have some sort of causal effect on the psychological state of his earlier self.

Imagine that at a certain point somewhere early in the game, adult Link has no idea how to operate a boomerang. Later in the game, however, his younger self learns how to use a boomerang. If the psychological account is correct, Link's older self should have already known how to use a boomerang because he learned it when he was younger. The oddities of space and time, at least in

Ocarina of Time, make it difficult to apply the psychological continuity account of personal identity.

There are also accounts that are hybrids of these two views. Some philosophers argue that psychological states are caused by physical states and so there must be some sort of continuity in both in order for identity to persist. This doesn't seem helpful in our analysis because the examples we have seen from the game demonstrate that Link's identity cannot be accounted for by either the psychological continuity model or the physical continuity model. It seems unlikely that a combination of these views would be any less problematic.

Other accounts reject the idea that identity persists at all. A group of philosophers known as 'mereological essentialists' argue that because a person at a later time cannot have all the same properties as a person at an earlier time, it's not coherent to claim one identity. So it's not true that they're really the same person.

Other views hold that what accounts for personal identity is indeterminate. If we applied either of these views, we would not be able to attribute a consistent identity to the characters in the *Zelda* games. This doesn't seem to be what is going on in the *Zelda* universe. It seems that when Link goes back in time or is able to control the body of another creature, we are still supposed to think of him as the same person. This may be a built in human assumption. Humans created the game, so there are built in intuitions about our metaphysics that can't help but to show themselves in the *Zelda* universe. I don't think such a view is necessary for understanding identity in the games. We can think of the *Zelda* games as having a distinct metaphysics that is unaffected by our own.

Solutions to the Problem: *The youth whose destiny it is to lead Hyrule to the path of justice and truth . . .*

As we've seen, the standard models of personal identity do not seem to apply in the *Zelda* universe. As a result, there are three kinds of conclusions available to us.

First, we can reject the idea that any clear concept of personal identity is possible. We may be tempted to do this in our own metaphysical world; however, this is not the conclusion which seems motivated by evidence from the games.

The second conclusion would be to look at each game separately and construct a model of identity for each. For example, problems for the psychological continuity account that are present in *Ocarina of Time* could be accounted for by appealing to a physical continuity model in that particular game. The physical model would have to be one which would allow for the body changing back and forth from old to young. Similarly, in *Wind Waker, Phantom Hourglass*, and *Twilight Princess*, we could appeal to the psychological continuity model to avoid problems with the physical continuity model in these cases.

There are problems with this kind of approach. All of the games are supposed to occur in the same metaphysical world. Some of them may occur in different dimensions or parallel universes, but there's no evidence in the games that should lead us to conclude that the basic laws governing things like personal identity are different in these realms.

And then, at least some of the games are supposed to be sequels to or at least occur on the same timeline as the other games. It would be strange to construct an account that would make Link's identity fixed in one game, but not identical to Links from other games. It would be odd if, in the sequel to a previous game, Link is an entirely different person.

But there is a third answer which I think is better. This solution relies on the concept of destiny which is omnipresent in all of the *Zelda* games. When the three goddesses, Din (the goddess of power), Nayru (the goddess of wisdom), and Farore (the goddess of courage) created the world, they left behind a Triforce which was capable of granting wishes to the user. If the person who found the Triforce had a balance of wisdom, courage, and power, that person would be able to wield the power of the united Triforce. If they did not, they would only be able to obtain the portion of the Triforce that embodied the trait they possessed.

Most of the games begin with the discussion of a great evil. The evil is Ganondorf, who is often portrayed as possessing or being destined to attempt to possess the Triforce of power. A boy is destined to thwart the evil because he is the embodiment of the virtue of courage. The Princess Zelda, on most accounts, is the embodiment of wisdom. These predictions, in every game, hold true—unless the player gives up on the game without completing it.

For the main characters the destiny they have is what picks them out as the same person within any given game and from one game to the next. The destiny that awaits them is a necessary and sufficient condition for the essential element that allows their identity to persist. This kind of account may also apply to non-main characters. Because the gods imbued the world with a balance of wisdom, courage, and power, all citizens have a role to play in the course of destined events. The role holds fixed, no matter what other characteristics change.

Admittedly, this is a strange view of identity. However, it seems to yield the correct conclusion. It allows us to identify all the characters as the same people from game to game and from one moment to the next within any given game. The essential characteristic we have identified is certainly not arbitrary. This may be an odd conclusion in our own world but, given the particulars of the metaphysical structure of the *Zelda* universe, it seems to be a very plausible answer.

Moreover, there is good reason for thinking that videogames would be governed by strange metaphysics and hence yield odd identity conditions: videogame universes are created by designers and therefore their metaphysical commitments are necessarily stipulative in a way that the metaphysics in our world are not. Given this, it seems perfectly okay for something such as destiny to serve as a defining characteristic of identity in a videogame.

Level 4

The CDi Games
Don't Count!
Timelines and
Miyamoto

8

The Hero of Timelines

SEAN C. DUNCAN and JAMES PAUL GEE

> And critique me that is the only way any one wil ever get this riht is
> to be critiqued!
>
> —LINK-FAN-242

In contemporary popular culture, it's increasingly common for
everyday people to "compete" with experts. As journalist Thomas
Friedman put the matter:

> When everyone has a blog, a MySpace page, or Facebook entry, every-
> one is a publisher. When everyone has a cell phone with a camera in
> it, everyone is a paparazzo. When everyone can upload video on
> YouTube, everyone is a filmmaker.

With the rise of the Internet, people carry these forms of everyday expertise quite far and often organize themselves into "communities of practice" in order to do so. Fan fiction writers organize
into groups and even form "colleges" in ways that have virtually
professionalized fan fiction writing. *Yu-Gi-Oh* players see and use
language on cards and websites that is as complex and technical as
the language in any academic domain. Players of *World of Warcraft*
"mod" (modify) the game by building and downloading models
which track and assess myriad elements of game play in highly sta-
tistical terms. Gamers make "machinima" movies from games,
involving the scripting, lighting, and direction techniques of professional film production. Pop culture now tends to stress production and not just consumption, as well as expertise certified and

earned within digital communities and not only via professional forms of degrees and certification.

One of the most interesting areas in which these everyday people compete with professionals is in the area of intellectual argumentation, the seemingly arid concern of philosophers and scientists. Online discussions around games can be quite complex and involved, so that, like science, they come to belong not so much to just one person but to a group as a whole. Some philosophers and sociologists of science have argued that, despite our "great man" conceptions of science as something that flows from the individual minds of smart individuals, science makes its real progress as a "conversation." The nature of this conversation is, of course, a matter of dispute, as well as its implications for *epistemology*, or the nature and construction of knowledge.

We see similarities between the kinds of informal discussions around *Zelda* and the kinds of argumentation that are often valued in other intellectual pursuits. But what could the point be—and what could arise from, say, discussions by *Zelda* fans about the chronologies of the multiple *Zelda* games? Do debates such as this mirror the ways that scientists and academics construct knowledge and, if so, how might thinkers such as Bruno Latour help us to understand them? Before answering these questions, let's first look and then wonder—wonder what it is all about.

Debating Chronologies: The Hero(es) of Time

Ever since players concluded *The Legend of Zelda: Ocarina of Time,* the role of time within the *Zelda* games has been a concern for many fans. The end of *Ocarina* left players with an adult Link, "The Hero of Time," who had saved the land of Hyrule from the domination of Ganon/Ganondorf. Link was then rewarded with a trip back in time to a point before Hyrule had been conquered. This plot device—the use of multiple timelines—was a way to achieve a happy resolution to the game and reset Hyrule to its pre-Ganon beauty. As more and more *Zelda* games have been released, the issue of reconciling the games' timelines has become a popular one to discuss on online forums, which, to the uninitiated, can seem surprisingly complicated, ranging in topic from how to employ game cheats to discussions of fan art. Let's look at some of the fan debates regarding *chronology* and potential timelines in the *Zelda* series, and their central problem—the role of time in these games.

On the Nintendo NSider online forums (http://forums.nintendo.com), this topic has been popular for several years—a series of threads on the topic was started in September of 2004 and has continued through the time of this chapter's writing. Several dozen different posters (participants) have written over sixteen thousand posts (contributions) to this series of discussion threads (subtopics), proposing intricate theories of overarching storylines for the entire *Zelda* series, critiquing other posters' proposals, providing evidence, counter-evidence, and developing new timelines as new games were released. The degree of involvement for some of the posters on these threads was quite high—one poster's contributions totaled several hundred posts.

The size of these threads and the extent of some posters' involvement hints at interesting intellectual content in *Zelda* timelines for debate. With fourteen officially licensed Nintendo *Zelda* games, a comic book series, and a cartoon series, not to mention the obscure BS Zelda and Philips CDi games, *Zelda* lore has many story elements to reconcile. Over the past twenty years, there has been very little clear information from Nintendo and the games' developers as to whether or not all of the *Zelda* games should be viewed as one large story, different versions of a common "legend," multiple storylines/timelines, or something else entirely. The "texts" of the games themselves are often ambiguous on these issues (other than a few games, such as *Majora's Mask* and *Phantom Hourglass*, which are explicit sequels to other *Zelda* games). We may not completely understand what motivates some fans to view it as their task to determine the "correct" organization of the *Zelda* timeline, but their activities show the complex ways argumentation and reasoning can occur in online communities.

Much like how fans in other kinds of media have taken ambiguity as a license to create elaborate new fan-written stories (like the fan fiction around *Star Trek* and *Harry Potter*), *Zelda* fans have taken this opportunity to elaborate and argue explicit *theories* of how the games are organized—that is, why might the events of *Ocarina of Time* occur after *A Link to the Past?* Do the events of *Majora's Mask* occur in the same timeline as *The Wind Waker* or are there multiple timelines? The nature of these arguments varies, but all have at their root questions of *chronology*—how one should order the events of one game relative to the events of other games.

Many proposals rely on simple chronological orderings of the games to do much of the speaking about theories of time in *Zelda*.

For instance, in the earliest days of the first forum thread, many posts were simply proposals for timeline organizations, such as this one from a poster named SEGA42[1] in September 2004 (with SEGA42's acronyms decoded in the brackets):

> Here is my timeline on the games:
>
> FS [*Four Swords*]
> OoT [*Ocarina of Time*]
> MM [*Majora's Mask*]
> TWW [*The Wind Waker*]
> FSA [*Four Swords Adventures*]
> TLoZ [*The Legend of Zelda*]
> TAoL [*The Adventure of Link*]
> ALttP [*A Link to the Past*]
> OoS/OoA [*Oracle of Seasons* and *Oracle of Ages*]
> LA [*Link's Awakening*]
>
> I'm too lazy to explain it right now (), but I've thought over it a lot, and I find only one flaw: the geography of FSA. Its Hyrule matches perfectly with the Hyrule of ALttP, yet TLoZ and TAoL do not. I'm working on it . . .>_>

SEGA42's timeline theory only included eleven games, since it was written before the release of subsequent games *The Minish Cap*, *Twilight Princess*, and *Phantom Hourglass*. The organization of the games into an intelligible timeline was a goal of many participants in this thread, and some, like SEGA42, started off by proposing their organization of the games, then opening it up for the rest of the forum to probe for flaws.

SEGA42 admitted that the geography of Hyrule might be a problem for his or her theory. For SEGA42, geography was apparently a marker for time in the game, indicating the time period in which the events took place. Since the *Zelda* games have featured quite different presentations of Hyrule (or, in the case of *The Wind Waker* and *Phantom Hourglass*, the Great Sea above a sunken Hyrule), fan theories have sometimes hinged upon "which Hyrule" was the setting for a game. For example, in September of 2004, another poster, SWORDM, described a chronological ordering of games based, in part, upon these differences in geography:

---

[1] "SEGA42," like all names of forum posters given in this chapter, is a pseudonym.

. . . the Hyrule found in these two games [*The Legend of Zelda* and *Zelda II: The Adventure of Link*] is, for the most part, a barren wilderness with spread out, isolated communities. This reflects the far-flung isles of the Great Sea in The Wind Waker much better than the close-knit kingdom of A Link to the Past and Four Swords Adventures. Observing landscape differences further brings to light the presence of a large sea bisecting the two halves of Hyrule, which was absent from Ocarina of Time or any game in the first timeline. This could reasonably be what remains of the Great Sea after the union of the lands by the Koroks.

In SWORDM's timeline, *The Wind Waker* was a much earlier game than in many other timelines (occurring well before the first two *Zelda* games), and the landscape's depiction ("barren wilderness" versus "close-knit kingdom") was used to hang certain posited events upon in the overarching story (for example, when the Koroks created a "union of the lands"). What's most interesting about the use of geography is not really geography per se, but the ways that it works as a stand-in for the passage of *time* in the game. Some posters (such as SWORDM) have put forward theories in which all of the games' narratives can be reconciled into a single timeline, while others refer back to the conclusion of *Ocarina of Time*, and argue that the future that the adult Link left behind continued in his absence and became the setting for future games' adventures.

One of the most popular conceptions of the games' timelines has been a variety of so-called "split timeline theories." Starting with the multiple timelines shown at the end of *Ocarina of Time*, fans have used elaborate means to organize other games based on the two timelines seen in that game. The conception of time as nonlinear and involving potential branches (with some games occurring in the world that the adult Link left and others occurring in the world that the child Link was sent back to at the end of *Ocarina*) has led to elaborate models of the games' overarching story.

Philosophers such as David Lewis have explicitly addressed this kind of issue—is it possible that multiple "worlds" (timelines or realities) may exist?[2] A common read of Hugh Everett's and later Bryce DeWitt's interpretation of quantum mechanics implied that, for every quantum event, all outcomes that did not occur actually *did* occur in a separate universe. That is, the universe was conceived not as a solitary universe but a "multiverse," branching into

---

[2] David Lewis, *On the Plurality of Worlds* (Blackwell, 1986).

separate realities with every event. This idea, in which multiple realities and timelines are potentially real, was popularized through various forms of science fiction, and likely influenced the *Zelda* discussions.

But, how are these conceptions of time *shaped* throughout the course of the discussion? As SEGA42 and SWORDM have shown, there are a variety of approaches a discussant may take in negotiating and arguing a theory of *Zelda* chronology.

Understanding Evidence: Opening the Treasure Chest

As you might have guessed, many kinds of evidence have been used to support *Zelda* fan timeline theories. How evidence is employed in these debates sheds light on the ways that reasoning occurs in these settings, as well as the nature of many fan arguments. We propose a way of organizing the types of evidence used in *Zelda* chronology debates, which include (but are not limited to):

- **Dialogue within the game (What did Midna specifically say in *Twilight Princess*?)**

- **Existence and naming of characters (Is the villain named Ganon, Ganondorf, or both in a particular game?)**

- **Existence and placement of objects within the game (Where is the Master Sword found?)**

- **Geography within the game (Is Hyrule a "barren wilderness" or a "close-knit kingdom"?)**

- **Information from game manuals (The print materials for *The Adventure of Link*)**

- **Relational game marketing (*Phantom Hourglass* was an explicit sequel to *The Wind Waker*).**

- **Game designer intentions (Interviews with Shigeru Miyamoto or Eiji Aonuma)**

- **Game mechanics and game design (Is the game rendered as 2-D or 3-D?)**

To understand how these arguments work, we'll need to dig into them in some detail, and carefully tease out the particular ways that arguments are formed, grounding our claims in the statements of the thread's participants. How do these discussions *work*? That is, how does the back-and-forth of a forum debate show how people use evidence and argue their claims? What "counts" as evidence, anyway?

The following is an edited excerpt from November 2004 showing the proposal of a timeline by poster LINK-FAN-242, and a discussion with another poster (SWORDM again). In this series of posts, several kinds of evidence were used and called into question. For clarity, we've broken the exchange into "stanzas" and each line from the original posts has been numbered for reference purposes, but the included text remains otherwise unaltered (typographical and grammatical errors have been kept in):

Stanza 1 (LINK-FAN-242):

1 - Ok so here is the TimeLine as I see it.

2 - TMC*TMC is first we all know that*

3 - FS*second*

4 - OoT*not sure*

5 - MM*know it is after OoT*

6 - TWW*know it is after MM*

7 - LoZ*has to be here because Ganon doesn't have the Trident*

8 - AoL*after LoZ*

9 - OoS*You'll se later*

10 - OoA*againg you'll see later*

11 - FSA*Ganon gets the Trident*

12 - ALttP*Master sword get put to sleep*

13 - LA*after ALttP*

14 - Ok well OoA/OoS are where they are because the Master Sword gets put to sleep in ALttP and the Master Sword is in OoA/OoS.

Stanza 2 (SWORDM):

1 - * You put The Legend of Zelda before Four Swords Adventures because Ganon doesn't have the Trident, but you also put Oracles before it. In Oracles, Ganon does have the Trident... It seems a bit inconsistent.

2 - * Why is Four Swords second?... especially since it seems to feature the same Link as in Four Swords?

3 - * How do you account for Twinrova's apparently difficulty-free revival, when Ganon, a much more powerful entity, had so much difficulty?

4 - * Back on Four Swords Adventures, how do you explain Ganondorf being human again, and alive, when he died in The Legend of Zelda and wasn't properly revived in Oracles?

Stanza 3 (LINK-FAN-242):

1 - About the Ganon humen thing I seem to think that there could be two Ganons but I'm still working on that one.. And critique me that is the only way any one wil ever get this riht is to be critiqued!

2 - And about the BS Zelda I'm not even going to call it a Zelda game I'm sorry but I'm not just like I dont call the CD-I games Zelda Games.

LINK-FAN-242 first presented a timeline with justifications for the placement of each game, followed by SWORDM picking apart that evidence and interpretation. LINK-FAN-242 responded, identifying the parts of his or her theory that were still in need of work, as well as delimiting the set of games that did not count as evidence (the BS Zelda games and Philips CDi Zelda games).

Take note that LINK-FAN-242 used several kinds of evidence to shape his or her timeline of the games' chronology. Initially, in Stanza 1, lines 2 and 3, *The Minish Cap* and *Four Swords* were the earliest games in the timeline without explicit justification ("we all know that" and "second"). Soon after, LINK-FAN-242 began to provide some justification for the timeline: In line 5, *Majora's Mask* was put "after *Ocarina of Time,*" since it was an explicit sequel, line 7 indicated that the lack of Ganon's trident put the original Zelda at an earlier spot in the chronology, and line 11 argued that *Four Swords Adventures* must have been later due to Ganon acquiring the trident in that game.

Most interesting, however, were the ways that SWORDM addressed LINK-FAN-242's timeline. Stanza 2, line 1 addressed an inconsistency in LINK-FAN-242's chronology (according to SWORDM, lines 9 and 10, Ganon's trident appeared in the *Oracles* games). Line 2 then addressed the assumption that games which have been marketed as sequels to one another and which are similarly designed (such as *Four Swords* and *Four Swords Adventures)* occurred after one another (much like how LINK-FAN-242 assumed that *Majora's Mask* followed *Ocarina of Time* in lines 4 and 5). Line 3 tackled the revival of characters in the game—the "Twinrova sisters," Kotake and Koume, from *Ocarina of Time, Majora's Mask,* and the *Oracles* games—and how this seemed inconsistent with their relative weakness compared to Ganon (who, more powerful, would presumably have less problem reviving).

LINK-FAN-242 then explained in Stanza 3, line 1, that there may be more than one character named Ganon in his or her theory, and that critiques were valuable—speaking openly about the social construction of knowledge in these timeline debates. Finally, in line 2, LINK-FAN-242 explained which games weren't "Zelda games," claiming that the BS Zelda game (an obscure 1995 game released only in Japan) was on par with the "CD i games" (three obscure, poorly-regarded games—*Link: The Faces of Evil, Zelda: The Wand of Gamelon,* and *Zelda's Adventure*—none designed by Nintendo and all released on the Philips CDi platform in 1993–1994). That is, LINK-FAN-242 dismissed the BS Zelda game as being on par with the games most often considered outside the "canon" of the *Zelda* games.

So, let's step back and try to understand this: In this short interchange, we saw a number of different kinds of evidence employed to both bolster and critique an argument. These included the presence of Ganon(dorf) and his naming, the existence of Ganon's trident, the location of the Master Sword, relational game marketing (*Majora's Mask* was an explicit sequel to *Ocarina of Time,* while *Four Swords Adventures* was perhaps a sequel to *Four Swords*), and the game design similarities found between explicit sequels. Finally, the borders of what "counts" as evidence in these debates

was discussed—the BS Zelda games were declared as being outside the realm of legitimate evidence.

The issue of evidence is an interesting one, but most interesting
was how LINK-FAN-242 *justified* his or her evidence. Obviously,
this does not happen in a vacuum in online forums, leading us to
wonder the manners by which evidence itself is socially constructed, and how that may resemble what we see in science.

Socially Constructing Knowledge: The "Legendary" Zelda

In the philosophy of science, evidence and the ways that it inter-
acts with theory has been a central concern from Comte and
Popper to Kuhn and Lakatos. Historically, an assumed distinction
between evidence and theory has had its roots in particular conceptions of science, but has been actively critiqued by philosophers
who have aimed to better elaborate the ways that science and scientific knowledge are created.

For Bruno Latour, the construction of knowledge loomed large
in his model of scientific practice. In *Laboratory Life,* Latour and
Steve Woolgar challenged traditional notions of science and the scientific method, via ethnographic observations of a neuroendocrinology laboratory.[3] The importance of the single, critical
experiment was devalued by Latour and Woolgar, and they empha-
sized the ongoing construction of knowledge through social interaction in a community of practice with shared norms. In *Zelda* fan
debates, the meaning of evidence is constructed through the arguments in the online forums. In the previous example, posters negotiated a particular chronology of the *Zelda* games through several
proposals and critiques of a theory. The very nature of these
debates involved a give and take in the development of the meaning of various pieces of evidence, and constructing timelines necessarily involved discussion to some extent. Evidence isn't simple
value-free information—it's shaped by practices and norms which
are held by those using it.

Therefore, what "counts" as evidence in these fan debates is,
like in many scientific settings, a *theoretical construct.* It is
unclear from the previous example whether or not SWORDM and

---

[3] Bruno Latour and Steven Woolgar, *Laboratory Life* (Princeton University Press, 1979).

LINK-FAN-242's believe that the BS Zelda games or the Philips CDi games have explicit reasons for not being legitimate evidence, but given the other posts in these forums, there is certainly an implicit social norm which denies that those games are legitimate. For example, a post from April 2005 by poster MEERKAT-MAN stated:

> I don't take [the BS Zelda games] as canon because they aren't available legally now, they are, in essence, remakes. The story is pretty ludicrous and generic IMO, and is pretty much just thrown on there for flavor. It is more like a mini-game than a real game.

The justifications for why these games are not considered evidence contain embedded value judgments—MEERKATMAN privileged the original creative work of Nintendo designers, the availability of the games, the quality of the games, and even aspects of the game design ("mini-games" vs. "a real game"). The combination of these factors seemed to influence whether or not a game could be considered evidence in a timeline debate; this mirrors Latour's emphasis on how evidence is theory-laden in constructing scientific knowledge.

To illustrate further, let's look at how and why the meaning of a particular piece of evidence can quickly change through debate and negotiation. The following is an exchange between posters GAMEFAN#1 and SGM2 from June 2004:

Stanza 1 (GAMEFAN#1):

1 - Okay, you remember that the first time when OOT Link pulled the Master Sword from the pedestal.

2 - Seven years later, he grew up.

3 - Then Sheik appeared to Link

4 - and said he really does look like the Hero of Time.

5 - So. . . How did Sheik know how the Hero of Time is supposed to look like?

6 - That implied that there was another Link before OOT who became the Hero of Time.

7 - That means OOT Link is the second Hero of Time.

Stanza 2 (GAMEFAN#1):

1 - Also, when Navi first saw the Master Sword,

2 - she said it was the legendary blade.

3 - So, what made it legendary in the first place?

4 - Unless another Link used it before OOT

5 - and that Link is the first Hero of Time.

Stanza 3 (SGM2):

1 - I am not saying there was not another hero before the game

2 - but it could of become legendary just because it was created by the sages

3 - and that it repels evil.

Stanza 4 (GAMEFAN#1):

1 - First off, it is not legendary if it hasn't done anything significant yet.

2 - For example: I forged a knife.

3 - Does that make that knife legendary right after I forged it?

4 - No, of course not.

Stanza 5 (SGM2):

1 - If you later do something famous

2 - that knife will become the legendary knife of GAME-FAN#1.

3 - The sages created the blade.

4 - They are also the protectors of the triforce.

5 - It would be lengendary just by being created by them.

Stanza 6 (GAMEFAN#1):

1 - Ah, but remember in ALTTP's backstory.

2 - The Master Sword was forged for the purpose of sealing the evil away.

3 - But... If OOT was the Imprisoning War,

4 - then why was the Master Sword already there as if it had been forged long time ago?

5 - That means there must be a game before OOT

6 - and that game is the true ALTTP's backstory.

Stanza 7 (SGM2):

1 - I'm sorry.

2 - I am getting mixed up in a conversation.

3 - I am just saying that saying it is legenndary is not great proof.

4 - I am not saying the IW was in OoT

5 - or if it was not.

6 - The thing is stuff can happen even if it is not in a game.

7 - The IW may not be in a game as we know it so far.

This series of posts dealt with the necessity of another Link predating the Link of *Ocarina of Time* ("OOT" to the posters). In Stanzas 1 and 2, GAMEFAN#1 proposed a theory based on two pieces of evidence: First, that Link in *Ocarina* was recognized by the Sheik as the "Hero of Time" (stanza 1, line 4), implying that there must have been an earlier Link who was called that and, second, that Navi referred to Link's Master Sword in *Ocarina* as "legendary" (stanza 2, line 2), meaning that the Master Sword must have been used by a previous, "legendary" Link. It is the interpretation of "legendary" that dominated the rest of the thread.

In Stanza 3, SGM2 presented a direct challenge to the understanding of "legendary" as proposed by GAMEFAN#1, stating (in lines 2 and 3) that "it could of [*sic*] become legendary just because it was created by the sages and that it repels evil." This is a very different "legendary" than GAMEFAN#1's: for GAMEFAN#1, the source of what makes a sword "legendary" was the original sword's owner's actions and thus the sword inherited this property from a previous, heroic Link. However, for SGM2, the source of what made the sword "legendary" was the provenance of the sword (in this case the "sages," mythical characters in the game's story), as well as the sword's properties (it "repels evil"). So, one interpretation of the term "legendary" meant assigning the "legendariness" of the sword to a hypothetical earlier hero, and one did not.

In other words, for GAMEFAN#1, "legendary" initially meant something about a character in the story: Link was recognized as being a "legendary" hero because there must have been an earlier hero who spawned the legend, implying that there must have been a game (or story) that occurred before it. In Stanza 4, GAMEFAN#1 challenged SGM2's reading of "legendary" by proposing a hypothetical situation in which GAMEFAN#1 (presumably not a "legendary" person) created a knife that was then "of course" (Stanza 4, line 4) not inherently "legendary." The intent of GAMEFAN#1 seems to have been to criticize the interpretation of "legendary" as having anything to do with who created it — at this point, GAMEFAN#1 argued that the *only* interpretation of "legendary" that made sense was one in which "legendary" referred to an earlier character's reputation being inherited by the sword.

SGM2 replied in Stanza 5 by incorporating aspects of GAMEFAN#1's original concept of "legendary"—by "doing something famous" (line 1), GAMEFAN#1 could pass on "legendary" qualities to the hypothetical knife. The concept of "legendary" was thus malleable for SGM2, unsurprising given the reactive stance he or she adopted to GAMEFAN#1's initial proposal. However, this was not a conciliatory move, since SGM2's point was still to address a flaw in GAMEFAN#1's reasoning; for SGM2, the adjective "legendary" still referred to a property of the sword, inherited from the "legendary" status of the creator of the sword.

In Stanza 6, GAMEFAN#1 took a different approach, retreating from further discussion of the term "legendary" and addressing why the Master Sword was supposedly created within the text of *Ocarina of Time* ("sealing the evil away," line 2). Here, the usefulness of "legendary" in the argument was essentially jettisoned; GAMEFAN#1 switched from relying upon "legendary" to indicate the existence of a previous heroic Link to acknowledging that if "legendary" was the property of the sword, there was still a need for an earlier event in the chronology. In Stanza 7, SGM2 tried to clarify his or her criticism over the entire "legendary" discussion (Stanza 7, line 3).

So, once more, let's step back and try to figure out what this means. First, we can see that evidence was, again, negotiated—but more than that, theories of the games' chronology actively hinged upon the negotiated meaning of evidence. If "legendary" referred to a previous Link's actions, then this implied a *Zelda* timeline in which *Ocarina* was placed early. However, if "legendary" referred to the influence of the sages (the creators of the Master Sword), then *Ocarina* would not necessarily need to be posited as an earlier game in the timeline. The interpretation of a single piece of evidence—in this case, a single *word*—can have a great deal of impact, driving the theories taken by participants in these discussions.

One can see that the social construction of *Zelda* timelines matches much of what Latour argued about scientific knowledge. Evidence isn't simply passive information; knowledge is *necessarily* situated and constructed. By the 1986 revision of *Laboratory Life*, the term "social" was so redundant with "construction" as to be unnecessary in the subtitle of Latour and Woolgar's text.

Putting Together the Triforce

The blurring of distinctions between theory and evidence, between agent and tool, and between individual and group knowledge are seen in fan discussions about *Zelda* like they are in the practices of science. The philosophical implications of this are considerable—if the kinds of issues that arise in the development of scientific theories are found even in fan discussions around videogames, perhaps new ideas of how knowledge is constructed should be entertained. This is a point that has significance beyond either science or game fandom and tells us something about *argument* itself.

With *Zelda* fans, the forms of argumentation and debate around timelines included complicated interpretations of texts, negotiations of evidence, and vigorous debate. Much like other intellectual pursuits, the construction of knowledge is *social*, contingent upon the specific uses of tools, interactions of participants, and even the ways that people use Internet discussion forums. Without a set of official Nintendo forums online, timeline debates would not have had the same character as they presently do (if they were to exist at all), and these examples show that, at the very least, the interplay between participants in these threads is often surprisingly constructive.

We don't argue that the typical *Zelda* fan is interested in debating about chronologies because he or she is inherently interested in elaborating a theory of time, nor because he or she is consciously trying to emulate an academic. Comparing *Zelda* timeline debates to those in, say, neuroendocrinology, physics, or sociology, it's clear that the game discussions do not rise to the level of broader significance that these established scientific fields often have. But, let's not forget that there are strong similarities in *form* and *practice* between what goes on in science and what goes on within fan debates.

In the GAMEFAN#1/SGM2 excerpt alone, the path of the social knowledge construction should appear familiar:

- **A theory was proposed, with evidence provided**

- **The evidence was critiqued and reinterpreted by another**

- **The proposer of the original theory defended the original evidence**

- **The original evidence was dismissed in favor of stronger evidence.**

Stripping the discussion of its context, we can see argumentation which is similar to that in scientific debates and other academic arguments in general. Time and again, fan activities around games have been shown to embed serious intellectual practices (or, at least, mirror them), and we find that to be the case here as well. The content of the debate may be quite different from one in, say, geology, but the nature of the debate is one in which evidence is forwarded, critiqued, and evaluated in service of developing a theory.

If we are to take the proposal of Latour and his colleagues seriously, this has implications beyond science—knowledge *in general* is constructed within and is dependent upon networks of tools, agents, and social/cultural commitments. Within this view, there is no sense in debating what "counts" as science any more than there is in debating whether or not chemistry and economics are both "science"; what's important for us to see are not the particular tools used in the construction of knowledge as much as the simple fact that this is how knowledge is constructed. Again, what science and *Zelda* fan debates share are common *practices*, and a common approach to discussing investigations of the world, though they differ in terms of application to real problems and the specific tools used to conduct those discussions.

Thus, we find ourselves returning to Latour and Woolgar's rather bold claim about epistemology—the conception that knowledge is formed "intrinsic to the mind" simply cannot be reconciled with the practices of how knowledge is constructed in real scientific laboratories nor discussions in fan communities such as *Zelda*'s. The *Zelda* timeline debates show that the construction of knowledge is *necessarily* mediated and shaped by the use of tools, interaction with others, and the use of discourse practices. Like all knowledge, *Zelda* timeline knowledge is constructed socially.

9
Linking to the Past: *Zelda* Is a Communication Game

CARL MATTHEW JOHNSON

All of the games in the *Legend of Zelda* series share certain similarities. There are puzzles, monsters, and dungeons; there's an evil to be vanquished. And most of all there's the rich mythos of Hyrule and its hero in green.

It's natural to think that these games are meant to be related to one another. However, due to various statements made in the games—such as *A Link to the Past's* stating at its conclusion that the Master Sword rested forever—the order in which the games were released can't possibly be the chronological order of events in the *Zelda* universe.

Until recently, the die-hard *Zelda* fan base was firmly split into two opposing camps concerning the relationship between different games in the series. On the one side were those who felt that all the stories in the *Zelda* universe could be treated as taking place in a single linear timeline and on the other side were those who felt that the conclusion to *Ocarina of Time* split the timeline into two parallel tracks, one following from the "adult ending" and one following from the "child ending." Both sides of the issue produced elaborate explanations of how the different games fit together by drawing up various bits of evidence from within the games, and from comments by developers.

The battle between the "splitists" and "linearists" was fierce until it was finally laid to rest by an interview comment from director Eiji Aonuma in the December 2006 issue of Japan's *Nintendo Dream Magazine*. In the interview, Aonuma states that *Wind Waker* and *Twilight Princess* story lines should be seen as taking place in parallel worlds branching out of the time traveling ending of *Ocarina of Time*. Fan reaction to the interview was intense, and though many fans questioned the quality of the translation for the interview or even the authority of Aonuma, in the end, group opinion came around, and now the split timeline is widely (if grudgingly) accepted as the consensus view of the history of the *Zelda* universe.

This debate raises several interesting questions. Why do fans expect that the games of the *Legend of Zelda* series can be placed into any kind of unified framework at all? Why are fans driven to make complex charts explaining how they see the various games linking up? Why do they scour in-game text and developer interviews for clues about the relationship between the games? Can it be that by going to these elaborate lengths, *Zelda* fans have created a new game on top of the *Zelda* series that is filled with puzzles almost as rich and complex as those found in the games themselves?

Why Should We Think the *Zelda* Games Can Be Linked Anyway?

Before thinking about how the games should be linked, let's note that there are numerous problems with supposing that there even is a coherent interpretation of the *Zelda* universe out there for us to find.

To begin with, if we're to take the series seriously as a story there are a lot of plot holes to which we must turn a blind eye.

- **How do the towns and villages in Hyrule support themselves economically with so few people in them?**

- **How does the Hylian royal family manage to live in a castle that apparently lacks toilets? (Perhaps the toilets are revealed by a lighting of torches in a particular pattern?)**

- **Why do all the keys in Hyrule seem to break after one use?**

- **Where do monsters' carcasses go after they are slain, and why do they often leave behind bombs, arrows, or rupees?**

- Why do Ganon's evil minions always arrange their dungeons in order of increasing difficulty and so that earlier dungeons can be beaten without the specialized tools found in later dungeons?

- Who hides the rupees in the grass?

- How do heart pieces work? (It would be a powerful medical technology if it could be adapted to our world!)

- Can the non-playable characters in the game hear Link saying things, or do they just not find his near constant silence bizarre?

And on and on goes the list of points where suspension of disbelief comes into play . . .

However, those questions about the series aren't actually all that bad as far as understanding the stories goes. An audience will accept fantastical, impossible details like talking animals or enchanted objects in a story, so long as the story has a consistent internal logic describing the way that the world of the story works, even if that logic is quite removed the working of our own world. The structure of the story's world need not be spelled out in explicit detail, and most fantasy stories skip over tedious explanations of how seemingly contradictory elements can fit together. The important thing is to create a vibrant structure that can engage the audience's attention and imagination, which is something that most successful games in the *Zelda* series clearly do.

Any interpretation of the game's plot must begin by assuming that what we see when we play is not meant to be seen as exactly what "really" happened in the game world. Instead the game structure relates the story without conveying everything about its world, just as when we read a fairy tale even if the narrator doesn't say, "The protagonist was in a room with normal flooring and ordinary walls and an average ceiling and . . .," we can still safely assume that the minor details of the character's world that are left out are as one would expect. Characters in stories have an eye color, even if that color is never mentioned. The story that the audience hears is not the fullness of the world of the story. In the same way, when we play a *Zelda* game, what we get is not the story of that particular *Zelda* game. Even though it helps to convey that story, the game is not what we are supposed to think "really" happened, just a window that conveys the plot in a roundabout way. The game we play shows us part of another world and invites us to fill in its details with our imaginations.

This approach to the suspension of disbelief allows us to resolve some other problems not mentioned above that are a part of the nature of interactive games. As a videogame, each time a *Legend of Zelda* game is played, it's different. Sometimes you go straight to the end of the dungeon, and sometimes you mess around with a side-quest first, and yet other times you just go fishing for hours and hours. If we imagined that the *Zelda* game we play is the same as the *Zelda* story we're interpreting, the problem wouldn't be how does *Ocarina of Time* relate to *Wind Waker*, the problem would be how does my game of *Ocarina of Time* relate to your game of *Ocarina of Time*, since in my game I named Link "Carl," but you named him "Thrillhouse," and in my game I got the arrow upgrades, but in your game, you collected all the Poes, and so on. Just by assuming that individual games are not the real story, only a version of the story, we can make a lot of our interpretive problems go away.

But new problems arise to replace the ones we remove. Since we have assumed that the game as played is just a window into the larger, "real" world of *Zelda*, there must also be some way for us to fill in all the gaps in that world if we are to work out the intercon-nected history of the *Zelda* universe. However, there are still two big problems that we must face before we can do away with those gaps.

First, when many of the games were made, the thought given by the writers and programmers to the placement of their individ-ual game within a larger *Zelda* cosmos was cursory at best, since different games present baldly contradictory versions of past events. Wise men, sages, maidens, and magical seals come and go as the means of ensuring that Ganon "dies" for the final time shifts from one game to the next. Of course, no matter how expertly sealed away at the end of a particular game, Ganon inevitably finds a way to come back in the next, with no explanation given for how this is possible or why the means of striking evil down keeps sub-tly changing from game to game. In interviews, developers will talk at length about the reasoning behind minor game play details like making broken signposts float in the water,[1] but spare no more

---

[1] *Iwata Asks* interview series, Volume 5, p. 10. "I Simply Want Everyone to Enjoy This World." <http://wii.nintendo.com/iwata_asks_vol5_p10.jsp>. Accessed July 2007.

than a dozen or so cryptic words about the relation of their latest game to the previous entries in the series.

When asked in an interview if there is in fact any internal agreement about the timeline of the *Zelda* series, Aonuma stated that while there is a confidential document on the company's PCs that purports to show the relationship between the games, "It's not as though when [the developers] go in to create a game that they know exactly where it will fit in the timeline." Instead, he states, "after it's complete they know more or less where it might fit in."[2] In other words, during the development process determining the relationship of the new game to others in the series takes a back seat to making the game fun and engaging. Thus, when we try to fill in the gaps between the games, it may be that we are venturing into territory that the game's designers never imagined, let alone fleshed out.

Second, not only do the makers of the games not care that much about meticulously linking their plots together, there isn't even one "author" that we can point to and say, "The author intended for us to interpret the game like this." Normally, when we read a book or see a painting or listen to a song, we reflexively ask ourselves, "What was the author trying to tell us?" To find out, we can go back through what the artist has said about their own work and what schools and influences bear consideration when thinking about the artist's past to gather together clues about what the right interpretation of it is.

To resolve questions about the *Lord of the Rings* universe, fans quite regularly sift through the letters of J.R.R. Tolkien looking for some written indication of his intentions on the matter at hand. For the *Lord of the Rings* universe, Tolkien's views are definitive, because the series as a whole is his attempt to express a coherent vision of "Middle-earth." However, with the *Zelda* games, there is no one author who was trying to tell us anything. Each *Zelda* game was made by a vast team of people working together, each of whom had a direct impact on the final product.

Sometimes, fans talk as though producer Shigeru Miyamoto or director Eiji Aonuma are personally responsible for every aspect of the games, but that's just not the case. In reality, different groups

---

[2] Aonuma, Eiji. "Video Interview (July 19th, 2007)." Question asked around minute 6. Transcribed from video at <http://media.wii.ign.com/media/748/748589/vids_1.html>. Accessed July 2007.

of people worked together to make each game, and each person probably had a different idea of what the game means and how we should interpret it. Since no one person wrote all the text in the games or designed all the dungeons in the games or even translated all the games into English, how are we as fans supposed to decide which of the many people on the team is "the" author whose vision counts for more than all the rest? No matter how great we may think Miyamoto and Aonuma are, without programmers, artists, and sound technicians working for them, they couldn't have accomplished anything. Isn't it odd then to give individuals all the credit for collaborative effort? Besides, the personal involvement of the pair with some *Zelda* games, such as *The Minish Cap*, was only slight, since those games were created by developers outside Nintendo. Taken together, it's odd to credit the vision of any one person, no matter how crucial to the development of the *Zelda* series, as final and authoritative. But, without an individual's vision to credit as authoritative, what are fans supposed to point to when trying to fill in the gaps in the *Zelda* world? All that is left is a multiplicity of competing interpretive visions. Some of these visions are from developers and some are from fans, but none is any higher than the others, or so it appears.

It seems then that there's just no possible way that fans could ever agree on a timeline for the *Zelda* games, because there is no timeline to agree on! . . . And yet, though the fans do debate the timeline quite passionately, they still agree with each other often. Even if they disagree on the specific order that the games are linked together, almost all of them at least agree that the games seem to be linked together. Particular games clearly offer clues that are meant to remind the player of other games in the series. No one goes on to Internet message boards to passionately explain their theory that each game is an island. Fans have persistently seen some connection between the games and intricately worked out the possible relationship between the many plotlines. They communicate and reach a new collaborative consensus together by arguing from evidence internal and external to the games. But how are they doing that?

Enter Hermeneutics: Parts and Wholes

The branch of philosophy that deals with interpreting texts or systems of meaning is called "hermeneutics." Books, paintings, plays, music, and videogames are all obvious candidates for interpretation, but philosophers like Martin Heidegger and his student Hans-Georg Gadamer went further and claimed that all of life consisted of the same sort of hermeneutic process that is engaged in when interpreting a text. Finding "the meaning of life" is a similar process to finding the meaning of a work of art. Interpretation is an activity that we are constantly engaged in, if only subconsciously.

Every waking moment, we take in what we see in the world around us and draw conclusions that allow us to act purposively. The goal of philosophers of hermeneutics is to describe how we actually interpret the world everyday in order to describe how interpretation ought to be done in difficult cases.

The central insight of the philosophy of hermeneutics is that interpretation is a circular process by which our understanding of the part informs our interpretation of the whole, and our understanding of the whole informs our interpretation of the part. Our knowledge that Ganon recurs as an enemy throughout many games in the series allows us to make sense of the references to previous attacks by him that are included in *The Wind Waker*. Our knowledge of the whole helps us interpret the part. On the other hand, some fans have speculated about a connection between the owl Kaepora Gaebora in *Ocarina of Time* and other owls in the *Zelda* series based on particular bits of text from that game, like a gossip stone calling him a reincarnated sage. In this case, their understanding of a part helps them form an interpretation of the whole. Without an understanding of the whole, we can't figure out where to put specific parts, but without an understanding of specific parts, we cannot grasp the outline of the series as a whole. The insight of hermeneutics is that we must iteratively refine our interpretation by incrementally improving our understanding of the whole from the parts and the parts from the whole.

One of the long standing debates in philosophy has been between the "empiricists" who claim we can learn about the world best by studying our experiences and the "rationalists" who claim we can learn about the world best by using our reason. Experiences without theories are blind, because we need theories to help us shape our experiences into a coherent whole, but theories without an empirical basis are empty, since we need experience to give credence to our theories. To give either exclusive emphasis is useless. Hermeneutic interpretation is a process that must draw on both.

So, we need to use a hermeneutical method to interpret the *Zelda* universe. But, if the hermeneutic process is circular, our problem isn't just with *Zelda*. We need to explain how anyone ever interprets anything if we need theories for our facts and facts for our theories. The process may continue to refine itself circularly once it has begun, but we need an initial basis from which to start the whole thing or else we may be draw into a vicious regress.

The initial set of facts from which to draw when creating an interpretation of the *Zelda* universe will be the experiences that emerge while playing the games. However, without an initial framework of interpretive theories in place, we will still be unable to refine our interpretation of *Zelda* over time. We will be stuck with facts without theories. Thus, the first task in our interpretive process must be to vet principles that can guide the selection of theories and facts, and select those principles that best advance the achievement of our aims. Since our aim is the creation of an interpretation of the *Zelda* timeline that will be accepted by the majority of the fan community on the basis of its support from evidence in and around the games, we must look for universally acceptable principles, so that our framework can be accepted by the fan community as a whole.

Underdetermination

Before explaining what those principles might be, let's illustrate the difficulties associated with having facts without a theory that connects those facts. Suppose we're playing a mathematical guessing game. I'll give you a series of pairs of numbers, and you have to guess the formula for the series. If I say, "one and two; two and four; three and six," you might blurt out, "the formula is '$y = 2x$', and next in the series is four and eight!"

But you would be wrong, because the formula I was using was actually '$y = 2x + 1 - (x - 4) \div (x - 4)$.' Normally, the last part of the equation drops out, since it is equivalent to one minus one. However, four minus four is zero, so if x is four, y equals $2 \times 4 + 1 - 0 \div 0$, but zero divided by zero is not defined in arithmetic, so there's no answer to this problem. It seemed obvious that my formula was just to double the first number in the pair, but in actuality there was another formula that fit the facts at hand just as well as the "double first the number" formula.

The larger problem is this: when we're given a set of pairs of points, it doesn't matter how many points we are given; we still can't say for sure what formula was meant to describe them because there are an infinite number of variations on the normal formula that one would expect to describe it. My formula excluded four, but it could just as easily have excluded any other number, making it just one variation of one method of describing the points out of an infinite pool of alternative functions. (In addition to variations on the same method, there are also many other methods to employ for mapping the points that use advanced mathematical functions like sine and cosine.)

The problem is called "underdetermination," and its first recognition as a serious problem is commonly ascribed to the philosopher and mathematician Leibniz. If his negative conclusion is that there is no one formula that best describes a set of points, at least on the positive side, Leibniz proved mathematically that every finite set of points, no matter how simple or complex their distribution, can be described by some group of mathematical functions. We don't have to worry that we will encounter a set of points without a corresponding set of descriptive functions. If these properties hold for the highly restricted process of mathematical interpretation, it should be clear that they will hold for interpreting other, less rigorous, informal logical systems as well.

When we interpret the *Zelda* series, we have an infinite number of choices for how to interpret anything in any game of the series. (Which is not to say that anything goes as an interpretation, just that there are infinite variations on what does work. Similarly, the formula above couldn't have been '$y = 3x$', though it could have been any one of an infinite number of other formulas.) Reflecting briefly, we can see the wide range of possible interpretive theories for the *Zelda* universe that are available to us: maybe all of the games are a dream by the Zelda in *The Adventure of Link*; maybe all of the games are the work of a powerful, but unseen wizard, who causes all of the seeming plot holes and inconsistencies; maybe hyper-intelligent Cuccos are the real power behind Ganon's evil magic; and on and on.

That there are an infinite number of possible interpretations may seem like very bad news since it makes reaching agreement on a single, correct interpretation even harder. And yet that there are an infinite number of interpretations for everything is also good news since we no longer need worry that, in their sloppiness, the game designers have made the games truly contradictory. Any apparent contradictions in the timeline can be resolved by just proposing a new and more complicated theory to explain away the seeming inconsistency. As the philosopher's cliché has it, "When faced with a contradiction, make a distinction."

The Trouble with Simplicity

Now that we know we have an endless array of potential theories, we must return to the selection of universally acceptable principles to choose from among those theories. William of Ockham famously endorsed one key principle of interpretation, now named "Ockham's razor" in his honor. He claimed, "entities should not be multiplied beyond necessity." In other words, the simplest explanation—one that cuts away all the unnecessary bits—is the best. This rule is still a central principle for hermeneutics, because it can quickly eliminate all but a handful of potential theories from the pool of consideration.

Occam's razor has its problems, however. As the counting example shows, it's not guaranteed to always give us the correct answer. Guessing that my formula was '$y = 2x$' is much simpler than guessing my formula was '$y = 2x + 1 - (x - 4) \div (x - 4)$'. Applying Occam's razor in this case will inevitably lead us away from what turns out to be the intended formula. In spite of that, '$y = 2x$' is still a good guess to have made even though it didn't turn out to be the right answer in the end. Since it's a simple enough formula for us to fit into our heads it has practical advantages as a hypothesis, such as that it makes it easier us for us to come up with the formula, remember it, and work out all its consequences. On top of that, with a simpler proposed formula, we are more likely to encounter test cases to contradict our guess, letting us know that we need to revise it. If I had been allowed to continue giving number pairs and said, "four and undefined," it would have been immediately clear to you that the formula '$y = 2x$' is incorrect and that a new formula is needed, whereas if you had guessed that my formula was like that but undefined for thirteen million five hundred and sixty, the evidence against this would not have shown up as readily. On top of all this, a simpler formula is more easily inferred by others, which makes it superior for collaborative purposes. Since our formula is simple, we can reasonably expect that others who are attempting to come up with an interpretation will create one similar to ours if ours is simple, and by working with them, we can point out bits of data that may require revision away from a simpler theory.

We have seen the difficulty of interpretation, because the part must inform the whole and the whole the part; and because any set of data points can be connected in an infinite number of ways, and so we recommended simplicity as a key quality for an interpretation, even though it may not always give the right answer. But what does it mean for something to be simple?

The philosopher Wittgenstein once worried about a related problem. Suppose that you show someone a set of examples to teach her how to count by twos, and at first she does so correctly—"2, 4, 6, 8 . . ." —but when she gets up to 1,000, she suddenly shifts to "1,004, 1,008, 1,012 . . ." while claiming she is still going on in the same way. What can be said to such a person? Because of the problem of underdetermination, she seems to have deduced the formula for counting by two incorrectly. However, if she thinks like a normal human being, we can tell her, "No, the formula you are using is too complex, since it treats numbers above and below 1,000 differently. You must use a simpler formula!" While it is a leap to conclude that everyone everywhere will agree with our assessment of what is simple, so long as our learner has a relatively normal human brain, in this case surely she will see what we mean and correct herself.

Can we always assume that everyone will see simplicity in the same way? What could we say to our learner if she stubbornly insisted that her way of counting by two seems simple to her? While it seems fairly clear that changing how one adds at 1,000 is less simple arithmetically because the formula to express it would be longer when written down, it is less clear that we can precisely define simplicity for other interpretations.

While it seems simpler to assume that the Master Sword of *Twilight Princess* is the same sword as the Master Sword of *Ocarina of Time*, is it simpler to assume that the flute from *A Link to the Past* is the same as the ocarina from *Ocarina of Time*? If we blindly follow Occam's razor, then we might be inclined to say that assuming they are different is a needless multiplication of entities. On the other hand, the flute in *A Link to the Past* is very different in its function from the ocarina in *Ocarina of Time*, to such a degree that it's difficult to see a real connection between the two other than their being similar in color and shape. Where does the simplicity lie?

Communities Shape the Perception of Simplicity

Simplicity is not an absolute, objectively quantifiable value. Rather, simplicity is relative to the properties of the system in which it is being measured. What is considered simple depends in part on what is considered complex. Given our shared mathematical culture as humans, we all agree that it would be strange to count by twos differently at 1,000. However, computer chip manufacturers routinely produce chips that can easily do math within some large but finite range but are incapable of doing math normally outside of that range, because these sorts of chips are easier to produce. (That is to say, they are simpler to make.) For those computer chips, what is natural is to say that 32,767 plus one is – 32,768, that is *negative* 32,768. The fact that humans find it simpler for arithmetic to work the same way no matter what its scale stems from the fact that in our human existence, we experience objects as adding continuously. Adding one more bead to a pile never causes the pile as a whole to disappear. However if we were to somehow live in a world like *Tetris* where putting enough things in a row causes the row to disappear, our species would find it simpler to think that nine plus one equals zero, rather than ten. Simplicity depends in part on the particular qualities of the world in which we find ourselves.

Even for humans living in this world, what seems simple depends on how you approach a problem. Using decimals, one third is 0.333 . . . repeating, an inconvenient number to work with. Using fractions, it is inconvenient to work with a number like 0.12345 which reduces to 2,469 over 20,000. In either case, the approach you use dictates whether a number is "simple" or "complex" to work with. Some numbers are easier to calculate with when written as decimals; other numbers are easier to calculate with when written as fractions.

Our assumptions about how the world operates shape how we think of certain situations. These assumptions in turn are based on our repeated experiences. If we run into certain situations again and again, our brains will regard that as an ordinary situation and come up with simple ways of explaining it. The cultural context of the interpreter will have an impact on what that interpreter considers simple. If you have played many *Zelda* games already, you need only see that a room has a group of torches in it to recognize that they need to be lit, but to someone who has never played *Zelda*, solving a puzzle by lighting torches may feel as arbitrary as if a room could be beaten by, say, walking around in a circle seven times or knocking on the wall with your sword in a particular rhythm. Thus, to a *Zelda* fan, a "light the torches" puzzle may seem very simple, but to a non-gamer this puzzle may seem quite arbitrary and complex. Part of the fun of mastering a *Zelda* game is to make the transition from being an outsider for whom *Zelda* puzzles are difficult to being an insider who solves them with ease.

If simplicity emerges from the needs of a community, then it should be clear that the reason simplicity is an important interpretive principle is that simplicity means nothing other than what a community already finds useful for achieving its aims. If the definition of simplicity is the recurring abstraction through which the community understands its world, then tautologically, simplicity must be the means by which a community makes decisions about the best interpretations. Thus, the fundamental principle of interpretation depends upon there being a community with unified aims and common experiences, though of course the community will still also have serious disagreements about how their aims and experiences are to be unified. Nevertheless it is the community which must precede the creation of any interpretation, if it is to be a meaningful one. Disagreements within an interpretive community are fine as long as the community has a central activity that creates a core of agreement among its members.

The notion of simplicity springs out of familiarity, which in turn springs from the recurring needs of a community. If we examine the fan community of *Zelda*, we see that the recurring need which *Zelda* fans share and which anchors simplicity of interpretation for them is their need to master the games. This need unifies the *Zelda* community around a common cause. Because of their unity of purpose, the community naturally develops the ability to rapidly interpret game play details and clues in order to overcome puzzles and challenges. By interpreting the story line surrounding the Master Sword's unique ability to banish evil, one will learn that the sword will be one of the key weapons to use in any final battle with Ganon. Similarly, fans use the numerous clues sprinkled throughout each game to find the many treasures and upgrades hidden within it.

Zelda Is a Communication Game!?

No single fan can reasonably be expected to find everything in one *Zelda* game the first time he or she plays it. New players must regularly go online or use other resources from outside the game in order to flesh out their understanding of the world which they seek to master. Indeed, the game's designers even expect that their fans will build communities as a part of the game itself. Though what happens inside these communities is separate from what happens when actually playing the game, online communities are nevertheless a part of the design of the game. Speaking at GDC (the Game Developers Conference) in 2007, Shigeru Miyamoto made the surprising statement that he considers *Zelda* to be a communication game—just like Nintendo's *Animal Crossing* series! In his own words:

> Some people view *Zelda* as [lacking a communicative component], but when I created it, I had a different idea in mind. Some people think that this single player game is one where you communicate only with the computer, but from the start I thought that *Zelda* could create a different kind of communication, centered around the game itself. And when I first showed an early prototype version of the NES version of *Zelda*, it did not go over well in Japan. People were confused. They didn't know their objective. They didn't know how to move from stage to stage. They couldn't even solve the puzzles. And a lot of people said well look, why don't you just make one way through the dungeon— no multiple paths. But of course I ignored them all. Rather than making it easier for players to understand, I decide to take their sword away from the very beginning. You do that then you know what you have to do. See, I did this because I wanted to challenge them to find that sword, because I knew that they would think about these problems. They would think before they go to sleep how am I going to do this? Or maybe as they're riding to work in the morning. And at the same time, I wanted them to talk with other *Zelda* players and exchange information, ask each other questions, find out where to go next, exchange information—that's what happened. This communication was not a competition; but it was a real life collaboration that helped make the game more popular.[3]

In other words, from the start the activity of fans has been an integral part of the *Zelda* experience! Naturally enough, as fans built the community that surrounds the *Zelda* universe, they didn't limit

---

[3] Miyamoto, Shigeru. "Keynote: A Creative Vision." Speech delivered March 8th, 2007 at the Game Developers Conference 2007. Conference details available at <https://www.cmpevents.com/GD07/a.asp?option=C&V=11&SessID=4886>. Transcribed from video at <http://media.wii.ign.com/articles/771/771717/vids_1.html>, part two, around minute 18 and onward. Accessed July 2007.

their hermeneutic activities to "beating" the game itself. Instead, the fans cast a wider eye and challenged one another not only to beat the game, but to thoroughly master its material and the *Zelda* universe itself. In their way, the fans who debate the connection of the *Zelda* games are as legitimate an interpretive community as any other, even if the universe they explore cannot be said to have a single unitary designer's vision at its core. By bringing their different perspectives to bear on the worlds, the fans create and refine interpretations that better fit the model of the *Zelda* world that they have jointly constructed. This too is a part of the *Zelda* experience.

To interpret *Zelda*, the community must come together to use the same ways of thinking that they used to beat a particular game to explain the games. Beating the videogame is training for beating the hermeneutic game. When Aonuma announced that he sided with the "splitists" in his *Nintendo Dream* interview, he wasn't merely explaining what the *Twilight Princess* story line is. He was adding another puzzle piece to the mix for fans to put together into a picture of *Zelda* world themselves. When he spoke, he didn't act as an author delivering an unchallengeable interpretation. He acted as game creator and added another puzzle piece to the interpretation game. His pronouncement changed the relative simplicity of the two sets of explanations for fans, but only because his pronouncements are considered by fans to be one element of the interpretation game. (Incidentally, the same applies to the quote by Miyamoto given above: its importance stems from the fact that as a game designer his comments are also a part of the meta-game surrounding each videogame. The comments do not work to impose an interpretation on us, but rather they are clues that suggest a new solution.)

Zelda demonstrates that a work need not have a single author with a unitary vision in order to have meaning. Meaning is the product of a group of people working together for some common end with common agreement about the sorts of things that count as evidence, principles, and progress towards the end, but disagreements about the best interpretation that unites it all into a whole. What the *Zelda* fan community does is to create a deeper and richer experience by investing meaning in the games they seek to explain.

Level 5

Time and Space
in Hyrule

10

Three Days in Termina: *Zelda* and Temporality

LEE SHERLOCK

We might say that as a series, *The Legend of Zelda*, and perhaps all of us players too, have an obsession with time. A simple glance at the history of titles indicates how central the idea of time has become to the series: for example, *A Link to the Past, Ocarina of Time, Twilight Princess*, and *The Phantom Hourglass*.

Endless debates rage among fans over the proper chronology of the series—which Link killed what villain in what order? Are there two parallel universes containing two distinct timelines? It's enough to make a Hylian's head spin.

This is made all the more confusing when the games toss away the idea of linear chronology. In *The Ocarina of Time*, Link opens the Door of Time leading into the Temple of Time, with an assist credited to the Song of Time (see what I mean about obsession?). The result is that the player skips ahead seven years to find an "adult" Link ready to take on the causes of sage-freeing and Ganon-battling. After Ganon's dismissal, Link goes back in time to return the Master Sword and happily discards those tacked-on seven years of age.

I'm most interested in looking at a *Zelda* game that makes no reference to time in its title but offers the most to think about philosophically in terms of time and temporality: *Majora's Mask* on the Nintendo 64. *Majora's Mask* is the spiritual successor to *Groundhog Day*, only Phil Connors is played by Link instead of Bill Murray. Before you start groaning, let me pitch it this way. Link has a measly three days to save the land of Termina from certain doom and destruction. This destruction is threatened by the Skull Kid, who is trying to force an anthropomorphic, deranged-looking moon to crash into Termina. Sound better than Punxsutawney Phil? I thought so.

Eternal Recurrence—It's a Long Three Days

Friedrich Nietzsche's concept of "eternal recurrence" or "eternal return" has generated a good deal of discussion on the philosophy of time, even though Nietzsche did not devote much space in his work to explicitly laying out the concept. In *The Gay Science*, Nietzsche frames the idea of eternal recurrence as a hypothetical construct in which one's existence in the world, and the world itself, are repeated infinitely under the same conditions. As Nietzsche puts it,

> What, if some day or night a demon were to steal after you into your loneliest loneliness and say to you: "This life as you now live it and have lived it, you will have to live once more and innumerable times more; and there will be nothing new in it, but every pain and every joy and every thought and sigh and everything unutterably small or great in your life will have to return to you, all in the same succession and sequence." (*The Gay Science*, Vintage, 1974, p. 273)

If you've played *Majora's Mask*, this should sound eerily familiar. *Majora's Mask* presents the player with a three-day cycle in which a number of heroic missions must be completed to save Termina. Why three days? Link is asked to grab Majora's Mask to give to the Happy Mask Shop owner, but apparently he's on a tight schedule. To further complicate the matter, these three days are actually *not* three days; rather, they are three simulated days that take less "real" time to elapse. As Jesper Juul notes, videogames often rely upon two parallel time structures, "*play time* (the time the player takes to play) and *event time* (the time taken in the game world)."[1] This distinction allows gamers to eat and get a wink of sleep sometimes, rather than having to devote actual years to build a city or raise an army. In the case of *Majora's Mask*, one day of event time takes up about eighteen minutes of play time, giving the player roughly fifty-four minutes to finish the entire game.

If that seems too little time to finish a *Zelda* game, Nietzsche is here to help us out! Assuming that the player goes back in time

---

[1] "Introduction to Game Time," *First Person: New Media as Story, Performance, and Game* (MIT Press, 2004).

before the three days are up, this time cycle then repeats itself over and over. Link is sent back to Clock Town, in the same spot in front of the Clock Tower, and the people of Termina go back to whatever business they were up to before. At the beginning of the cycle, the message "Dawn of the First Day—72 Hours Remain" appears. This and subsequent messages every twelve hours of event time not only serve as temporal reminders to the player, but also suggest the entire chronology as repeating itself within the same frame of reference; this is "the" First Day, not "another" or "a different" First Day.

Why Eternal Means You

The intellectual "test" of Nietzsche's eternal recurrence is one part of the concept. His basic argument is that in a system with a finite number of forces, if we allow for an infinite amount of time, a point will be reached where the same events happen in the same way and the same order, repeated infinitely. However, using this as a thought experiment is not exactly how Nietzsche intended it. As Graham Parkes argues in the introduction to Nietzsche's *Thus Spoke Zarathustra*,

> the thought of eternal recurrence is not to be taken as something to think about intellectually (Can it be true? Does everything really recur?), but rather as a possibility that can inform and clarify our existential choices: 'Rather than looking towards distant unknown bliss and *blessings* and *reprieves*, simply live in such a way that we would want to live again and want to live *that way* for eternity!—Our task steps up to us at every moment.' (Oxford University Press, 2005, p. xxv)

The existentialist spin means that all of us, as individual agents, are responsible for determining what meaning to take out of our own existence, and this meaning is created from individual *choices*. If we go back to Nietzsche's demon from *The Gay Science*, the existentialist choice arrives in how one responds to the demon's proclamation of eternal recurrence:

> Would you not throw yourself down and gnash your teeth and curse the demon who spoke thus? Or have you once experienced a tremendous moment when you would have answered him: 'You are a god and never have I heard anything more divine.' (pp. 273–74)

Eternal recurrence is a good place to start thinking about temporality in *Majora's Mask*, because the temporal structure of the game relies on the idea of repetition, of Link going back in time to re-encounter the same three days over and over. In this way, the game resists the conventions of linear, serial narrative; playing the Third Day after logging twenty hours of gameplay is not "later" than a Third Day played near the beginning of the game, at least in the narrative sense. The three-day cycles are not sequenced one after the other, but rather it is implied that they temporally coexist.

Despite the grand and bold efforts of Nietzsche, I would be remiss if I left the discussion of temporality here. A number of philosophers have raised interesting ideas about the philosophy of time that can be used to productively question and challenge Nietzsche's version of eternal recurrence, and the structure and design of *Majora's Mask* likewise present elements that complicate a mapping of eternal recurrence onto the game's temporality.

Putting That Ocarina to Good Use

The first item complicating the matter is the very thing that allows the three-day cycle to happen in *Majora's Mask*: Link's Ocarina of Time. After learning the Song of Time, the player can have Link play the song on his Ocarina to save the game and go back to the beginning of the First Day. The Ocarina, though, can also be used to *manipulate* the flow of time, thus disrupting the three-day cycle. Play the Inverted Song of Time, and the flow of time is changed to half its normal speed. The Song of Double Time skips directly ahead to the next evening or morning, depending on the current place in the cycle.

Unlike other games where the player can select the game speed or even control the pace of event time mid-game (as in various versions of *SimCity*), *Majora's Mask* allows the player to manipulate the flow of time entirely within the diegesis of the game. The player is not simply intervening with a controller or interface to change the pace of the game; rather, we can read this as a narrativized event with Link playing his Ocarina to somehow alter the progression of linear time.

What this suggests is that each iteration of the three-day cycle is *not* a repetition, in the sense that the same events occur in the same order. Additionally, three days is no longer really three days. With the player's ability to manipulate time in this way, the "day" cannot represent a stable period or amount of time—it could take more or less time to elapse. The illusion of repetition is still here; the same clock at the bottom of the screen runs, and the player still gets the same reminders to serve as notification of how many hours are left. However, the player knows that time in this context functions more as a commodity to be controlled ("out of time, better withdraw some from the Bank of Time") than an absolute limiting factor.

This presents an alternative scenario to that of the Eternal Recurrence Demon. The addition of an unstable, day-hopping, forward-backward, slow-fast mode of temporality throws into question the idea that events must eventually occur in the same, infinite sequence. The very idea of sequentiality is no longer reliable. Similarly, while some philosophers have gone along with Nietzsche's formulation of eternal recurrence, some have found it more problematic. For example, David Wood writes in *The Deconstruction of Time*,

> As it stands, I am not persuaded either that a finite number of elements could not generate an infinite number of qualitatively different states, thus making the necessary infinite repetition of each state a non sequitur. Nor, if everything were to be repeated infinitely, is it clear why it must take the form of exact cycles of complete sequences of permutations." (Northwestern University Press, 2001, p. 16)

The ability to manually manipulate time, as presented in *Majora's Mask*, is just another theoretical problem tossed onto the heap.

Might this also problematize the existential implications of eternal recurrence? After all, is Link really faced with the pressure to affirm a life repeated infinitely, which might lose all significance? Nietzsche argues, "The question in each and every thing, 'Do you desire this once more and innumerable times more?' would lie upon your actions as the greatest weight" (*Gay Science*, p. 274). With control over the flow of time, this "greatest weight" loses its command. It seems a new existential crisis is in place for Link in *Majora's Mask*, one that questions not one's desire for eternal recurrence, but whether the meanings of experience and self are even identifiable within the interrupted flow of time—whether the fragmentation of time represents an unrecoverable loss.

Can I Keep This Cool Stuff?

In *Majora's Mask*, Link doesn't have to sacrifice all of the goods he's accumulated when he goes back to the beginning of the First Day. Many of the less significant items, such as Deku Nuts, are lost during the time warp, but Link gets to keep major items such as masks and weapons. Rupees are lost as well, but Link can deposit them in the Clock Town bank and withdraw them after returning to the beginning of the cycle.

True, it would be an incredibly frustrating experience to accumulate all those amazing items only to surrender them an infinite number of times. The implication of this, though, is that each iteration of the three-day cycle is again marked as a *non*-repetition. As the player gradually accumulates items, the "past" can be recognized as an absence of those materials. For example, when Link didn't have the Hero Bow (referenced as an earlier state), he would have killed various enemies using alternative means and items. Each iteration of the cycle becomes an effort to gain affordances in the game through items and materials, and at the same time, create a historical account defined in context of the items taken (or given back, as the case may be). The player's save game file works in coordination, creating a player history that is rewritten as the game is played, with gradually more items completed and more quests fulfilled. The save game is a linear construct, and even though the three-day cycle moves the game events and narrative forward, there is ultimately a return to linear time when the player walks away.

In *The Deconstruction of Time*, David Wood draws attention to Jacques Derrida's claim that "there is (and could be) no alternative concept of time, no nonmetaphysical concept of time" (p. x). As metaphysics is concerned with the nature of the world and attempts to define a basic reality, we can consider the possibility of time being abstracted outside of the world, its reality, and our experiences and thinking within the world. Derrida doesn't think it's possible, and I would suggest that *Majora's Mask* points to a few conditions that lead down the same path.

The presence of material items that Link takes across time cycles suggests that time is marked by materiality in some way; even if we were to conceive of a "pure" repeating time cycle, that cycle still depends on the materials within it. In this case, time cannot be separated from the metaphysics of Termina. To collect things takes time, and time is represented by the objects themselves as a form of Link's and the player's investment. Time also depends upon its own representation in the game.

There needs to be some way of marking out time, of keeping track of it, even in the face of an unstable time flow. The clock at the bottom of the screen keeps constant track of time, and the Clock Tower visibly ticks away. Time is also invoked with the messages and warnings given to Link, serving as a reminder of how much time is left before the moon crashes into Termina. Even the choice of days as the unit of the repeating time cycle reveals the necessity of imposing some kind of representation.

The Material Value of Time: Why Time Is Money

Even though *Majora's Mask* uses the concept of an infinitely repeating time cycle, there's not just one but two endpoints that the player must negotiate. The first endpoint is that of the cycle: Link must return to the beginning of the cycle before seventy-two hours have passed, or the moon hanging over Termina wins the game, and *no one* wants that to happen (well, maybe the Skull Kid). The other endpoint is that determined by progress in the game, including items collected and dungeons cleared of evil forces. The player plays with the understanding that the game events are not really infinite and will not allow for unending repetition. This establishes a hierarchy of values, for both the economy of in-game items and for the treatment of time as negotiated by the player.

Let's face it: some items are just more fantastic than others. Would you rather face Ganon equipped with the Master Sword or the Slingshot? In *Majora's Mask*, the value of items is determined not only by their various functions and affordances, but by the amount of time the player has to invest to get them and whether they will be erased by the jump in time cycles. What's the point in spending two days digging around and stockpiling extra Deku Nuts if they're going to disappear anyway? Thus, time functions in the game to create a system of values whereby some items are privileged just because of their "permanent" materiality, but removing the limitations in play would fundamentally change the relationship between time and value. Rupees act as a special case, because they do not themselves aid Link in any way and are lost at the end of each cycle. However, Link can store them in the bank and later withdraw them to buy shop items. Given this unique position,

rupees act as a kind of *deferral* where the player can alter the normal relationship between time and value—rupees can be deposited
over time until the player might decide to cash them in, either inter-
mittently or all in one moment.

Event time in the game is also given value, although certain
moments in the narrative take on more value than others. As part
of the time cycle, people in Termina go about a routine that is
repeated over the course of three days. Characters will arrive in
specific places at specific times, and this becomes predictable after
observing characters and their interactions with the environment.
Link also has a Bomber's Notebook, which serves as a kind of
schedule to plan out where and when to meet people and accomplish game objectives. The result is that the player needs to keep
an eye on the clock for time-sensitive game events, because if they
are missed, Link needs to somehow get back to that point in the
cycle.

Although there's quite a bit to do in Termina, there are often
cases where the player is simply "killing time" while waiting for a
specific part in the cycle to come up. Time is entirely devalued in
these intervals despite the urgency of the seventy-two-hour clock;
there is the sense that time is of the essence yet not worth much
more than trimming the bushes or occupying it in some other
menial way. What we have here is an existential alienation, opposite from the desire that Nietzsche proclaimed one could affirm for
eternal recurrence—this is more a subjugation to time and the ways
in which it controls life.

Although repetition seems at work here, it's not repetition itself
that creates such boredom, but rather having to kill time to get to
the "important" moments. Juul points out, about the experience of
time in videogames, "repetition or triviality of choice will make
time be experienced as unimportant, *dead* time (time will drag)" (p.
139). In either case, time is experienced as death, which is represented not by a temporal endpoint suggesting a final loss of life but
by the loss of the meaning we assign to time as a form of value.

An Uncanny Sense of Time

As I have suggested so far, temporality in *Majora's Mask* is charac-
terized by a series of tensions, if not outright contradictions, that
challenge familiar notions of time. The same three days recur over
and over, yet this reveals itself as a *non*-repetition; time is urgent

and of the highest value, yet there are moments where time is dead. Temporality also figures into issues of identity—for example, the "existential crisis" that Link faces is tied to the fragmentation and disruption of time.

These challenges to naturalized notions of and associations with time work to defamiliarize our experience of time, introducing an element of the *uncanny*. I would argue that *Majora's Mask* operates with an uncanny temporality, one that not only introduces alternative time structures but makes the idea of time unfamiliar (yet familiar), strange, and frightening. Sigmund Freud, in his essay "*Das Unheimlich* (The Uncanny)" notes the link between the uncanny and what is unfamiliar: "the German word '*unheimlich*' is obviously the opposite of '*heimlich*' ['homely'], '*heimisch*' ['native']—the opposite of what is familiar; and we are tempted to conclude that what is 'uncanny' is frightening precisely because it is *not* known and familiar."[2] Freud goes on to complicate the argument beyond this semantic analysis, claiming that "this uncanny is in reality nothing new or alien, but something which is familiar and long-established in the mind and which has become alienated from it only through the process of repression" (p. 217).

In their discussion of the uncanny, Andrew Bennett and Nicholas Royle argue that the uncanny "has to do with a *troubling* of definitions" and with "making things *uncertain*: it has to do with the sense that things are not as they have come to appear through habit and familiarity, that they may challenge all rationality and logic."[3]

In the opening sequence of *Majora's Mask*, the representations of time used throughout the game (for example, the clock that appears at the bottom of the screen) have not yet appeared. The sense of urgency and the "moving forward" of time are directed by Link's chasing after the Skull Kid, who has just pilfered his Ocarina. The uncanny moment comes in where the Skull Kid transforms Link into a Deku Scrub. The aesthetics of the scene are pervaded with hauntings and notions of the uncanny: darkness, the multiplicity of other Deku Scrubs surrounding Link, and a reflection of Link's new Deku face. Although the Deku Scrub is clearly an unfamiliar bodily form for our hero, Link simultaneously maintains

---

[2] *Writings on Art and Literature* (Stanford University Press, 1997), p. 195.

[3] *Introduction to Literature, Criticism, and Theory* (Harlow: Prentice Hall, 1999), pp. 36–37.

familiar parts of his appearance, such as the green cap. Shortly thereafter, the Skull Kid taunts Link by saying, "You'll stay looking that way forever." The Skull Kid's remark uncannily plays on the double senses of "looking," as both Link's personal appearance and the act of looking or gazing upon an object.

The Skull Kid also makes reference to time here—this transformation of the body will last forever, and it has a quality of permanence that transcends time itself. At this moment a few different forms of the uncanny converge. Link's bodily transformation is connected to his anxiety over a loss of identity as well as the temporal dimension of this loss. There seems to be no possibility of recovering Link's identity because of the permanence linked with "looking that way forever." When Deku Link later approaches the Happy Mask Shop owner, the owner says, "I know of a way to return you to your former self. If you can get back the precious item that was stolen from you, I will return you to normal." Link's identity is once again connected to time here; his anxiety over his new form is addressed through the idea of returning, of going *back*, to a self of the past.

The way Link is introduced to the idea of controlling the flow of time is also marked by the uncanny. The scarecrow Pierre addresses Link by saying, "Yo! Hey, baby! I'm a stylin' scarecrow wandering in search of pleasant music. Time will pass in the blink of an eye if you dance with me. If you like, baby, we can forget the time and dance 'til dawn!" There's a double loss present in this scenario: the loss of time as it is collapsed into a single moment, and the loss of awareness as one "forgets the time," or even losing oneself *in* time. This possibility resists the urgings of Link's fairy, Tatl, and other characters, who constantly remind Link of the value of time and the need to be hyper-aware of the status of time.

If talked to again, Pierre informs Link of a song he can teach him on the Ocarina: "By the way . . ., I know of a mysterious song that allows you to manipulate the flow of time. . . . Do you want to learn it?" If the player selects "yes," Pierre continues, "If you play that strange song backward, you can slow the flow of time. And if you play each note twice in a row, you can move a half day forward through time." The descriptions of these two songs (referred to as the Inverted Song of Time and the Song of Double Time) invoke the uncanny with the usage of "mysterious" and "strange," suggesting deviation from the familiar. The structures of the songs also disrupt the familiar, especially the repetition that constitutes the Song of

Double Time. Bennett and Royle argue that "the uncanny involves, above all, strange kinds of repetition: repetition of a feeling, situation, event or character" and note the "idea of the double" as being one form this repetition can take. The idea of time being double not only manifests itself in the game in various ways, but can also be considered in the relationship between event time and play time, where cyclical and linear time operate simultaneously.

These two songs are the only songs in the game that are "hidden," that is, the player does not need to learn them to advance major events in the game narrative. Bennett and Royle discuss the idea that "alternatively, the uncanny is—in the words of the German philosopher F.W.J. Schelling—that which 'ought to have remained . . . secret and hidden but has come to light'." (p. 40). The act of discovering these two songs and enacting these forms of control over temporality is thus an uncanny event. In effect, the "secret" of time has been unlocked, which holds amazing power but also threatens an unthinkable loss, of both self-identity and time itself. If time is lost, Termina is lost.

The Triforce Holds a Prosperous Future

Time is one of the great themes of the *Zelda* series, and I have only covered a fragment (nay, a shard!) of the possible discussions of temporality here. Introducing the philosophical implications of time might help us arrive at some new conclusions. Once that's done, we'll have a whole set of defenses against the petty accusation that we waste too much time playing *Zelda* and other games. Trust me, the day will come. Soon. Just wait.

11

Constructing NESpace in *Zelda*

JOAQUÍN SIABRA-FRAILE

Here we are.

We have explored deserts. We have climbed mountains and crossed oceans. Spiders have bitten our bodies, stone statues and laughing skeletons have attacked us. We have discovered secret passages. We have fought and defended ourselves. We have discovered a world. Finally, here, in the deep, the last door. Behind it, the fierce and not so good-looking Ganon awaits. He isn't going to allow us to rescue Zelda that easily, and we know that. But we have a made a choice. We aren't afraid of those moldy skulls on the floor from the heroes that came before us. We aren't worried at all about the shapes the torches make or those echoes coming from the deep. We aren't. Are we?

We open the door. We open the door and step into . . . a ministerial office?

"Come in," says the official to Link without standing up. He is staring at him through his big glasses, while stamping application forms.

"Excuse me . . . I wish . . ." stammers Link. An office in the dungeon? Well, this is really astounding. The official is signing documents, papers fly here and there.

"I'm in hurry, you know? What're you looking for?"

"Well . . . I want . . . I want to rescue Princess Zelda from . . ."

"Wait. Have you already filled the form 48? If she's from a Royal Family, you must bring the Royal Communication FG3, and the Family Book too."

"I only have this magical sword . . ."

"It's useless. Come back tomorrow with all the forms filled. From nine to two. Have a good day."

"All right . . . See you tomorrow . . . Wait! Who are you?"

"Smith, Level 9 Official, Tax Inspector."

"What are you saying? But . . . Something's wrong . . . This can't be happening. . ."

"Why can't this be happening?"

"You can't be a Tax Inspector . . . You must be a deadly monster with blooded-eyes!"

"I do my best . . ."

"But you can't be here!"

"Here? Where?"

"In Hyrule!"

"Really? And *where* is Hyrule? You know, this is a videogame and I can be wherever I want . . ."

"But you can't . . . you can't . . . be here" says Link scratching his head under the green hat.

That's the question. Why can't he be there? What can Link say to show him that a Tax Inspector is out of *place* in Hyrule?

Hyrule . . . Where?

What are we looking for in *The Legend of Zelda*? We only want to reach the place where Princess Zelda is waiting for us (quite patiently). But if an adventure is something more than a walking through, it's because it costs some effort to get there. If there weren't any obstacles, Zelda would be rescued at the very beginning of the adventure, and this would be a very short, very poor videogame. So what's an obstacle? What does "effort" mean in *The Legend of Zelda*? Keep in mind that Link is only a sprite (that is, a two-dimensional animation or graphic) moving on the screen— only a sprite: truth is sometimes hard. In order to become an adventure, the movements of sprites like Link and others should make things happen. And we, by virtue of our control over Link, should help those things to happen (after all, *Zelda* is not a film, but a game). So, again: what does it mean "to make something happen" in a videogame? How do those things that happen force us to make an effort? And *where* are we, when we are with Link?

With these questions in mind this chapter will explore the difference between physical space and logical space in the original

Zelda for the Nintendo Entertainment System (NES), eliciting further questions. How are things in *Zelda* related? What is the nature of the logical space in *Zelda*? How is the logical space in *Zelda* and the logic of language related? Can Ludwig Wittgenstein's famous notion of "language game" help us out at all? Can playing *Zelda* be a language game?

Physical Space and Logical Space

Let's imagine that Hyrule is an apartment building. Zelda is our next-door neighbor and her door is open, so it isn't very difficult to enter her apartment. The distance between Zelda and us is zero. But what if the door is locked and Zelda has lost the key? Physical distance between her door and ours is the same, but now we have to go to the locksmith and ask him very gently (it is 2:00 A.M.) to come with us.

The obstacle (a locked door) has forced us to look for a solution in another place. The distance between our door and the locksmith's has been added to the distance between our door and Zelda's. Now let's imagine that the locksmith is stubborn and wants us to pay him a hundred rupees. Now the locksmith has himself become an obstacle, so we must go to the street and chase some confused oktoroks for rupees (they aren't used to the city). Then we go back to the locksmith's store, we pay him for the key and, finally, we return to Zelda's door. The physical distance between our door and Zelda's is always the same; however, a different sort of distance between her and us is growing and growing. . . . Each obstacle moves Zelda further from us, but each obstacle is actually a requirement to be satisfied. A locked door is a condition met by the key. But the key is another requirement: we need the locksmith. But, surprise, the locksmith adds a further condition to be satisfied: he needs money. As the requirement links increase, the *distance* between Zelda and Link increases too.

What kind of distance is that? We can't measure it in meters or inches, but, more accurately, in the number of requirements that must be met. Instead of a physical distance, we are dealing with a logical distance.

A locked door requires a key. A key requires rupees. Rupees are obtained by hunting oktoroks. Hunting oktoroks requires, at least, a wooden sword. The wooden sword is given to us by an old man. This requirement chain is what creates the experience of effort, and this chain also allows the progress of a storyline (the plot of *The Legend of Zelda*).[1] It allows a virtual space to be built, a logical space that works, in some sense, like a physical space.

Things and Conditions

The chain of conditions, from the start until the end, is the game. These conditions are not abstract, but concrete: a locked door, a merchant that wants money, a magical sword to be found. Each thing in the game is in fact a condition, a restriction on Link's movements and, consequently, on the player's. What kinds of things does *Zelda* have to deal with? There are objects, characters and items.

Objects are those things used for drawing the scenery: trees, rocks, bridges, stairs. But there are objects that block Link´s movements (trees, rocks, locked doors, or rivers), and there are objects that allow them (bridges, stairs, opened doors, and caves). Combined properly, objects on the screen draw a path and lead our movement.

Characters move in a concrete way: an octorok moves every direction but diagonally; a leever comes out of the ground and moves around a bit, then goes back under it for a few seconds; a keese flies around like a bat, slowly and diagonally. Enemies make the area they inhabit dangerous to Link. And friendly characters, likewise, make the space they inhabit safe and secure.

Items are things that Link can carry (keys, rupees, hearts) or get from a friendly character (bombs, potions, bows, swords). And, of course, they can be used. Items don't determine Link's movements as objects or characters do, but they also construct the space of Hyrule by improving Link's abilities.

Objects

Without rocks, trees, or locked doors Link could move freely around the screen with no restrictions; he could go everywhere. Unfortunately, this everywhere is nowhere. The space would be empty, and if we could move in any direction, there wouldn't be

---

[1] Yes: the Wiimote controller is tiring. We aren't talking about weariness, but about effort. Effort has a purpose, and we can make a story with purposes, but not with weariness. Maybe it seems impossible, but there were videogames before the Wiimote.

any reason to move in a concrete direction. If we found an empty screen, we would throw down the controller, annoyed. But what if there's a tree, only one, in the middle of the screen? Some spatial relation will be created. This is the point.

Link can be near the tree or far away from it, on the right side or on the left. If there is a tree row, we have a path. If there are a lot of trees, like a forest, Link will be lost in a maze. Notice that each tree added on the screen is a possibility of movement subtracted for Link. So if we continue filling the screen with trees, we'll have completely blocked Link. he won't be able to move anywhere because there won't be any empty space. Such a thing in a videogame wouldn't likely be a great success.

Therefore we have, on one hand, the empty space, that allows free movement (and this is boring). On the other hand we have a blocked space in any direction (and this is boring too). The videogame designer has to decide how many objects and enemies to put in the screens, because the way they are distributed gives us different movement possibilities. A screen is a concrete space configuration.

- The tree and the rock are Link-sized, so they block Link's movements in the same manner and he must go around. Trees and rocks stop the enemies' shots, but also ours. Sometimes, a secret passage is hidden under them, and we need to burn the tree or to bomb the rock. If the function is the same in both cases (blocking Link's way), why didn't the designer use only trees or only rocks? What is the reason for distinguishing them by coding different sprites? A game programmer doesn't like to waste any effort, if he or she can. Well, Hyrule is so wide that there are forest areas, mountain areas and even ocean areas. But what makes a tree different from a rock isn't only the way they look, but also (and that's the point in a videogame) their functionalities, the actions we can do concerning those objects. A tree and a rock are more than atrezzo and are different from each other in *Zelda* because the tree burns and the rock explodes. And that means in terms of Link's actions we need a candle to burn a tree, and a bomb to explode a rock. Bombs and candles are obtained in different ways. So trees and rocks need to be distinguished using different sprites, because Link bears a different relation to each.

- The Hollow Tree blocks Link's movements, as trees or rocks do, but it also allows us to go to underworld. So, it merges some functions of the tree sprite with some of the door's. Note that both stairs and hollow tree lead us to an underworld place (caves, dungeons) in contrast to the overworld. But stairs must be discovered, whereas hollow trees are visible. In other words, stairs require bombs (if hidden by rocks) or candles (if hidden by trees), but hollow trees don't force us to use any object as a condition to go down. Why? Because stairs lead into an old man's cave, and this is good (he gives us presents), and the hollow tree leads us into a dungeon, and this is bad (it's full of dangers). So, the stair requirements are a form of price. And the hidden place the stairs leads into is then qualified as valuable. Therefore, both stairs and hollow tree connect underworld and overworld, but in a different way. And that's why they have different sprites.

- We can only cross the water areas through bridges (over a river) or if there is a dock (at sea). The difference? Well, oceans are wider than rivers, but this fact is translated into *The Legend of Zelda* as follows: Link can use the bridge freely, but using the dock requires the raft. Quantity of water is not as important for the player as the conditions he is forced to meet. Similarly, water and mountains are almost the same thing because both block our way into wide areas of the screen. Again, the difference? On the water surface zolas can appear (they pop up, shoot and dive avoiding our arrows) and nobody else but zolas; in the mountains we can found tektikes jumping, or there can be hidden caves or, sometimes, rocks fall and roll from above. So, because of that, water and mountains are different things in *Zelda*. They allow different things to happen. It isn't useful for game playability trying to imitate all the characteristics of real water by copying it into Hyrule; it's wiser to select those characteristics that are interesting for, and relevant to, Link's adventure. In real life, water freezes and we can walk over it. In *Zelda*, water doesn't freeze or boil, nor is it even wet. Water in *Zelda* is that thing with a blue appearance that blocks our movement, that has zolas in it, that can be crossed only through certain points (bridges, docks) and only if certain conditions are met (rafts). This is the meaning of "water" in Hyrule, and nothing else.

- Doors, stairs, and docks are peculiar. We said that trees, rocks and rivers block our way, inside a single screen. Doors, stairs, and docks block the way or allow passage, but between different screens. Therefore, as we'll see, they are working on another level regarding the construction of space. Some objects are used for building screens, others for connecting screens.

So, sprites are something more than graphics imitating a landscape: they can be seen as a summary of the things we can do with them. Sprites are the sign (in short, the name) of those actions (the meaning). And we usually use different names for different meanings. A tree is different from a door in *Zelda* because they restrict Link's movements in different ways. We can think about putting various sprites together. A combination of ten trees, two rocks, and one bridge will determine a concrete path, different from a combination of nine trees, one rock, and two bridges. There are a lot of possibilities regarding the construction of spatial relationships, using only a handful of sprites.

Characters

Suppose we are in a screen with some trees, some rocks, a river, and a bridge. Link has to walk around the trees, avoid the rocks, and cross the river. So Link's movements depend on the space configuration, and this configuration is the screen. But trees, rocks, and rivers affect Link's movements. On the other hand, enemies affect Link himself.

If a tektike manages to bite Link, a life heart will be lost on the life-meter. If Link dies, he certainly won't move: that's the strongest limitation to his movements. Consequently, we (as gamers) try to avoid the enemies. So, objects are directly limiting Link's movements by blocking the way, but enemies do it indirectly by threatening his life. An area with an enemy in it makes that area dangerous, and so we avoid it. This dangerous area is alive with the enemy. Therefore, if dangerous areas are moving, secure areas in the screen can't remain always the same: when an oktorok goes up, the lower area in the screen becomes safe; when the oktorok goes down, Link will be secure in the upper area.

And if this weren't enough, there are usually a lot of enemies in a screen. The distribution of safe and dangerous areas inside a screen (the restrictions to Link's movements) is never static but always changing. In this way, what could have been a mere atrezzo turns into an alive, dynamic, interesting space.

Some characters are friendly. The old man, the merchant, and the medicine woman all allow us to obtain items (as a present or by paying some money). They aren't harmful, so the caves where they live are secure places. Differences? The old man gives us items for defending ourselves, the merchant sells us items for unblocking our way (bombs), and the medicine woman sells us... medicine. Their functions aren't the same. The place where they live is defined, in fact, by these functions: the old man's cave is the place where we can obtain the sword or the bow; the medicine woman's, where we can get potions. In other words Link goes to the old man's cave because he wants the sword, not because he wants to visit the old man. The old man is only the symbol of the cave function: a place for getting arms.

So a place is defined by the objects in it (rocks, trees, water) as well as by the characters that live there. Oktoroks and ghinis appear only in Hyrule overworld, whereas keeses and likelikes live only in dungeons. In this easy way, two big areas are defined: the overworld and the underworld. At the same time, in the overworld ghinis stroll near graveyards and oktoroks watch the mountain areas: they don't mix. In the underworld, keeses and likelikes inhabit different dungeons. The differences between overworld and underworld concerning the characters are also related with the differences between objects. In some way, each character requests a scenery type, and each scenery type suits concrete characters: a zola only makes sense in the water, a leever only on and in the ground, and a ghini near graves. But in what way?

Think about a book. In English we can say that the book can be read or flicked through, bought or lent, criticized or praised. Some actions suit a book well, but others don't suit it at all: we can't drive a book on a road, nor use it to make a whole in the ground. It is the car that can be driven. It's the shovel that can be used for making a hole. Not a book.

Each word is related with some others; they have some sort of familiarity. A set of words with this familiarity is called a semantic field. This is important, because we usually can't link words from different semantic fields. The words 'spoon', 'fork', 'knife', and 'pan' belong to the semantic field of kitchen tools (and so too do the verbs about cooking) and don't belong to the semantic field of swimming. The words 'fir', 'sock', and 'reindeer', as different as they are, belong to Christmas. Realize that in the semantic field of Christmas, verbs related with a fir (we can decorate it, or illuminate it, or put gifts around it) are far different from verbs belonging to carpentry (we can cut it, polish it, varnish it, build a chair with it).

The way characters and objects are related in *The Legend of Zelda* is similar to the way words are related in semantic fields. Characters make movements and perform actions in certain places and not in others. A zola that pops up out of the water, attacks, and then dives can't live in a tiled dungeon floor because nobody can dive into a tiled floor. The videogame designer has to decide where the characters live and how they behave. The designer has plenty of rules to choose from, but once the decision is made, the videogame must obey them. Otherwise, the gamer won't be able to play: nothing will make any sense, and no virtual space will be built—there will only be colored things moving on the screen. And Hyrule in *The Legend of Zelda* is a well built, well designed world.

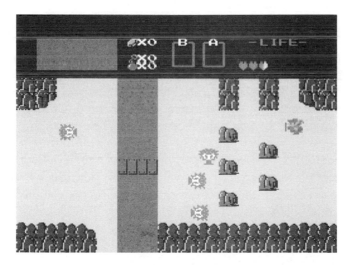

Link Explores the Overworld (The Legend of Zelda, *Nintendo, 1986)*

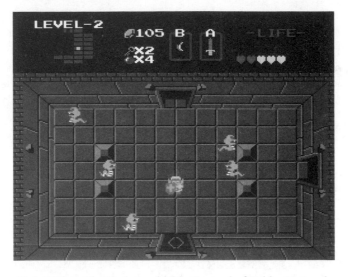

Link Explores the Underworld (The Legend of Zelda, *Nintendo,* *1986)*

Items

Items modify Link's abilities. We can see this on the score (number of hearts, rupees, bombs, and keys) and the inventory. Both are a measure of the power of Link, because each item allows Link to do certain things he can't do without them.

- The Key, the Bomb and the Candle are used to open a blocked way. A key opens doors (surprise!), a bomb destroys rocks blocking hidden passages and a candle burns trees blocking hidden stairs (well, now yes: surprise!). But in *The Legend of Zelda* we find locked doors, and we do know where the keys can be used, whereas we don't know where candles or bombs can be used (only few rocks and certain trees are correct, not whatever). If keys *only* were available in Hyrule, Link could open doors, but there couldn't be hidden places such as passages or stairs, because we couldn't reach them without bombs or candles. So the Candle and the Bomb allow space to be qualified.[2]

---

[2] Similarly, the raft and the ladder. The raft allows Link to cross the water and get to another location from a dock, turning a blocked space onto a free space. It is therefore equivalent to the key, but in other context: the overworld of Hyrule and, more precisely, the aquatic areas. The ladder allow us avoid narrow obstacles, precipices or rivers, inside the screen.

- The Map and the Compass don't concern Link movements, but they concern the gamer's conception of Hyrule. The Map and the Compass give us a representation of Hyrule's spatiality. The map shows the level layout. The compass points, on the map, to the screen in which the level boss is hidden. This seems like only an aid for the player, but in fact map and compass are also tools for the construction of Hyrulean virtual space. Think about a city map: there are bus stops, museums, schools, the city hall . . . Well, the bus stop is in the map? Not at all, only its symbol. The representation doesn't have to be similar in appearance to a school or a town in the city, but it has to give us a diagram, an outline of the spatial relations between the real schools, museums and bus stops. Those relations are what we need to find our way: distances, streets names, symbols. The map of Hyrule in *Zelda* is representing the virtual space of Hyrule as a real space. And it works. It works because we look up this map in order to be guided through the dungeons, as if those dungeons had the same structure in reality that the map is showing, as if those dungeons in *Zelda* were there (but, where?) even before we reached them . . .

- The sword, the shield, and the bow change the way Link faces the enemies. Armed with the bow, Link can attack from a distance remaining in a secure area. The magic sword is more powerful than the wooden sword, and so it takes Link less hits to kill an enemy. Thus he can spend less time in a dangerous area. The shield simply turns a dangerous area into a more secure area. We said that enemies made an area secure or insecure, so modifying the relation between Link and oktoroks, moblins or ghinis is changing the way Link lives in this space.

Three Ways of Building Virtual Space in *Zelda*

Objects, characters and items are related in a way that makes sense for Link's movements. Because of them there are dangerous or secure, hidden or obvious, valuable or common, populated or uninhabited, underground or surface places. Objects, characters and items are the bricks that the space we call Hyrule is built with.

But in the way that bricks, beams, and tiles cannot be mixed when building a house, objects, characters, and items can't be mixed either. In the house, foundations come prior to the beams, beams allow walls to be erected—then the roof can be tiled.

If we don't pay attention to this order, erecting the walls first, or using beams as bricks, the house will fall. A house requires a certain structural order. In *Zelda*, objects, characters, and items must be regulated in a similar way—that is, if we want the space created to support itself and make sense. In terms of the player the space has to be playable—it has to understand our actions and it has to be able to respond to them in a coherent way. Space must follow some meaningful rules, so that our actions can be meaningful. But these rules build a functional space aimed at our actions, more than a representational space aimed at the appearance, at the resemblance to reality. There are some videogames, maybe graphically not very appealing, but creating a complex world inside of them, much more absorbing, fun and immersive than other 3D games, plenty of cinematics but deadly boring because they can't recreate successfully an interactive world. We all know some of those infamous remakes . . .

So objects, characters and items are organized in different ways in *Zelda*. Each organization, each structure, is a screen. There are screens for mountains, woods, desserts, caves, and dungeons. Each screen is different from the others. And all these screens aren't mixed anyhow, but are connected following a concrete order, a logical order. Other kinds of order, of course, respecting the order of objects, characters, and items follow *inside* a screen. In the English language, words are combined with an order (not just any order) to build phrases. Those built phrases can be combined into paragraphs, and the paragraphs into a whole discourse. Usually, words are a grammar topic; phrases, the subject of syntax; paragraph and discourse, rhetoric. Grammatical order, syntactic order, and rhetorical order follow different rules. But note how syntactic order uses words from grammatical order, and how rhetorical order uses phrases (like bricks) from syntactic order. In the English language three levels can be recognized (word, phrase, and discourse) that work together.

What has this to do with Hyrule? Think about objects, characters, and items working like words. When properly combined, a screen results—something similar to a phrase. Screens are connected in levels in a similar way that phrases are linked in paragraphs. Finally, all the levels, sequentially ordered, are the map of Hyrule as a whole, as discourse is composed of paragraphs.

But this is only an analogy. Language is used to say something, and space in Hyrule, although constructed according to rules, doesn't say anything. We can't properly align language with these rules used by the designer for articulating objects, characters, and items in a screen, screens in levels, and levels in a map. But they are rules, so the designer can't be arbitrary or chaotic in his construction of space. On the contrary, these rules make the Hyrule space coherent and sensible. We *understand* this space.

Regarding the rules, we can't call them a language, but there is a similar principle in operation. Maybe we should call it, in Ludwig Wittgenstein's words, a "language game." This term is "meant to bring into prominence the fact that the 'speaking' of language is part of an activity, or form of life." Wittgenstein used "language-game" to designate simple forms of language," consisting of language and the actions into which it is woven", and unified by family resemblance. Some examples given by Wittgestein are: "reporting an event; giving orders, and obeying them; describing the appearance of an object, or giving its measurements; constructing an object from a description (a drawing); presenting the results of an experiment in tables and diagrams; making a joke; telling it; solving a problem in practical arithmetic."

The point is that using a language is seen as a sort of action, and therefore actions (not only words) could be meaningful. How many kinds of language games are there? "There are 'countless' kinds", says Wittgenstein, "countless different kinds of use of what we call 'symbols', 'words', 'sentence'. And this multiplicity is not something fixed, given once for all; but new types of language, new language games, as we may say, come into existence and others become obsolete and get forgotten."[3] If Wittgenstein had played *Zelda*, he would surely have called it a "language game."

We've seen how objects, characters and items are organized inside a screen. Let's go to the level. Now the bricks for building space aren't objects, characters, items, but each unitary screen built previously with objects, characters and items. How are these screens organized?

---

[3] Quotes are taken from Wittgenstein's *Philosophical Investigations* (Malden: Blackwell, 2001), sections 7 and 23.

The Level

Like parts of a puzzle, some screens fit with others. There are two ways of fitting: in the underworld, the door, and in the overworld, the path (in some cases, the dock and the stairs). So we have four-way screens (four doors, one at each side; or three paths at south, east, and west, and a dock to the north . . .). And we have three-way screens, or two-way screens. But we need at least one way, because a screen with no ways at all—well, how can we enter it? It's sort of like thinking about a square puzzle piece: it won't fit with the other pieces and it can't be part of the puzzle.

We are talking about puzzles, and not by chance. In fact, in *Zelda* all the screens in a level form a layout: an eagle (first level) or a skull (ninth level). We don't realize it when we are exploring the dungeons—we are busy avoiding enemies and trying to get the next door. But if we manage to obtain a map (or we draw it patiently on some paper as we move from one screen to the next), we'll notice that underworld levels take on the shapes of wizard hats, spirals, helixes, snakes, or letters.

In order to be connected, two screens must share at least one access (if Link goes out of a room through a door on the left, he will come in the next room through a door on the right of the screen). This rule seems obvious. A four-ways screen can be connected with four screens. A three-ways screen, with other three . . . A lot of different levels can be built by combining four-ways, three-ways, two-ways, and single-way screens using this simple rule.

The second rule says that enemies we have killed or items we have picked up in a screen never appear again in that screen. It seems like a rule for constructing a screen, but in fact it's a rule for constructing a level since it's a restriction regarding the things we find when we return to a screen previously visited. And every rule concerning links between screens also concerns level building (going from one screen to another). This rule achieves some sort of permanence in space.

According to the third rule, a level is completed only when a boss is defeated. In the dungeons of *Zelda* are hidden Aquamentus (first level), Manhandla (third level), Gohma (sixth level), or Ganon himself (ninth, last level). Each boss has different movements and attacks patterns. Unlike tektikes, oktoroks, ghinis, zolas, and leevers, the bosses are unique. By defeating a level boss we get a Triforce fragment. When we join all the Triforce fragments the game ends. So, when we get a fragment from a boss, we have nothing else to do in that level. We have passed the dungeon. That space is no longer a challenge; now it is conquered. This rule allows us to feel a sense of achievement.

By applying only a handful of rules, levels of many variations can be constructed.

Because of these rules the space in *The Legend of Zelda* is coherent, and we can act with consistency in this space, foreseeing the consequences of our actions.[4]

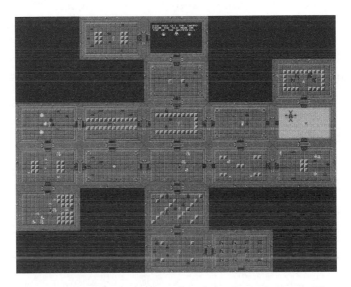

This representation was produced by Daniel Engel (The Legend of Zelda, Nintendo, 1986).

The Map of Hyrule

How are the levels themselves organized? One behind the other. First level, then second level, then third level. We can't reach a level if we haven't completed the previous levels. It's that simple. The nine levels are underworld dungeons. We need to return to the overworld when we complete a dungeon. So, in total, there are ten levels: the overworld is the main level and the nine dungeons are

---

[4] Nowadays "screen" should be applied to the playable space between two level-loading points. Note that the structure sprite-screen-level-map was a good solution to memory shortage and slow processors in old consoles.

levels linked one-to-one with the main level, but not connected between themselves. This is the classic star-organization, found in so many adventure videogames: a central level links all the others. Of course, a lot of layouts are possible (tree layout, net layout). Think about the high number of possibilities when creating the space of a world, even if the screens are very similar or the levels are uniform. And we get this high number by applying only a few, simple structural rules.

So, where is Hyrule? If we think about space as a set of things, then Hyrule isn't anywhere and can't be anywhere. If we think about space as a set of requirements for our actions with things, then Hyrule isn't *in* a place; instead, Hyrule itself *is* a place. It's a place, as virtual as you want to describe it, but real. It's real because we can act in it based on the constraints of various rules.

Hyrule Regained

"So, Mr. Smith? You can't be here because you don't meet any condition in this world." "I do! I'm Smith, Ninth Dungeon Official-That-Stamps-Deadly-Photocopies! Don't cheat me!"

"You're wrong. No character stamps anything here. A character can bite, as tektikes do, or can throw arrows as moblins do, or can use boomerangs like a goriya. But nobody stamps here in Hyrule of *The Legend of Zelda*."

"Are you sure?"

"What could a character stamp? Items in this world are swords, keys, shields, rafts, ladders, rupees and things like that . . . Don't ask for more, we are in a NES! Where could I find, here, a birth certificate? If you wanted me to give you one as a condition for freeing Zelda, I couldn't rescue her, and this videogame would be nonsense!"

"I see . . . Then, go ahead. Zelda is waiting you behind that door."

"No! A boss battle is required for completing a level. And you should be the final boss!"

"I'm getting tired . . . Let's fight, then, if it's necessary."

"Are you going to fight with a rubber stamp? Fool! You should be more . . . Hyrulean."

"Can I throw fire balls? That's the dream of my life . . ."

"Good idea. Anything else?"

"Yes. Now I become invisible, and I'm going to attack you from behind . . ."

"Of course. Just a little question . . ."

"Whatever you want . . ."

"May I call you Ganon?"

"Certainly."

"Much better," says Link, drawing his sword.

Level 6

Treasures of the
Hyrulopolis

12
Zelda as Art

LUKE CUDDY

Any English scholar will tell a classroom full of students about the genius storytelling of Faulkner, or the expert character development of Dickens. Art Historians will, likewise, impress upon you the beauty of a Monet, a van Gogh, or a da Vinci. But if you're a gamer sitting in one of these seminars, your thoughts may go back to the four hours of *The Legend of Zelda: Twilight Princess* you played the day before. And you just might start making the comparison between Faulkner's *The Barnburner* and the *Zelda* story-line, or between van Gogh's *Starry Night* and the Zelda backgrounds.

To protect your grade, you should keep your mouth shut; the fact that a student played *Zelda* for four hours isn't going to impress most ivy-league professors. But maybe you're onto something. Before intellectual rotten fruit is pitched at me, realize I'm not advocating that a comparison actually be made between *Zelda* backgrounds and a Monet, or between *The Barnburner* and the plot to *Twilight Princess*. But I am saying that there is a way the *Zelda* games can be considered art.

Most of us, probably, think of paintings and museums when we think of art. Maybe we think of what might be called new age or contemporary art: red cubes, paintings of nothing, steel bars, metal constructions—objects sometimes scornfully referred to as "the turd in the plaza." How, if at all, can videogames eke their way into this illustrious category? Bearing in mind that many people already do consider videogames art (as evidenced by their inclusion in the subcategory "interactive art"), I'll also remember that this is a book of philosophy, and that philosophy, in particular the philosophy of art, has neglected videogames.[1]

Games and Paintings

Some philosophers say that in looking at paintings, and other art objects, we play a game of make-believe, much as a child plays games of make-believe. In a child's game of "Pirate" a flagpole might become a ship's mast. It's in some sense a rule of "Pirate" that the flagpole be a mast, the stick in the child's hand be a sword, a piece of cardboard be a shield, and so forth. Appealing to rules and the fact that such games create a world separate from the real one, these philosophers find striking similarities between games and art.

Kendall Walton discusses the resemblance between looking at pictures and looking at things.[2] When we look at things in the world we pick out certain visual features. Some things are harder to recognize than others and, therefore, require more time and patience. When I look outside my window, I see the doors of other apartments, but to see whether or not the doors have panels, door-bells, or eyeholes, I will have to look closely.

Similarly, when we look at a painting we pick out certain features, and others take more time. With a van Gogh, for instance, I might at first see a hat and a bottle, but only by looking closely do I see the red of the label on the bottle, or the black band around the hat. We look in a particular way when we look at a painting. We play a visual game of make-believe. We willingly enter a fictional world and this world changes depending on the sort of painting we are viewing.

In looking a particular way, and in picking out the relevant features, we play by rules—a similar principle is in operation when a child's hand becomes a gun due to the fact that he's playing "cops and robbers." Depending on what style of painting we're looking at, there are rules that determine the way we look at that painting. Styles can thus be understood as the rules or instructions for play-

---

[1] With the exception of Aaron Smuts who also notes the failure of aesthetics and the philosophy of art to deal with videogames. "Are Videogames Art?" in *Contemporary Aesthetics* 3 (2005), available at www.contempaesthetics.org/newvolume/pages/article.php?articleID=299, accessed May 4th, 2008.

[2] In *Mimesis as Make-Believe* (Harvard University Press, 1991), pp. 304–313.

ing a particular art-game, and different kinds of rules go with different kinds of paintings. We would never look at a Realist painting the same way we look at a Cubist painting. If we assessed a Cubist painting with Realist rules, Cubism would have failed as a style since, in Cubism, a table simply doesn't look like a real table. This is the sense in which we play a game of make-believe when we view a certain style of painting; we play by the rules of that style.

It isn't that there are rules *in* the painting. There are two worlds. There's the world in the work (what is actually happening in the painting), and there's the everyday human world we all live in, from which we formulate the rules of the game we play in relation to the painting. Once you recognize the rules of the game (that is, that you are dealing with a Cubist painting) you start playing.

Games and Zelda

When we play any of the games of the *Legend of Zelda* franchise, we're clearly playing a game. But does this playing relate to a game of make-believe? Is there a similarity between the way we look at paintings and the way we look at Zelda? Are there rules that tell the gamer how to look at a Zelda game?

There is a similarity if we modify the word "look," if we take "look" to refer to a mindset or perspective that the gamer allows to govern his playing of Zelda. Isn't it true that there is a way of playing Zelda games that's distinct from playing, say, sports games, or fighting games? A brief story will show why I am inclined to say yes.

A friend of mine with minimal gaming experience recently started playing videogames. The other day he happened to be playing *A Link to the Past* on my old Super Nintendo (SNES), and he couldn't figure out where certain things (like the heart pieces) were. What he didn't understand was that to play a role playing game such as *A Link to the Past*, you need to explore and try out newly acquired items everywhere you can.

For example, if you just got the hookshot in a dungeon—and you know that its primary function is to pull Link across a hole he would otherwise fall into—once outside the dungeon you should explore different areas of the game with the hookshot. When you come across holes, you should experiment with the hookshot to see if there is something on the other side of the hole to pull Link across. This guarantees that you use the hookshot to the fullest and acquire all the possible heart pieces it can get you. You might find other interesting items or places by exploring with the hookshot, or by exploring with any newly acquired item. What you find may not be crucial to beating the game, but, first, the items may be useful (as opposed to necessary) and, second, the experience of exploring uncharted areas of Hyrule can be rewarding in itself.

In *A Link to the Past*, once you get the flippers you can begin to swim in the water that you couldn't otherwise swim in. Without exploring the water with the flippers you could never find the bottle underneath the bridge. You can store potions and fairies in bottles and, though they are useful, missing one is certainly not going to prevent you from progressing in the game.

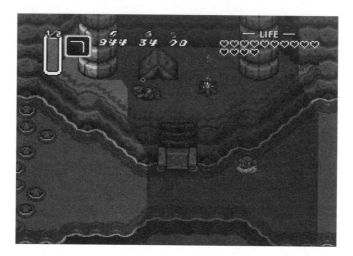

*Link comes across a secret area only found after exploring with the flippers. The character sleeping by the tent has a bottle (*A Link to the Past, Nintendo, 1991*).*

But the experience of inadvertently swimming under the bridge to find a man with a bottle sleeping in a tent is a rewarding experience in itself. Unless you understand the need to explore and experiment with newly acquired items, you're not going to get this experience. If someone tells you where to go it won't be the same; if you look it up on a walkthrough it won't be the same. And if you play the game like a sports game—your primary objective being the stealthy defeat of an opponent—you're certainly not going to get the full experience of the game.

What my friend didn't understand in his playing of *A Link to the Past* is something that most role-playing gamers *do* understand before playing. In this sense his playing of *Zelda* is similar to a person's viewing a Cubist painting with a Realist set of rules. As long as we remember to modify the meaning of "looking," there is certainly a way that gamers "look" at *The Legend of Zelda* before they play it, before they enter the onscreen Hyrule.

Most experienced gamers will not play, say, first-person-shooters like the games of the Doom series in the same way they will play a *Zelda* game. Although exploration is important in Doom (since there are secrets) it doesn't take precedence the way it does in *Zelda*. When a gamer plays Doom, she's mostly concerned with shooting up monsters and not getting killed. And getting an item like the Rocket Launcher in Doom does not demand that the gamer explore its possible uses to the degree it does in *Zelda* with the hookshot or flippers.

This exploration-factor might be appropriately labeled *freeplay*. We can tentatively define freeplay as gameplay not directly connected with the goal of beating the game. How far removed from this goal one has to be to achieve freeplay is a good question, one that is probably impossible to answer conclusively. Still, this impossibility doesn't rule out the fact that there are clear-cut cases of freeplay.[3]

Sometimes freeplay is even encouraged. In *Ocarina of Time* the gamer is told by townspeople to "kill some time on Hyrule Field." The point of this is so that when you come back to the town something is changed, allowing you to progress further in a small series of puzzles. But the gamer doesn't have to experience it as a means to an end, and perhaps this is, in some way, what the game designers intended. After all, they put all this work into making Hyrule Field visually appealing and, maybe, they don't want it to go unnoticed.

The Blue Candle Not the Red: Games in a New Light

Leon Rosenstein, like Walton, discusses games and art.[4] Rosenstein's take is a little different. He discusses viewing an art

---

[3] Freeplay probably falls somewhere in between ludus and paidia—see Chapter 6 in this volume.

[4] "The Ontological Integrity of the Art Object from the Ludic Viewpoint," *Journal of Aesthetics and Art Criticism* 34:3 (1976), pp. 323–336.

object (for example, a painting) as tantamount to playing by the rules of a game like soccer or baseball. Both the artwork and the game set up a world that is spatio-temporally distinct from the real world. This is like Walton's game of make-believe. But for Rosenstein, the work has integrity when it sets up or creates a world that is sufficiently distinct from the real world—unfortunately, a work does not always do this successfully.

Rosenstein uses the terms "transparent," "translucent," and "opaque" to refer, basically, to how well the sensuous medium of a given artwork breaches the gap between the world in the work and the real world—how well the sensuous medium brings the world to us (the viewers).

To understand what it means for a work to "bring the world to the viewers," consider the following example. In a van Gogh painting, the physicality of the paint is thick and raised, and this effectively brings the world of the painting to our attention in the real world. If we are willing to play by the rules—if we look at a van Gogh according to the rules of the van Gogh, and not as we would look at a Salvador Dali painting—we will be able to receive that world. The physical medium is neither too distracting (too sensuously present so that we cannot get beyond its physicality) nor irrelevant (too insignificant so that its presence and nature pass us by as if non-existent); the medium is "translucent."

When the sensuous medium fails to successfully breach the gap between the world in the work and the real world, it is either "transparent" or "opaque." A transparent work fails to create its own world because it is more message than anything else. Think about war propaganda. Even if such propaganda is poetic, by virtue of its intention to coerce, it is transparent; its message overrides the medium. An opaque work is at the other end of the continuum; it's too much a part of the world to be separate from it and create its own. An example of this is Duchamp's infamous *Fountain*—a disconnected urinal placed in a museum.[5]

By broadening Rosenstein's idea of the "sensuous medium," I think his ideas can be made to apply to *Zelda*. The sensuous medium can, in addition to referring to the physical medium of an artwork, also refer to the onscreen world of Hyrule. Thus, the bal-

---

[5] Actually, *Fountain* is also transparent since it is an art theory masquerading as an art object. I am grateful to Leon Rosenstein for bringing this to my attention.

ance between transparency and opacity takes on a wider scope, and translucence can be produced in a videogame.

Think about early videogames like *Adventure*. We can call this medium (the onscreen world) "transparent" since it seems to be nothing in itself but a vehicle for communicating a message. It's only slightly removed from a written explanation of character movement.[6] And we can call a game that is too lifelike "opaque" since it doesn't separate itself from the real world.

We're reminded here of *Second Life*, a virtual environment which allows users to engage in real-life activities like attending school lectures, dancing, or exercising. Is this opaque? Probably, but since many do not consider *Second Life* a game, and it's videogames that we're considering here, I will not come to any conclusions about its status as art. If the growing complexity of videogames causes them, at some point, to become indistinguishable from reality, then they aren't going to produce the same sort of gaming experience. A game that is opaque behaves as though it *is* life. Friedrich Nietzsche, in fact, thought art was *better* than life.

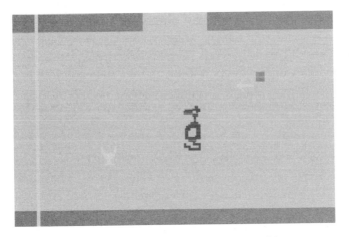

The avatar—the little grey dot in the upper right of the screen—encounters one of the chicken-like enemies (Adventure, Atari, 1979).

---

[6] I acknowledge the importance of *Adventure* to the development of videogames, but its seminal value in this respect and its value as an art object are two distinct investigations.

Features of Hyrule

The previous section brings up an important question: what are the features of the onscreen world of *Zelda*? Some of the more salient features of the *Zelda* games are the following: the avatar, the music, the exploratory terrain, the characters, the enemies, the bosses, and the story. A game's translucence, seemingly, depends on these features. But what's special about them? Why do certain features appeal to people? Well, why is a mountain more appealing than a cement driveway? And why would some people (admittedly a lesser number) say the opposite?

I'm not going to pretend I can list the objective qualities that make some features of the world "beautiful" or "appealing" and others not. Most significantly—though the features taken separately might also be appealing—it's the *combination* of the features that makes a game translucent. A combination of appealing elements leads to a translucent game. We can at least discuss what some of these individual features are for clarity, without going into detail about the nature of their appeal.

Beginning with the avatar, we have the exalted Link. Whether it's the Link from the original *Zelda* or the graphically detailed Link of *Twilight Princess*, something drives the gamer to control that little green-hatted, elflike character. It seems like there's a reason gamers are driven to control Link, beyond the fact that he's the sole avatar in the game. One possibility is that Link *is* a little elf-looking creature in green. Our culture typically associates elves with escape from reality (even if the only reason for this is that elves do not, in fact, exist). The opportunity to play as an elf, due to its connection with fantasy, is more inviting to the player, the player is more likely to be drawn into the onscreen world.

The *Zelda* music is incredibly appealing. I have friends unwilling to power on their Nintendo consoles unless they know the music will be heard. The music draws the gamer into the game; it brings the world of the game to her by setting up the appropriate atmosphere. There are some movies in which the music is indispensible, without which there is no movie—the Johnny Greenwood–composed Paul Thomas Anderson movie, *There Will Be Blood*, for example. It's the same with *Zelda* games. How does the music do this? In the original *Legend of Zelda* there are two primary tunes: one for the outside world and one for the dungeons. The tune for the outside world is more uplifting in that it utilizes

major musical keys. The dungeon tune is darker and more mysterious in its use of minor keys. In both cases the music sets up an
atmosphere that can, potentially, draw the gamer in.

The backgrounds and exploratory terrain are especially pleasing
to the eye in the newer *Zelda* games due, of course, to the
enhanced graphics. But even the earlier *Zelda* games have their
moments. *A Link to the Past*, for instance, is only the third game of
the franchise and yet the terrain the gamer gets to explore is often
visually appealing, as in the case of the waterfall area of the light
world where the flippers are found. But newer games such as *The
Legend of Zelda: Wind Waker* have long drawn out sailing
sequences where it's hard for any gamer to ignore the beauty of
the surrounding ocean and sky.

Characters, enemies, and bosses run the gamut. There may have
been a deficiency in the first two games of the franchise in terms
of characters, but beginning with Sahasrahla from *A Link to the
Past*, the characters acquired more complexity and personality.
Sahasrahla is a wise master who communicates with Link telepath-
ically. Figures of the wise master type typically carry an air of mys-
tique and command respect. The gamer is therefore drawn to
Sahasrahla out of mystery and reverence.

There are many other characters with some sort of similar appeal
(eccentric townspeople, witches, rambunctious children). From the
first game on, there were appealing enemies continuing throughout
the rest of the franchise. In the original, the red and blue Darknuts
(the shielded knights) were challenging, but interesting to fight
based on the attack sequence required to defeat them (that is,
attacking them perpendicularly). There were also appealing bosses
from the beginning of the franchise. It's hard for a fire-breathing
dragon not to draw the gamer in, even if out of fear or awe.

Then there's the story. What could be cooler than trying to
defeat an evil guy named Ganon, rescue a princess, and find scattered pieces of a once united Triforce in order to save the land of
Hyrule? Moreover, the story draws one in more effectively due to
the fact that the gamer can participate in it. Once the gamer defeats
a level, she's usually given some sort of indication from one of the
characters that there are other parts of the storyline which can now
be attended to (sometimes this is referred to as "unlocking" the storyline). The gamer has *control* over the story to the extent that she
can decide when, and to some extent in what order, to unlock elements of the story.

I already expanded the reach of translucence to apply to the onscreen world of a videogame in addition to the sensuous medium of a painting. Thus, a videogame is translucent if the relevant features of the onscreen world *together* can bring the entire world of the game to the gamer, if the gamer "looks" in the appropriate way. The less appealing the features of the onscreen world as a whole, the less likely the game is translucent. Although the features individually can be appealing, it's the features of the onscreen world together that, in Rosenstein's terminology, make a game translucent, transparent, or opaque.

So *Adventure* is not transparent just because it's simple graphically, but because together its backgrounds, music, avatar, and characters do not satisfactorily create a sufficiently distinct world. The world the gamer experiences comes across as little more than information in the form of shapes, sounds, and movements. Of course, a *Zelda* game, too, is a form of information but the appeal of Hyrule as a whole keeps this fact out of the gamer's psyche.

All the Nintendo-developed games of the *Zelda* franchise create an onscreen world that is translucent, a world that is transferred to us by means of its translucency, that is neither opaque (like adventure) nor transparent (like a game that is too real). In the case of games like the original *Zelda* where the backgrounds and exploratory terrain are less appealing (probably due to simpler graphics) and, therefore, contribute less to the translucence of the onscreen world, there are other features, like music and enemies, that make up for the lack of appeal in terms of backgrounds and exploratory terrain.

Zelda and the Aesthetic Experience

All of which is to say, if you haven't seen it coming, that playing the games of the *Zelda* franchise can lead to an aesthetic experience, on par with an excursion through the modern art museum.

Introducing the idea of the aesthetic experience also introduces the problem of defining it; it's notoriously hard to define. Some might say they had such an experience at the Opera; others might say it happened at a Metallica concert. Some might say they had the experience when they dropped acid; others might say it happened while looking at a Monet painting. Chances are if you try to get any of these people to put their experience in words it's going to come out like gibberish. "I felt one with the universe," "My body was a vessel," "The truth of the world was revealed to me," are some typical responses.

There are philosophers who will tell you that this experience is simply heightened perception or heightened emotion. Some say it's nothing but paying very close attention to an object, and that there is no aesthetic experience at all.[7]

But even if what everyone calls the aesthetic experience is no more than paying attention and can be broken down into emotion and perception, it's still one hell of an experience (at the level at which we experience it). Anyone who has had one can verify it. Maybe it's different for everyone. Maybe it can't—and shouldn't— be broken down into parts; that is, maybe it's subjective. But the subjectivity of the experience itself does not entail that what produces it is also subjective. Erwin Panofsky argues that there are objective properties in art objects that demand to be experienced aesthetically.[8] Basically Panofsky says that even if the aesthetic experience is subjective, there are objective qualities in certain objects that demand our subjective attention. So maybe we sound like a delirious drunk when we try to put into words our experience at the Metallica concert, but this doesn't mean there wasn't something demanding to be experienced aesthetically when Metallica went into the "Orion" solo.

Do any of the games of the *Legend of Zelda* franchise have objective qualities that demand to be experienced aesthetically? I think so. Based on what's been discussed thus far, I would posit three objective properties of art. Drawing from Walton, the first property is the ability to be "looked" at in a particular way. We look at van Goghs differently than we look at Dalis. The second property is translucence. A work must set up a spatio-temporal world that is sufficiently distinct from the real one. And the third objective property is the clear possibility of freeplay. While there isn't enough space here to fully develop this notion and its role in other artworks, freeplay is clearly present in some videogames. Typically, role playing videogames have large gameworlds to explore and thus they allow the gamer to engage in gameplay not directly connected with beating the game (freeplay tentatively defined).

---

[7] See George Dickie, "The Myth of the Aesthetic Attitude," in Phillip Alperson, ed., *The Philosophy of the Visual Arts* (Oxford University Press, 1992), pp. 30–40.

[8] See "The History of Art as a Humanistic Discipline," in *The Philosophy of the Visual Arts*, pp. 469–477.

The games of the *Zelda* franchise have the ability to be "looked" at; we don't "look" at *Zelda* the same way we "look" at *Doom*. *Zelda* is translucent; all the games of the franchise create a spatio-temporally distinct world that draws the gamer in. And *Zelda* clearly has the possibility of freeplay as elucidated by the discussion of the flippers from *A Link to the Past* above.

A Win for *Zelda*?

So does this settle any possible debate about *Zelda* and art? The next time we stick our heads in an art museum should we see a Nintendo Wii console and TV positioned strategically next to a da Vinci? For that matter, does this mean videogames are art? Has the gamer won? Should the ivy-league art historian walk away in shame, pathetically clutching his print of *Starry Night?*

It might be objected that I have simply defined *Zelda* into its art status. And yet, the framework I've developed here is rather restrictive. There are many paintings which are not art according to this framework—many realist paintings, for example, might not make it as art. And not all videogames fit the bill. Think about games like the original *Super Mario Brothers* for the NES. Where is the freeplay in this game? Clearly, the gamer has to beat these side-scrollers left to right, one level at a time. Sure, warping is possible, but this can hardly be argued to distinctly establish freeplay. The gamer is bound by a time limit and can't even go backwards. She is constrained by the game (*Super Mario Brothers 2*, however, might count as art). What about *Tetris?* How much freedom does the gamer have here? This doesn't mean such games are not fun, fulfilling activities. But art? It doesn't seem likely.

The take home point is this. The question as to whether videogames are art is a more in-depth question than the traditional aesthetician might imagine. Just as some paintings are art and some are not, so some videogames are art and some are not.[9]

---

[9] The ideas in this chapter are more fully developed in my dissertation, "Videogames as Art: One Interpretation Using *The Legend of Zelda* as a Case Study." Master's Thesis, San Diego State University, 2008.

13

Hyrule's Green and Pleasant Land: *The Minish Cap* as Utopian Ideal

PAUL BROWN

In the beginning God created the heavens and the earth.
Now the earth was formless and empty, darkness was over the surface of the deep, and the Spirit of God was hovering over the waters.
And God said, "Let there be light," and there was light.
God saw that the light was good, and He separated the light from the darkness.

—*The Holy Bible: Genesis*

A long, long time ago . . .
When the world was on the verge of being swallowed by shadow . . .
The tiny Picori appeared from the sky, bringing the hero of men a sword and a Golden light.
With wisdom and courage, the hero drove out the darkness.

—*The Legend of Zelda: The Minish Cap*

In 1516, the writer (and Saint to be!) Thomas More used the word 'Utopia' for the first time. It was the title for his fictional tale of a faraway land. The word means, literally, 'no-place'—from the Greek '*ou*' ('non') and '*topos*' ('place')—but, as the faraway land was pretty much More's idea of a perfect society, the word has since become a catch-all term for a "better" or "ideal" place.

Thinkers have explored numerous variants of this ideal from Plato onwards. What is perhaps less well documented, however, is that utopias have also been explored by the likes of Shigeru Miyamoto and Eiji Aonuma. Their Utopia simply takes another name. Usually Hyrule. Well, Utopia by any other name would smell as sweet. So before we take a close look at the worlds of *The*

Legend of Zelda and in particular the world of *The Minish Cap*, let's take a little time to consider Utopia's characteristics.

The Order of Utopia

Despite its literal meaning, Utopia has, at its heart, a physical presence. It is this physicality that facilitates the lofty ideals suggested above. This is why most imagined *nowheres* have very clearly been *somewheres*. The idea of physical Utopia is at its most concrete in the concept of the city, or ancient Greek state of the "polis" discussed by the early Greek philosophers Plato and Aristotle. In the writings of these philosophers, the structure of a city allows for an ordered, ethical way of living.

This is certainly something that survives in more recent Utopian thinking. Utopian scholar Robert Fishman, for one, suggests the place of the city simply cannot be overestimated: "The ideal city is a working plan for the total transformation of society in order to achieve a natural harmony—*the* natural harmony—of man, society and the environment."[1]

While portions of Plato and Aristotle's visions have drawn criticism, particularly the advocating of slavery and the state's near-totalitarian sphere of influence, much of the more praiseworthy elements can be found in the towns of *The Legend of Zelda*.

A Platonic Relationship

Plato's Utopia is presented to us through the dialectics—the elaborate, back-and-forth dialogues in his famous work, *The Republic*. Here, the ideal city-state is broken down into three classes: producers, auxiliaries and guardians. As 1940s critic Lewis Mumford put it, there's no chance of social advancement for those in any of these classes: "Plato makes his Republic immune to change: once formed, the pattern of order remains static, as in the insect societies to which it bears a close resemblance."[2]

The "best" become the leaders (guardians), those who don't quite make the grade become guards (auxiliaries) while the rest become the workers (the producers). It is on the whole, however,

---

[1] Robert Fishman, "Utopia in Three Dimensions," in *Utopias* (Duckworth, 1984), p. 95.
[2] Lewis Mumford, "Utopia, the City, and the Machine," in Frank Manuel, ed., *Utopias and Utopian Thought* (London: Souvenir Press, 1973), p. 7.

a just society, with the guardians gaining no more material profit than the producers. Notably, for the first time in such thinking, women were at least considered as equals. Such a consideration is evidenced in this question posed in Book V:

> "Are dogs divided into hes and shes, or do they both share equally in hunting and in keeping watch and in the other duties of dogs? or do we entrust to the males the entire and exclusive care of the flocks, while we leave the females at home, under the idea that the bearing and suckling their puppies is labour enough for them?"[3]

The Minish Cap shares something of this social structure, albeit rather loosely. The Royal Family and its inner circle (The King, Princess Zelda, and Minister Potho) could be seen as the guardians. The guards which patrol the castle, the castle gardens, and (once Vaati makes his evil intentions known) Hyrule Village, could be viewed as auxiliaries. Lastly there are the workers, most of whom are, literally, producers: the market traders Beedle, Brocco and Pina, the blacksmith Manon, and other artisans such as the shoe-maker Rem. While this last category has been broadened to allow for other professions in this only-just post-agrarian society, its spirit remains true.

Also, while it may not be quite the fifty-year program of study recommended by Plato (for the guardian class only, mind you), education is clearly important in Hyrule. There are in fact two educational establishments. The school, presumably, caters to academia and its importance is signified by the generous size of its allotment of land. The Sword School provides the practical skills required by Hyrule's many guards and, of course, its Hero of Men, Link.

Hyrule, then, is something of the Platonic ideal. In other ways it is much more. Here, there is no slavery and, as indicated by Princess Zelda's high status, there is absolutely no ambiguity regarding sexual equality.[4] The greatest positive departure may be Hyrule's porous social structure. There may still be no firm move-

---

[3] Whether Plato actually believed in equality is a debate that still rages. While Plato believed that women and men had different strengths and weaknesses, some scholars detect misogyny in the words of the *Republic* and question whether its author believed in true sexual equality. For readers wishing to join the debate, Book V of *The Republic*, from which this extract comes, is a good place to start.

[4] For a more elaborate look at Princess Zelda's sexuality, see Chapter 19 in this volume.

ment between classes, but there *is* a sense of easy integration. As noted in the dialogue between The Princess and Master Smith, Link is Princess Zelda's childhood friend. She visits him at the start of the game, and there is the feeling that such a thing is a common occurrence, as evidenced in Master Smith's words to the princess, "The Minister is sure to be worried about you. You know how he gets." This is reinforced by the fact that a "lowly" artisan such as Master Smith can deliver goods to the King in person: "I do have an errand at the castle"

Most telling of these fluid social boundaries is the ease with which Princess Zelda can move about the festival. She is left alone. No one asks for her autograph, no one crowds her and the paparazzi are nowhere to be seen. Furthermore, the carefree manner in which she walks among her people shows she is accepted as one of them: "Link, there's a storyteller here! We should stop here and listen to—Oh! I wonder what's over there . . ." Can anyone think of any real-world situation where this would be so? Even in other games with similar settings, this ease is unusual. Master Smith might note that the Minister will be worried about Princess Zelda leaving the castle, but Chrono Trigger's Princess Nadia, for instance, is kicking against much more restrictive bonds. So overprotected is she that the court is quick to put on trial for abduction someone she befriends while out on a jaunt.

Indeed, the state's authority, or control, in this, and for that matter all instalments of *The Legend of Zelda*, is extremely relaxed. It is comprised of a two-tier structure of Crown and Local Government: the existence of Mayor Hagen suggesting at least some democracy at work within the guardian, auxiliary and producer template.

The movements of the people help to reinforce a sense of easy living and personal freedom: Hylians wander the streets at will, sip milk at Mama's Cafe and in at least one corner of the town, between Romio and Julietta, romance is in the air.[5] There's also an abundance of evidence that personal economic enterprise is encouraged—the traveling salesman at the fair, the machinations of the property developer Gormon, and Malon with her handcart of Lon Lon Milk all help to suggest that Hyrule is a place where the free market flourishes. This would be unfortunate and anti-Utopian

---

[5] Adding to the charm of this situation is their waiting on their pets' approval for the match.

of course if the nature of such business was morally suspect. However, none of this enterprise encroaches on the freedom or happiness of the people. The proprietor of the treasure game shop, Barlov, uses anything but the hard-sell ("It's ten Rupees for one try, if you still want to throw your money away on such a terrible pastime . . . I would really just save it if I were you."). Also, those managing to rent from the landlord are delighted ("Oh fabulous! And it's so clean and new!")

Hyrule is also a place where people desire to be. This is evidenced by the spacious and welcoming—with a free gift for every guest!—Happy Hearth Hotel, the aforementioned house-hunters and, perhaps most tellingly, the words of the inhabitants themselves: "I've been on the road for a while. I came back in time for the festival. It feels wonderful to be back in Hyrule again in this joyous time," and "I love festivals. It's like seeing your town transform into another world. It really gives you a chance to think about how well we have it here."

Hyrulopolis

This lack of totalitarianism and the happiness of the citizens to some extent run parallel with Aristotle's vision. Although there are guards everywhere, there is never the suggestion that they are there for anything but the security and well being of the populace. Perhaps even more than these factors, however, is how much in common the *design* of Hyrule town has with Aristotle's Polis.

More so than Plato before him, Aristotle was clear about the physical design of his polis. It should, he felt, be large enough for independence yet small enough to engender a feeling of community and identity. It should be near water so that it can have ports for sea trade and sound defensive measures.[6]

In almost all of these respects, *The Minish Cap* is faithful. Hyrule town occupies one area out of seventeen and can be traversed in a few hundred strides. Yet despite this middling size, it manages to contain everything its inhabitants need: post office, school, library and a multitude of retail outlets all sit comfortably within its walls. That there is also a sense of community here is both implicit in the very existence of the fair and explicit in the following comment made during it: "Phew, preparing for the festival has left me exhausted. Still, I'm just enjoying watching people have fun."

---

[6] See *Politics*, Book VII for more detail.

In terms of security, Hyrule town is also a walled space, allowing for easy defence. The town has only a superficially symmetri-
cal design—invaders who manage to breach the walls will
undoubtedly be confused by a polis that places its market square
so left of centre. There is a river here but no port, indicating con-
fident self-sufficiency and prudent forward thinking. It is enough
for now that this powerful force of nature powers the mill: trade
and military routes can always be opened later if necessary.

In a more general conception of 'the ideal' however, the idea of
Utopia as a town or city is a little limited. There needs to be something more than the polis, something above government, guards
and city gates. This something is in fact some *things*: the natural
and the spiritual.

The Nature of Utopia

If the town, city, or polis is a functional, ordered Utopia, then
nature is Utopia untamed, a delight for the eyes, ears and soul.
Perhaps the philosopher most associated with theorizing the beautiful is Immanuel Kant. Though he wasn't the first thinker to turn
his attention to aesthetic appreciation, he wrote extensively on the
topic and his *Critique of Judgement* is, arguably, the subject's most
influential work. In it, Kant discussed the notions of the beautiful
and sublime. Unlike other things that bring us pleasure, explained
Kant, we don't want to possess, or *do* something with beauty; we
simply want to appreciate it. This simple appreciation he, perhaps
misleadingly, termed "disinterestedness."

All three of Kant's critiques were presented as a method by
which to evaluate our own mental faculties. However, that such a
significant portion of this influential philosopher's words relate to
the beautiful, in nature in particular, underlines the importance of
beauty to mankind. Philosophers and, latterly, psychologists have
often discussed this need for beauty. Indeed, the German
Philosopher and writer Friedrich Schiller, inspired by the horrors of
the French Revolution, noted that exposure to beauty was key to
improving man's moral character. The beautiful, he said, can unite
the seemingly disparate qualities of sensuousness and reason,
famously stating that, ". . . it is through Beauty that we arrive at
freedom."[7]

---

[7] Friedrich Schiller, *On the Aesthetic Education of Man* (New York: Dover,
2004), p. 27.

It's not surprising therefore that the beautiful should be a key element in many fictional Utopias and perhaps even less surprising that the idea of the beautiful Utopia has existed long before philosophy was even 'invented'. Perhaps one of the earliest, well-known literary examples of this is the Garden of Eden. Man was placed in an area of great abundance and beauty:

> Now the LORD God had planted a garden in the east, in Eden; and there he put the man he had formed. And the LORD God made all kinds of trees grow out of the ground—trees that were pleasing to the eye and good for food. (*Genesis* 2:9)

Here, Utopia is a beautiful garden. This is something echoed in many examples that followed from Henry Neville's *The Isle of Pines* to Samuel Taylor Coleridge's *Kubla Khan* and, of course, Miyamoto's concept of Hyrule, which in various interviews he has likened to a miniature garden.[8]

The more developed notion of the natural Utopia, like the concept of the polis, also has its source in ancient Greek thought, in the writings of the poet, Theocritus, and the "bucolic" (Greek for "cowherd") poetry he penned. Though Theocritus and his bucolic form first celebrated the simple joys of pastoral life, this theme was most notably explored in the work of those he inspired. Roman poets Virgil and Cattullus, and much later the English Alfred Lord Tennyson produced paeans to the notion of the Idyll or Golden Age, a mythical time and place where man was in harmony with the natural world. The early twentieth century historian Martha Hale Shackford best articulates the source of this blissful union: "An idyll is a picture of life as the human spirit wishes it to be, a presentation of the chosen moments of earthly content."[9]

Much of *The Legend of Zelda* series has this whiff of the Golden Age about it. The environment of the first game is almost completely untouched by the manmade, instead being a world of forest, river and mountain. All subsequent instalments have instances of civilization in the shape of Hyrule town and its satellites, and, as

---

[8] Shigeru Miyamoto has spoken often about his inspiration for *The Legend of Zelda*, referring to Hyrule as a "miniature garden." For a fuller discussion of his creation, it's worth tracking down the recent fan translation (by Zentendo) on the making of the series: *The Video of Zelda: Everything about Zelda*.

[9] Martha Hale Shackford, "A Definition of the Pastoral Idyll," *PMLA* 19:4 (1904), pp. 583–592.

has been noted, this is important. It's equally important that a large portion of this natural world—Miyamoto's ever-blossoming garden—remains. While it's most immediately obvious in the lush grass and dancing pollen of *Ocarina of Time*, the natural world is just as abundant in the lands of *The Minish Cap*. Even though the town is of a perfect size to function effectively, it is the natural landscape that dominates. There are isolated instances of civilization dotted throughout: Master Smith's shop, Lon Lon Ranch, and Percy the Poet's cottage. However, of the seventeen areas in this particular overworld, only two, Hyrule Town and Hyrule Castle Garden, bear significant marks of the manmade. Even then, the constructs are in keeping with the landscape in which they sit: not here the scars of modern architecture that show so little regard for context. Here it can be believed that everything is locally sourced—that the wood and stone that form the foundations of Hyrule town and Castle come direct from Mount Crenel and The Western Wood, an instance of the natural world reaching out to shelter its children. The rest of Hyrule county is a pastoral landscape of creamy pastel shades, a vista of meadow and woodland. It's perfectly possible to imagine finding Comatas—a character from one of Theocritus's untitled idylls—leaning against a tree in The Trilby Highlands, extolling the virtues of his surroundings: "Here be oak trees, and here be the galingale, and sweetly here hum the bees about the hives. There are two wells of chill water and on the tree the birds are warbling . . ." (Theocritus, quoted in Shackford, p. 587)

Even these place-names are important in evoking a sense of romantic solitude. Who can help but wonder about the origins of these names: The Trilby Highlands, The Castor Wilds, and Veil Falls? Their etymology is seemingly lost to time. For the Hylians who wander this way now there remains the beauty of a rugged, rustic paradise found, unspoiled by even the monsters that roam here.

Also, unlike some other instalments of the series—think of the thunderstorms that open *Link's Awakening* and *A Link to the Past*, or the one which accompanies the escaping of Princess Zelda in *The Ocarina of Time*—this world is forever bathed in sunshine. In the world of *The Minish Cap*, night never falls. This is a paradise of eternal light, a permanent summer of love where darkness is reserved for the deepest of dungeons, where only heroes go.

The Spirit of Utopia

The final aspect of this consideration of Hyrule as Utopian ideal is the spiritual or religious. Aristotle pondered the soul and Plato certainly believed in Heaven and Hell in some form, the concepts being central to his idea of justice. In fact, spirituality and religion factor into the work of many philosophers, though very few of them could be said to be in agreement with each other. Some, like Georg Hegel and Søren Kierkegaard, held diametrically opposed views, the former believing God could be understood only through logic, the latter, anything but. For Kierkegaard, God was beyond reasoning and could be reached solely through faith. Even Immanuel Kant, who took pains to ensure that the beautiful in nature was not interpreted as proof for the existence of God, was still a believer.

Religion also crops up both in pastoral idylls, with Pan, the God of shepherds and flocks being most common, and later literary ideal world narratives. Religion is a key feature of More's *Utopia*: the conceit of rewards and punishments for the immortal soul plugging directly into Plato's theories. In such imagined Utopias, and in real life, the purpose of religion is often twofold: societal and personal. It firstly helps to maintain a good and just society, and secondly provides a comfort blanket for the populace: no matter the horrors of this life, a better one awaits. It could be argued that the less defined and rule-bound the religion, the better these purposes are served. The more an attempt is made to dot the i's and cross the t's of a doctrine, the more it is exposed to the rigour of reason and the burden of proof. It is better, perhaps, when religion is vague, fuzzy, and almost out of sight.

This is largely the case with *The Minish Cap*, where artifacts and echoes of religious imagery and myth tug at the edges of the experience. Unlike, say, that other giant of the genre, *Dragon Quest*, the world of *The Legend of Zelda* never presents the practicalities of organized religion. While the former has a chapel in every town providing formality and regularity, the latter has occasional temples that serve as comforting, fragmented hints of something more. *The Legend of Zelda* series also has that mythically suggestive backstory of Din, Nayru, and Farore, which remains in the player's memory, regardless of when she took her first baby steps in Miyamoto's Garden of Eden.

There have been numerous flashes of religion throughout the series—hints at Gods, Angels, and Demons: The Wind Fish from *Link's Awakening*, The Deku Tree from *The Ocarina of Time*, the ubiquitous heart fairy and the near-satanic imagery of *Majora's Mask*. It is in *The Minish* Cap, however, that this suggestion of the spiritual is at its strongest: from the opening prologue (given as the epigraph of this chapter), through Link's numerous dealings with the Picori, to the quest for Earth Elements, and the portals to the world of the Gods themselves. The preferred reading of the prologue is clearly that the Picori are the Godhead, working with Link—himself endlessly reborn—to save mankind. Here is the crux of what makes religion so pleasing a part of this particular Hyrule: the unquestionable goodness of these Gods.

In *The Minish Cap* we have unambiguously benevolent beings, working for the good of humanity: "We thrive on making humans happy. It gives us energy." It is telling that the only instance of negative Picori actions we see relates to the punishment of one who was once their own: Vaati. Ezlo's assistance in helping Link defeat Vaati, the only Picori ever to have fallen, is a symptom of the shame felt by the Minish when humans are harmed at their hands.

The sheer multiplicity of the Picori is also pleasing. This is a God made flesh many times over: the Picori are cheerful pint-sized Christs that, like the secular society over which they watch, walk among all classes alike, albeit largely unseen. This God proffers quantifiable physical help rather than vague and aloof intervention from afar. Here are Christs that inspire such feelings of love, that they have even been afforded the honour of a nickname, the Minish, a sure measure of the affectionate esteem in which they are held. These feelings of love must be inspired by many sources: knowledge of their fight against the darkness; the "good" things that happen when Kinstones are fused; and the abundance of rude health bestowed upon the people. After all, it seems obvious that such otherworldly items such as Kinstones, hidden Rupees and hearts can only be gifts from the Gods.

This religion is also Utopian in its lack of an originating prophet or, beyond occasional fragments, any sacred text. (Judging by the aesthetics, such fragments can be found in the stained glass windows of Hyrule's occasional temples.) Without a prophet or sacred text, no one in Hyrule will suffer religious persecution on account of his or her color, creed, or sexuality. Moreover, here is a religion purged of almost all superstition and absurdity with the attendant injustices and horrors such things can bring. In the final analysis, no leap of faith is necessary. Not only does God exist, but he is also one of the good guys.

The Gateway to Utopia

The Utopian ideal is a slippery thing. Far from creating states of happiness and equality, the majority of attempts to realize real-life utopias has resulted in anything but. Lest we forget, Hitler's Germany, Stalin's Russia, and Mao's China were all visions of societal perfection. Fictional utopias have fared much better. Harmony is much easier to achieve in imagination. Even then, though, there is a problem: such worlds can remain far away. We can follow where a narrative leads us, or stay within a painting's restricted frame, but we can't quite touch. In one Utopia however, this isn't true. In *The Legend of Zelda: The Minish Cap*, through our connection to Link, Utopia is there to explore. This happy Hyrule, with its ordered town, loving God, and eternal summer, is indeed Utopia achieved.

Paradise Found

Issues of time and space notwithstanding, it's tempting to see our oft-quoted philosophers settled in this Utopia.

The man who gifted us with the term, Thomas More, would find plenty that appealed, not least of all the small size of the population—in his Utopia no city has more than six thousand households—and the clear work ethic of its citizens. Any minor quibbles he did have he would seek to resolve, understanding that fine ideals were useless unless put into action. It wouldn't be surprising, therefore, to see him use his astute political mind to stand against Mayor Hagen in the next election. His primary aim? To work towards an *even* fairer, *even* more idyllic Hyrule.

Plato and Aristotle would take a cottage in the west of town, close to its pulsating heart and the *new* university but within spitting distance of the river. Here, after a hard day lecturing, the founding fathers of philosophy would discuss the nature of reality from the comfort of their cottage garden, in a climate close to that of their beloved Greece, while gazing out across the perfect polis. Whenever the debates reached a temporary stalemate, Aristotle, a keen and accomplished biologist as well as philosopher, would collect amazing aquatic specimens from the river. Plato, meanwhile, would take pleasure from fresh dialogues, in Mama's Café, with the ever-accommodating Hylians.

Kierkegaard and Kant, though never sharing a timeline in this world, would make happy housemates in Hyrule. Both men rarely left their hometowns of, respectively, Copenhagen and Königsberg, preferring the ordered, metropolitan life, which Hyrule town offers in spades. It's pleasing to think of them, newly arrived in Hyrule, engaging in a late-night discussion on the existence or otherwise of God, both blissfully unaware of the irony. For God *does* exist. He's there and closer than they could ever imagine. He's in the fields and in the forests, on their rooftop and in their rafters. He's dressed in red and blue and is looking down on them, and on everyone else in this green and pleasant land, with affection, benevolence and love.

Yes, I think these and, indeed, all our philosophers would like it here. Wouldn't *you?*

Level 7

You are Nearing
the End of Your Quest . . .
Grumble, Grumble . . .

14

I Am Link's Transcendental Will: Freedom from Hyrule to Earth

DARIO S. COMPAGNO

I am Link.

> *I know I should not travel so late at night . . . every time I do a bunch of creepy zombies tries to eat me . . . But, what else can I do? Time seems to go so fast since I have left the Kokiri forest (where as long as I remember days seemed much longer, maybe because I did not have so much to do after all). Anyway, I've got something important to do and the undeads are not a problem for me. Well, here comes one! It's better that I go and teach him some good manners . . . "Hey Navi! Would you please make some light for me here?" Which weapon do I use? I could grab my sword, or I might pull out my slingshot. I draw the sword; it's better.*

Who's thinking all this? Is it Link who lives in Hyrule, trying to do what the Deku tree told him right before passing away, who has undertaken a moral path that sometimes seems pre-determined?

Most of us have duties, often leading towards something unclear. We act and make preferences, the consequences of which seem out of our control, following a prescriptive *inner voice*. Does Link feel inside him a consciousness, deciding among the possible paths along his adventure? From our point of view Link's inner voice is not his deeper will and self (the 'true him'): his true self is . . . another's.

Is a player, then, thinking the thoughts at the beginning of this chapter? A player who lives on Earth, trying to do what that weird Deku tree said? Who has just a ludic aim that sometimes looks like destiny (we can't survive for long without games), but who probably also has a job waiting to be done, a family to care about, a favorite show on TV? This player surely feels inside him a consciousness, making choices among the possible decisions that face him throughout the game, an *inner voice* constantly telling him what to do next. And from our point of view this inner voice is his deeper will and self (the 'true him').

Any chance we have something in common with Link? That our will is not so clearly within our control, comfortably inside our consciousness? Whenever the word 'I' is used in real life, its use seems so straightforward. And yet, when someone describes a game of *Zelda* using the word 'I', it becomes ambiguous. It can point to Link in the gameworld, the character who actually slays monsters and explores dungeons, or to his player out of the gameworld, the person who does not physically move from his chair, but who must be held responsible for slaying monsters, exploring dungeons and finally saving Hyrule. 'I' inevitably points simultaneously to two beings: to Link as a consciously perceived body (however virtual), and to the player as a ruling will. Does the word 'I' really avoid an analogous ambiguity in real life? Pointing at the same time to a consciously experienced body and to a will we cannot see, but that has us under its control?

The Adventure of Will

I can hear you saying: "You can't talk like that! Link has nothing inside, he *is* nothing inside. He has no consciousness but that of the concrete gamer controlling him; he has no will but the one his players share with him. It is this emptiness that permits gamers to become his will. Instead *we* have both a unique consciousness and will. There is no invisible gamer playing us."

Let's think about Navi, Link's lovely talking cricket in *The Ocarina of Time*. She has no voice talking inside her and no gamer guiding her from outside Hyrule. She always performs the same acts, always utters the same sentences—actually it's not even she who expresses those sentences. It may seem so, but actually it's *The Ocarina of Time* speaking—I mean, the game as a whole. Alternatively we can say that it's the Nintendo staff that wrote Navi's words. There's a similar situation with narrative books where there are textual characters *inside* the text and a fully featured man (or staff) *outside* the text. Nothing else. Characters in books depend on the book's paper, people reading books, people writing books. They have an individual life inside the book and in culture, but this life depends on real people.

We humans don't require as much. First, I am my character, living in the real world. Second, I perceive by myself this world in which I live; in a certain sense I am my own reader. I am a pretty autonomous being: at least much more autonomous than a character in a book. Third, and most important, I am the author of my own choices. I do not feel someone else programming or playing me, and this is my *freedom*.

Link instead has a weird identity. He's still a fictional character (like Navi), but he has something 'inside' or 'outside' (the player). Shigeru Miyamoto, the creator of *Zelda* and *Mario* himself, said Link was named so because he is the link between the player and the game. *Nomen omen*, Romans used to say: the name is a destiny. Link is the spectacles that the person playing *Zelda* puts on to get access to Hyrule.

Hyrule revolves around Link and his player and recreates itself at every game. Link is the means for the gamer to manifest his or her will into Hyrule. Michel Foucault wrote that man is an "empirical-transcendental doublet," because of his twin existence of thing among things and of knower of those things.[1] Link too is a doublet between a virtual body and a player. Or, to put it differently, there's a connection between Link in Hyrule and the Player on Earth. But to understand all this we will have to clarify what we mean by *transcendental*.

None of the other characters in the gameworld know that Link is guided by another being, that outside Hyrule there are real people. The most they can know are the actions of Link as a game entity, and so how to react if Link behaves in a certain way. With all this in mind, with respect to Hyrule's dimension, Link's will (the player's) is necessarily too much 'inside' him or too much 'outside' Hyrule to be understood.

In certain respects our condition as human beings is not *that* different from Link's. Of course, Link and Ganon never wonder if something outside Hyrule really exists, if they are free to act as they want or if something or someone is ruling their lives. It would be fun to hear Link arguing with Ganon that he sometimes feels *something* inside, and then listening to Ganon's reply that it is just an illusion . . .

---

[1] *The Order of Things: An Archaeology of the Human Sciences* (Random House, 1970).

Will's Awakening

History of will begins with someone trying to put something into his (or her) mouth because *damn* he wants it *full stop*. He does not really know why—he doesn't even care—but *he knows that he wants it*. With time, he will be able to get the thing he wants, to take control of his body and of his actions and to satisfy his will. Having many ways to get the thing he wants, *he can choose the one that looks best*. He would then feel *freedom of action*.

Some people believe that freedom of action is also freedom in general, freedom in the fullest sense. But often in saying that we are free we mean that we can *choose what to want*. A person is free not only if he knows what he wants, but also if he can consciously determine his desires—in other words if he has *freedom of will*. Someone who saw this distinction between freedom of action and of will very clearly (and who did not quite believe that we humans have both of them) was the German philosopher Arthur Schopenhauer.

According to Schopenhauer, at first glance, I am a consciousness obeying a will (and all of you reading are too, sorry). What makes a man out of me is knowledge: I know, therefore I am a man. And the more I know the better I can understand what happens around me. I see things differently than a mosquito, so I'm not a mosquito. But I'm not completely different from it; if it could understand things as I do (or if I could share my knowledge with it) it would behave exactly like me. This happens because in both me and in the mosquito there is a *will* of the very same nature.

What do I know about myself? Do I know that I am choosing what to want? For Schopenhauer the answer is a clear no. I know what I want, and I try to obtain it in the best way I can, but I never actually feel within my consciousness the moment when a decision is made. It's simply an illusion to find a decision in my consciousness. I only hear my will choosing. I feel the outcomes of my will, and I confuse them with the process of decision.

My internal life is somehow like a strange painter's studio, where the painter draws a few lines, then a helper from a distance observes his results and describes them accurately back to him, and then the painter draws a few more lines. Who's in charge is the painter: he is the *will*. The helper is consciousness, and the work would be far worse without him. But he does not really choose what to draw. A mosquito would be something like a painter with a poorly skilled helper.

The distinctive way we humans act is by knowing, but what we share with all other living beings is much more important. At a deeper glance *I am what I will*, even if then I must admit that *I do not know who I am*. The word 'I' shows again, in a clearer way, its double meaning: the knower and the known. Schopenhauer tells us that the known is will, and that it is never *really* known.

The Schopenhauerian Console

For Schopenhauer decisions are taken away from consciousness. I can foresee the consequences of my actions, but I never observe the causes of my decisions nor the decisional actions themselves. Nevertheless, I *am* those decisions.

Isn't it true that sometimes we guess exactly what a person is going to do? We know his or her *character*, we see the situation's *motifs*, and then we accurately predict his actions? Sometimes we perceive noticeably what causes others to behave in a certain way. And this isn't a particularly amazing feat; if John's being an ass again then he's probably going to offend someone at the party—quite predictable.

Not to mention *Zelda*'s characters. I've had some problems figuring out how to hit the spiders in *The Ocarina of Time* without being hit back (I know, I suck); but after I figured it out, the spiders gently let themselves be killed. The game characters in particular have very stable characters (if you allow me the play on words), even if in some cases it may not be that simple to find out regularities of behavior, patterns of interaction.

We have to infer others' wills from outside—in order to know others' characters we must work them out using clues. But when it comes to ourselves things are different; we have a direct feeling of will proper. We listen to its 'voice' forthright; we have to infer nothing, we need no clues. We simply listen and act accordingly (pretty much as it happens whenever Link is given a command).

To Schopenhauer this is a key to fully understand who we are, what we want. We hear our proper will as if it is *another's*. Because of this, its decisions are not transparent to us. Either we want to discover what our character is, and we have to carefully observe the way we make decisions, or we directly pay attention to our inner voice. In both cases we must recognize ourselves as strangers. This is because will is *not* consciousness.

Daniel Dennett criticized what he called the *Cartesian theater*, a theory of the human mind stipulating that inside our brain there is a theater (an *I-max* theater maybe!) where our conscious self attends to the spectacle projected by our senses, and then chooses how to behave.[2] French founder of modern philosophy René Descartes (from whom 'Cartesian' comes) believed that man is made of body and mind; while the body is ruled by physical laws, as any other material entity, the mind is absolutely free to will whatever it wants. The problem with this approach is to explain how a completely constrained body and an absolutely free mind can coordinate to cause one and the same act every second of life. It seems like one man is too small for both of them.

In a similar fashion we could talk of a 'Schopenhauerian Console', where consciousness projects the world to will, to *a will that is outside this world*. This outside will then gets the joypad into its hands (a *wii-ll* mote? Any takers?) and plays our life. What is the originality of the Schopenhauerian Console with respect to the Cartesian theater? That consciousness and will are here two distinct entities in interaction. It's not a matter of mind and body as in Descartes. Our body is itself felt in two ways, consciously as part of the world we live (what we usually call the material body, that could eventually be substituted by a virtual body like Link), and also as the source of will. To Schopenhauer there is the world in which we consciously live and a 'real' world from which will communicates with us. For that matter why must we differentiate the player's consciousness and his will?

Maya's Mask

Schopenhauer wrote that having freedom of action means that "I can do what my will wants"; while having freedom of will means that "I can choose what to will."[3] He claimed that we have freedom of action, but *we do not have freedom of will*. In fact we cannot consciously choose what to will; will is independent of our consciousness. But still *will is free*. It is free because it is not influenced by worldly causes and effects, it is outside of the world.

One way to express this idea is by saying that others' actions are *immanent* to my conscious representation of reality, while my per-

---

[2] *Consciousness Explained* (Little, Brown, 1991).
[3] *Prize Essay on the Freedom of the Will* (1838; Cambridge University Press, 1999).

sonal will is not. Immanent means pretty much 'inside', 'within' something, and its meaning is opposed to *transcendent*, meaning 'outside' that something. The gods of the ancient philosopher Epicurus are completely transcendent to the world because they don't care at all about men and the Earth.[4] The philosopher Baruch Spinoza, on the other hand, imagined a totally immanent god, identical to empirical, physical reality—to the point that he simply *is* nature. Not entirely happy with these two weird words (immanent and transcendent), Immanuel Kant took from medieval tradition the term *transcendental*. By this he meant what applies to everything, what encompasses all that exists; but he gave a new verve to this concept.

Kant felt that things are not in themselves as they appear to men. Actually this is not exactly breaking news: since Thales (the first recognized occidental philosopher) almost everyone in the field of philosophy pretends this world is a cover for a *transcendent* 'real reality' we are not able to see directly—and, typically, almost everyone adds that philosophy is the medicine you need to get beyond.[5] But Kant believed that this fake world we live in depends just on the limits of our mind, of our capacities to know. Then, even if we cannot know anything about the transcendent 'real reality', we can know something about our cognitive faculties, about how we construct the world we live in.

Two points Kant made were important for Schopenhauer then (and for us now). First: a fundamental condition of knowing is a place from where things are organized altogether, and Kant called this the *transcendental subject*. The subject is neither in the world he lives, nor somewhere else far from it. It stays right on the border of experience.

Second: one of the means by which our mind builds the world we live in is *causality*, a never ending series of causes and effects. Everything has a cause, and this cause surely has another cause, and so on. To the point that it's not easy at all to understand what the word *free* means.

---

[4] From this belief Epicurus drew one of the four maxims of his 'spiritual medicine' (the so called *Tetrafarmakon*): Don't fear gods.

[5] Schopenhauer called this world of appearance "The Veil of Maya," referring to the partially illusory reality in which we live according to the Hindu tradition.

Twilight Will

Schopenhauer was a fan of Kant but he saw things *a little* differently. The world I see is built by my mind, true. I could never find freedom in such a world because I've built it up myself using causality as cement, true. But *will* is not a part of this ordered and squared world, not at all. Will lives in the all-singing all-dancing *transcendency*.

If Kant had always respected the limits of knowledge, what our minds try to reach but what necessarily stays out of sight, Schopenhauer instead found in *will* a direct access to the true essence of the world, a bridge to seeing beyond experience. As a living being I can feel my will speaking in me at any time, and this will is true, 'really real'. My self-consciousness gives me the opportunity to observe will subjectively and directly, instead of objectively and indirectly as when I look at another's actions. And, if we are careful observers, it comes clear that this will is *prior* to consciousness, it is its background and condition of possibility.

Did Schopenhauer take a step forward or backward in respect to Kant? Did he walk again into the transcendent (so into something no one can really be sure to know) or did he actually stay on the transcendental line? Is *will* a crappy, inevitably obscure concept or not? Michel Foucault wrote that will is an "objective transcendental" (pretty much a contradiction in terms). This means that will actually *is* still a condition for existence to be such as we know it—so in this sense it's transcendental; but at the same time it's situated in the unknown 'real reality'—so it is objective.

Whether or not he followed his master's philosophical method, Schopenhauer pushed Kant's ideas to their limit, and after having rationalized all of the world as a conscious representation, he found the abrupt dark side of man. Schopenhauer taught us that the unknowable, the raw will, has a massive role in life. We can't understand ourselves only as rational cognizers; we have an obscure nature that shows up at our rational consciousness.

But what can we know about will then? At least that it is *free* from any possible cause, because causality is part of the problem (the experienced world) and not of the solution (the 'real reality'). What we cannot know is free *because* it's not known. Apart from this, we feel its urge, and we can do nothing about it.

Schopenhauer wrote:

This freedom, however, is *transcendental* . . . it does not emerge in the appearance but is present only insofar as we abstract from the appearance and all its forms in order to arrive at that which, outside all time, is to be thought of as the inner essence of the human being in himself. (*Prize Essay on the Freedom of the Will*, p. 86)

I am my will, and this will is free because it cannot really be known. So I don't know myself. But we cannot have *everything*. *I am free* as long as we mean the right thing with this expression: I want what I want, and not something else; I'm free to act conforming to my will. The only thing *I am not free* to do is to will what I don't will. But carefully looking, that would be a bit uncomfortable.

A Link to the Present

Let's go back to Hyrule and try to understand what would happen in loading an episode of *The Legend of Zelda* into a Schopenhauerian Console. We have seen that Schopenhauer split consciousness and will. There is the consciously experienced ('immanent') world, the 'really real' world ('transcendent'), and the subject that is somehow in between ('transcendental').

In playing *The Legend of Zelda* we can identify all these three aspects. First, *Link* is a character in Hyrule (*immanent* to it). He lives at the same level of the game's other characters, and can be seen as a virtual body of the player. Second, there's a *transcendent* will outside Hyrule, the real person's will playing the game.

Last, there is a bond, a *transcendental* subject. It is the point of view from which Hyrule exists, the conditions for a real person to enter Hyrule. It's not a virtual body (Link), but a perspective, a competence the real player has to grasp. The real person is unknown to Hyrule's characters. He or she accesses the game's world only squeezing inside Link, becoming *Link's player*. In this way his or her will, the will that the player truly is, can have an effect on the game through Link's actions.

It would be incomplete to talk about Link only as a character, saying that the sentence "I finally defeated Ganon" applies just to Hyrule. It would be also incomplete to say that the player defeated Ganon without any mediator in Hyrule (you can't beat Ganon without Link doing so too). The representation of Hyrule is connected with *the true will of the player*. I *really* manifest my will in the game. Whenever I play, *I am Link* because my will is Link's will, and Link is my consciously perceived body in Hyrule.

'*I' is a link* that allows communication between two worlds: the will of the speaker and an expressed intention. And all the kids must learn how to use this word properly. In Zelda there's something permitting a similar communication. There is an '*I*' of the game, a role the game requires to approaching 'the borders' of Hyrule.

To become *Link's player*, the gamer has to respect some constraints, some rules. For example, any gamer has to grasp the alternation of side-scrolling and top-down perspective in *The Adventure of Link* or the mapping of Link's movements on the Wii-mote in *Twilight Princess*. But becoming Link's player is not just a matter of learning the game's interface, it also brings a model of behavior. If I get to the end of any *Zelda* game it means that I have impersonated Link in a good way. It means that I have managed to follow a possible path built up by the game's creators.

There are some particular strategies to be fulfilled to go forward in the game: Link has to find secret doors and objects in dungeons (characterizing all the installments of *Zelda* from the very beginning), or he has to talk to someone (or rather, listen) to allow particular events in the game to occur. In Semiotics there is a concept called Model Player, and what we have called until now *Link's player* is pretty much *The Legend of Zelda's* Model Player.

So Link's life, within the game, is fated, already chosen; in many episodes he *has to* find the Master Sword before he can save Zelda. To become Link's player requires the gamer to feel these limitations and follow Link's destiny. But the gamer must also feel will to give energy to this destiny. *Zelda* has always been an adventure game where the gamer has to discover things for herself and get into the game's story. There is a high involvement in completing Link's fate because the player has the sensation of 'being there', of being *himself* part of Hyrule. His decisions are effective there. This parallelism of determined life and free will is what was taught by Schopenhauer.

The adventure of Link and the Princess Zelda within Hyrule has been decided *long ago*, once and forever, and repeats itself at every game. But at every game Link's acts get repeated in a time that for the player outside Hyrule is always a *now*. Link's inner voice, at the same time inside him and outside Hyrule, speaks in a time that is *present* both to Link and to the player. The real person becoming

Link's player lives in Hyrule for a while. What permits this connection is the *transcendental*: having consciousness in Hyrule and will on Earth.

So, you see, Schopenhauer and *Zelda* do have something in common! How have you played until now without knowing Schopenhauer?

15

Zeldathustra

MICHAEL BRUCE

It's been over twenty years since *Zelda* was first introduced to the world. Yet every time you insert that original gold cartridge into the console and hear the enchanting music—after blowing on it and meticulously adjusting it, of course—it takes you back. You as the player have changed, but the game itself, the original adventure, is always the same.

One of the novelties of the old-school, original *Zelda* is that, unlike other games of the time like *Super Mario Brothers*, it does not utilize a game clock. There's no rush till the end, no desperate leaps or infuriating buzzers. Furthermore, while there is a distinct plot and direction to the game, Link has the ability to move in multiple directions, progressing in a fashion that could be called "out of order." In contrast to side-scrollers (games played from left to right), *Zelda* has a top down perspective which enables Link to navigate the terrain in a more adventurous way. (*Adventure of Link* has side-scroller dungeons and caves, but it, too, makes use of a top down perspective in the overworld.)

One of the effects of not having a nerve-wracking game clock is that you're able to explore Link's world, experiment with weapons and items, and, generally, play the game in a different way than you would if you did have a clock. With the freedom of unlimited time and the ability to restart the game, you as the player can make Link act in various ways—hero, villain, test dummy. In the absence of a game clock, the only time constraint is the one projected onto the game by you, the player. While you may have to break for dinner or homework, Link could journey forever. The ability to save your progress is a remarkable and necessary feature of the game; Hyrule is a vast wild space and this watershed technology enabled the player to project more meaning and value onto Link. When you've traveled so far together, days and nights (and now twenty years) it makes you wonder whether you've played a million different Links, each one divided between attempts, or if you've been playing with one unified Link that has evolved and got better or worse as you both co-authored the game.

Some variation of the following is generally taken to be the story of the original *Legend of Zelda* game:

> Ganon, the King of Evil, breaks free from the Dark World and captures Hyrule's beloved Princess Zelda. Before she is caught, Zelda manages to shatter the Triforce of Wisdom and scatter its eight pieces throughout Hyrule. Link swears to recover the Triforce pieces and rescue Princess Zelda from Ganon's clutches. (http://www.zelda.com/universe/game/zelda)

We're told one myth, *The Legend of Zelda*, but the game can have divergent interpretations. There is not one Link, but rather an infinite number of ways Link can maneuver, each as diverse as the player pushing his buttons. Each time you play there's an opportunity to change Link's relationship to the game, and because the game is not time-dependent, you ultimately decide what kind of sensibility Link will have. The lack of a dependency on time allows for enhanced freedom and feeling of control for the player who projects personality onto the avatar, leading to a stronger association with the character than would normally be found in a game that pushes along the action.

People understand value in different ways. One of these easiest ways to assess a particular value is to ask questions like, "If I had to eat this meal every night for the rest of my life, would I still like it?" or "Will I still love my wife in fifty years?" or "If I had to work at this same job forever, would I still do it?" I asked myself just these kinds of questions as a freshman in college sitting in a boring general education class. I questioned whether I really wanted to read these kinds of books, study with the personalities in these kinds of classes, and take on this kind of career later in life. The answer was a robust no!

This line of reasoning and psychological experimentation is what the German philosopher Friedrich Nietzsche proposes we undertake, not only for school but for our entire lives. Nietzsche writes:

The greatest weight.— What, if some day or night a demon were to steal after you in your loneliest loneliness and say to you: "This life as you now live it and have lived it, you will have to live once more and innumerable times more; and there will be nothing new in it, but every pain and every joy and every thought and sigh and everything unutterably small or great in your life will have to return to you, all in the same succession and sequence—even this spider and this moonlight between the trees, and even this moment and I myself. The eternal hourglass of existence is turned upside down again and again—and you with it, speck of dust!"—Would you not throw yourself down and gnash your teeth and curse the demon who spoke thus? Or have you once experienced a tremendous moment when you would have answered him: "You are a god and never have I heard anything more divine!" If this thought gained possession of you, it would change you as you are or perhaps crush you; the question in each and every thing, "Do you desire this once more, and innumerable times more?" would lie upon your actions as the greatest weight! Or how well disposed would you have to become to yourself and to life *to crave nothing more fervently* than this ultimate eternal confirmation and seal? (*The Gay Science*, Vintage, 1974, pp. 273–74)

The Returning *Legend*

In *Zelda* we have a similar structure to what Nietzsche calls the "eternal return" or "eternal recurrence." The game repeats itself each time you turn it on, and you must choose how to play. Each time a player starts the game from the beginning, the same videogame emerges in terms of the inherent structure that makes *Zelda*, *Zelda*. The fact that the player can start over or that there is no game clock does *not* mean that what you do doesn't matter. If you take Nietzsche's experiment seriously you might come to the conclusion that if your life were to repeat itself, it does not matter what you do; this is the exact opposite of what Nietzsche proclaims! If your life repeats itself endlessly, every instant counts drastically! For every subtle move will relive itself eternally, so take on this life and love your fate!

Repetition can be understood in two ways concerning *Zelda*: first, the lack of a time clock makes each moment of play eternally present, not passing away or surging forward; secondly, but with the same result, the structure of the game remains constant while there is the ability to replay and restart (saving) gameplay, which is in fact necessary to play the game. This second understanding revolves around the fact that while there are many different ways to play the game, Link and the player continually encounter the same underlying structure and limitations.

Nietzsche sees the world as a dynamic collection of forces, and this flux of energy or "will to power," permeates all levels of reality. From the smallest quanta of energy to the cosmos at large, existence can be interpreted through this lens of power, the sum of which ensures an eternal return.

Why would Nietzsche think that a world made of changing force and energy would eternally repeat itself? Relying on the second law of thermodynamics (conservation of energy), Nietzsche reasons that since there is finite "stuff" and infinite time, it follows that over time everything will re-occur. The game *Zelda* is finite; there are a fixed number of ways that Link and other characters and enemies can move. There are rules (written into the game's code) that govern gameplay and dictate the possible actions—though there can be many interpretations of the game's meaning and narratives. An example is the timeline theories.

Now suppose that you play *Zelda* for the next twenty years (infinitely); it seems to be the case that a single game—every action, command and outcome—would be repeated. Given *Zelda*'s 8-bit limitations, I think this is actually quite common. Just remember playing it for the first time and dying quickly, only to repeat that short game again.

But what does it mean to have the "same" repeating itself forever? If the world is in constant flux as Nietzsche writes, how are we to understand the concept of "sameness" or identity? There are two ways of understanding a recurrence of the same: the way I describe above, a more cosmological reading concerning the conservation of energy over time and an exact reproduction of the history of existence, and a second view which says that the underlying interplay of forces continually returns (are the same) but manifests *new* things, identities, perspectives, etc.

This second view, which is more coherent with the rest of Nietzsche's philosophy, may cause us to see *Zelda* in an entirely different way. While the forces at work in *Zelda* are constant— everything from the Nintendo itself, to the Triforce, and even your brain depends on, and in a sense is, energy—the spirit of the second interpretation of the eternal return of the same would say that new things or orientations to the game are coming into being. For example, while the *Zelda* game may be essentially the same each time you play it, you as the player are continually changing, thus changing your relationship to the game.

Taking this interpretation to another level, a program called "Zelda Classic" allows amateurs to effectively change the game and, therefore, surpass the original formulation of *Zelda*. Zelda Classic users can create their own *Zelda* game. Consequently users are able to manipulate all aspects of the game, like moving walls and structures, enhancing the abilities of the characters, and beyond. However, the creation of this new adventure is still bound within the logic of the original game. At the lowest level the programming code is still binary, but a new game or at least a new version of the game is born. On an even larger scale, you can think of the progression of the *Zelda* games from the original to the present as new creative manifestations emerging out of the same dynamic forces that have always pervaded our world.

The Necessity of Looped Time

In *Zelda* there's nothing that indicates a passing of time, only looped time as seen in the reccurring pattern of enemies and obstacles. *Zelda* was designed to be played many times, and this requires a level of predictability to ensure that the gameplay progresses through interpretation of patterns, yet stays challenging and continues to engage the player.

Timing in videogames is crucial. We only need to think to a normal time-dependent game, like those of the *Super Mario Brothers* series, to remember how running for a long enough distance and then jumping at precisely the right time is the sole way to master a certain part of a level. In this sense, looped time is the lifeblood of many successful strategies; this form of time allows the player to anticipate the coming challenge. Moreover, the return of the same hurdles enable the player to practice and hone these required skills for future levels of increasingly intricate scenarios.

Repetition is a way of training and experimenting, a way to take on a new perspective for the case at hand. Nietzsche writes, "A thinker sees his own actions as experiments and questions—as attempts to find out something. Success and failure are for him answers above all" (p. 108). Will the run-and-gun, all out, fast-as-you-can strategy work? Perhaps. Will a cautious and calculated tact yield victory? Maybe. You must take these masks and try, saying yes! to the challenge in the face of possible death and promised struggle.

Saying Yes to life even in its strangest and hardest problems, the will to life rejoicing over its own inexhaustibility . . . *Not* in order to be liberated from terror and pity . . . but in order to be *oneself* the eternal joy of becoming. . . . Herewith I again stand on the soil out of which my intention, my *ability* grows—I, the last disciple of the philosopher Dionysus—I, the teacher of the eternal recurrence. (*The Anti-Christ, Ecce Homo, Twilight of the Idols, and Other Writings*, 2005, p. 109)

One of the features that makes *The Legend of Zelda* such a popular game is the demand for players to employ creativity in different facets of gameplay. The game is not formulaic, not brainless fodder, but a medium that begs for artistic solutions. *Zelda* is saturated with logical puzzles that necessitate lucid discernment. In some of the later games that involve the gamer *himself* playing music (first introduced in *Ocarina of Time*) it becomes clear that the world of *Zelda* is intrinsically artistic and aesthetic.

The After-Worldly

Nietzsche despises the philosophy presented by Plato and Christianity for their two-worlds bifurcation, the sensible and the intelligible, heaven and earth. Plato envisioned another world that encased the eternal forms or ideas informing each of the particular things in our everyday sensible world. For example, the reason we can identify different things as belonging to a group—say, how we can tell that a chair is a chair even when there are many different kinds of chairs—is because the particular chair participates in the eternal form of the chair. Because of this relationship with this second world of fixed essences, we can understand the world of continual change. Plato's theory of the forms is complicated and for our purposes the importance is the basic two-world structure. This can also be seen in other belief systems which posit a world other than the world from which the system itself arose, namely for Nietzsche, Christianity's heaven.

The eternal return is Nietzsche's anti-venom to the prophets of the after-worldly. Since this present moment will forever survive, the meaning(s) of life and all our careful concentration is redirected back down to earth, to this life and moment. Imagine living your life as if you were just an alien visitor passing through this terrestrial rock on your way to a super Disney Land. From that perspective, this life has little meaning since it is not the land which houses Plato's eternal forms of Truth, Beauty, and the Good, nor the perfection of the Christian heaven. The sole (or maybe soul) purpose of this life is to get somewhere else, somewhere beyond this world of illusion and sin. Actions performed in this life are preparations for a death that promises redemption, love, and reward in the other realm.

Now imagine that life was lived without this schism of reality, and there was only one world, one life. The orientation to life and the meaning experienced in the world take on a radically new importance. If there is no other world after this, if this world is in a sense the true world for which we are not strangers on a train, but rather that we have evolved from and emerged out of this earth, then this life is saturated with meanings and purposes. Compounded with the idea of a life that eternally returns, value becomes placed on the concrete experiences of the life, of experimenting and exploring, of self-overcoming and the life affirming heroic impulse of those willing to take on this life as it is.

In the two-worlds philosophy there exists our normal world of change and becoming that is less real and therefore less valuable than the true world of Being and eternal fullness. The brilliance of Nietzsche's thought experiment is that an amazing thing happens when you overcome this schizophrenic worldview; namely, that if you release the idea of another world, of the things-in-themselves, you also deflate the chimera of "appearances." This world is not illusory or deceiving so that we can never get to its core essence—this is the world as such!

An important facet of *The Legend of Zelda* is that there are no directions or divine laws. While in some of the later installments characters are given some form of instructions, in the old-school *Zelda* games, for the most part, Link is able to explore wherever he wants, whenever he wants. Link can go into castles out of order, and there is no guide (or Bible) that dictates the one true way (Oh sure, there's the magic book, but what use is that without the wand?). Again, the absence of a time clock that pushes the avatar down a linear path opens up the possibility of non-linear time, like cyclical or looped time. Many ancient cultures and the philosophies they produced did not express linear time; like the seasons, the tides, the rising and setting of the sun, time was understood as a circle of life and death, abundance and dearth. With the inception of Christianity, which plotted a beginning (God created the world in six days) and an end (Armageddon and Judgment), a different understanding of time and history flared forth.

Will-to-Triforce

If we go back to the initial premises of *The Legend of Zelda* we find that Link must recover the Triforce:

> In the original game, the Triforce of Wisdom and Triforce of Power are described as "Magical Golden Triangles" that grant their holders great power. The game begins with Ganon in possession of the Triforce of Power, and with the Triforce of Wisdom split into eight pieces hidden in the dungeons beneath Hyrule. Link must fight his way through the eight dungeons to recover the pieces of the Triforce of Wisdom, and then battle his way through Ganon's stronghold to defeat him and recover the Triforce of Power. (http://zelda.wikia.com/wiki/Triforce)

The division between wisdom and power is an overriding theme throughout the work of Nietzsche. He sees what he calls the "unconditional will-to-truth," or truth at any cost, devastating to a healthy culture. For Nietzsche, untruth is a necessary condition for life, as untruth or created fictions often successfully promote life affirming actions and beliefs. Power, or the will-to-power as Nietzsche names it, is the underlying drive that informs and propels all forms of life. The will-to-truth is a veiled attempt to express the lurking will-to-power that is trying to find an outlet for its satisfaction.

Viewing the world in terms of power moves, of "might makes right," is easy to do. It's quite reasonable, yet can be depressing, to be able to come to an understanding of a person's or country's motivations in terms of power alone. The Holocaust and the shameful actions carried about by Hitler and the Nazis can all be described in terms of power and force. Nevertheless, power is not to be considered solely as negative or dominant; the will-to-power can also be seen in acts of great generosity. Rich and powerful leaders may express their overflowing power by giving to the poor and needy; in this act the feeling of power and nobility is heightened. At one point Nietzsche writes that an increase in the power of the people who are weaker than you ultimately increases your power as well. If you own a computer that is able to download files faster off the internet, not only the computer has an increase in its power, but you do as well since you have power over the computer.

Beyond simple dominance over others, the will-to-power can be understood as personal strength and moral courage. Nietzsche demands that the depths of our psyche be investigated, that the *values* of our own cultural values be unearthed, that we walk dangerously close to the abyss. All of these tasks require an immense bravery and power to cut into your own beliefs and assumptions, and to recognize that even the deepest and most profound "truths" of your life are but interpretations in a certain perspective that have been put forth by the will-to-power of others. The task then is to become aware of the man made values and ultimately become the creator of new life affirming ones.

As Link crusades through the eight original dungeons and acquires the broken pieces of the Triforce, he is engaging not only in a macrocosmic journey to save Zelda, but also in a profoundly personal expedition to overcome the inner treachery of life-denying values, obstacles that must be overcome to embrace the full brilliance of the unified Triforce. Link starts the game as a young boy full of raw courage, who slowly multiplies the strength and vigor needed to triumph over Ganon: this is one of the ways Link can be viewed in terms of will-to-power.

The will-to-power and the eternal return are interconnected in Nietzsche's Philosophy. In the strong reading of the eternal return, everything from the smallest atom to Mount Everest to your random thoughts repeats again and again. In Nietzsche's notebooks, which are controversial since he did not publish many of the ideas in them, he plays with the idea that the world is made up of "quanta" of power or energy. In this manner, power is the structure of all reality; not only is the NES Zelda Cartridge subject to the will-to-power, but also the player's psyche and the avatar's pixels. The idea that the cosmos is made up of small packets of power or energy coalesces with some of the advances in twentieth-century physics, namely quantum theory.

Will You Say Yes?

It would take an enormous amount of strength to live and play according to how life actually is, and not according to how you envision it. To affirm life, and to battle, struggle, and overcome is the expression of will-to-power; to not only want life to follow through as it has, to love your life in the face of pessimistic and world negating moralities that you have to rally against—this is *amor fati*, and this is one way Link soldiers onward. Link's bravery (and consequently the gamer's bravery) is just the sort of moral fortitude that Nietzsche envisions, a free spirit with the abundance of personal strength to will his life eternally.

At the end of the day, though, the force of Nietzsche's eternal return and its relation to *The Legend of Zelda* comes down to one question: this life as you now live it and have lived it, this game as you now play it and have played it, do you will to live and play once more and innumerable times more?

Level 8

The Triforce—
Need I Say More?

16

A Link to The Triforce: Miyamoto, Lacan, and You

PATRICK DUGAN

First there's darkness, then a chime, "Nintendo Presents" blips onto the screen, and then you see them: three triangular polygons float from different corners of the screen, spinning towards each other, accompanied by the cascading harp. The three triangles converge, touching at every third corner, leaving an empty inverted triangle in the middle. The logo comes up: *The Legend of Zelda: A Link to The Past*—the Triforce has lit up the darkness, there is a lake, woods, a castle.

"Ah", you think to yourself, "this is it."

The Miyamoto Framework

When you play videogames your mind is split into three. In addition to you, the player, with all the experiences and processes that compose your mind, there is the dynamic system you're playing in, and there is an agent that you control in order to affect the system. In most games, the agent you control is quite literal: a person or object that you directly control. Independent game designer Paul Eres describes games based around such an avatar as the "Miyamoto Framework," which he characterizes by five elements:

1. The player controls a character directly, and can move that character around.

2. The player has to get somewhere, find something, or kill some enemy to win . . . achieved by getting the player-

moved-thing to the goal through a long series of obstacles. Once done, it's the end of the game.

3. The player can die or lose by doing the wrong thing, such as falling into a hole or walking into an enemy or losing a battle. If they do so, they have to try again.

4. Everything in the game exists in space, with coordinates (in either 2D or 3D).

5. There's a gradual increase in the player's capabilities over the course of the game. (http://rinku.livejournal.com/1211360 .html)

A clean +99 percent of commercially made games since 1982 have worked within the Miyamoto framework; while this tradition may not have originated with Miyamoto, his early work established it as the predominant form of game design. You could say Miyamoto established the game design philosophy of an avatar-based game.

What philosophical system does Miyamoto subscribe to, if any? Can the guy behind *Mario, Zelda, Metroid,* and *Wii Tennis* be a philosopher? In interviews, Miyamoto has described games as gardens that one must tend, taking an almost Zen Buddhist perspective on the cultivation of dynamic systems. But if we look deeper, at the fundamental mental process that is involved in Miyamoto-frameworked games, we need to go to the West, to the psychological philosophy of a Frenchman named Jacques Lacan. The Triforce is the key.

Egos, Dyads, and the Social Symbolic

Lacan believes that human minds attribute meaning to themselves in relation to other persons or objects. An ego in a vacuum isn't much of a human mind, and we don't have any frame of reference to judge such an ego—even the hermit on Death Mountain has his Magic Mirror. So we reach and relate to whatever: a mother, a partner, a friend, a delicious chunk of sharp cheddar, and we connect to it, forming what Lacan calls a "dyad."

Growing up—coming into being you could say—is, to Lacan, about realizing what dyadic relations you depend on and reaching beyond their infantile comforts, to grasp the larger world of the "social symbolic." Language, culture, politics, religion, all these things belong to the social symbolic, as do relations beyond a one-on-one dyad, such as a company, family, church or nation. Human interactions, whether with other people, objects, or complex systems like games, follow this process: the mind will connect to an anchor that gives it some kind of positive response; pleasure, security, a feeling of empowerment—through that anchor the mind can explore a wider world of third-party symbols.

You could say that the dyad is the content of a mental process, what it's preoccupied with, and the social symbolic provides the context of that interaction. In game development, we commonly refer to things like level designs or missions, things that preoccupy the player and give a game "meat" or "volume" as being "content"; good content will keep you content. Therefore, using Lacan's model, you can analyze minds as being made up of these tangled triangles. This is particularly useful when looking at how people play games.[1]

Intransitive Relationships in Game Designs

To game designers, a triangular tangle of relations is a fundamental structure used to make dynamic systems; it's called it an intransitive relationship, or while drunk, the "Rock-Paper-Scissors love triangle." It's a bread-and-butter sort of structure, our three-pointed ninja star. Many games, both inside and outside the Miyamoto framework, utilize the structure. Fire, Ice, and Lighting magic in *Final Fantasy* fit the bill; as does *Starcraft*'s balance between unit power, cost, and deployability; while in *Halo*, it's a contest between the aim, power, and maneuverability of the player controlling the personality-less suit of armor.

In addition to designing tangled triangles of systemic factors to make interesting gameplay, every designer working in the Miyamoto framework has been working with a psychological triangle between the player, the game, and the player's effect on the game. Miyamoto's framework, with its emphasis on the player-character or avatar's spatial and internal advancement, treads close to Lacan's psychological theory. We, as an ego, are put into a dyadic relationship with our avatar; we play with our avatar, we

---

[1] This information appears in Jacques Lacan, *The Language of the Self* (Johns Hopkins University Press, 1968).

play *as* our avatar, and it's fun. The rest of the game then, the places we go and the people we meet, the world we explore, constitutes the social symbolic. We control the avatar, the avatar manipulates the world, the world changes and we adapt, adjusting our control of the avatar. That's interactivity Miyamoto-style.

Breaking Down the Triforce

Nothing in Miyamoto's whole ludography (his body of work as a game designer) better explicates this theory than the *Zelda* series. In interviews, he's admitted that he gave the avatar the name "Link" not because it's some Nordic name that's evocative of swords and sorcery, but because the little guy is literally our link to the system. Playing *Zelda* is about playing with Link, mastering that dyad, and then exploring more and more of the surrounding gameworld. As you encounter obstacles, you have to master a new aspect of your dyad, so you can explore new areas and encounter further obstacles, and so on until the big pig squeals. Once you've completely mastered all dyads and overcome all obstacles, the relations come together perfectly in the Triforce, your ultimate prize.

Nothing in his entire body of work epitomizes Miyamoto's philosophy better than the Triforce. I'm going to go over each third of the Triforce, point by point, so that you too can feel it's every corner weighing in your hands. Once you've grasped the Triforce, you will possess the golden power.

The Triforce of Courage

The Legend of Zelda—the legend itself, involves a youth born, and apparently from all the sequels, reborn, to the world in a time of crisis, and in his soul is the Triforce of Courage. Link is you, and if he's the embodiment of courage, that means you, as the player, are similarly emboldened.

The truth, of course, is that you're sitting on a couch, with jaw slackened and eyes glistened, moving your thumb slightly, just slightly, to march Link hundreds of miles without rest, risking his life repeatedly in the process. It's easy to be courageous when the Reset button is a few feet away. Link is our embodiment, our envoy and vessel in Hyrule, and he represents the potential for our decisions to manifest into action. Courage, in the sense of being able to kill monsters and explore dungeons at no risk to bodily harm, is what links us to Link. The Triforce of Courage is like the anchor that completes the two-way relationship that puts you in the game in the first place.

When you sit down and commandeer Link's body, you're entering into agreement to play the game according to that role—successfully doing so allows you to advance, to get more heart containers and items, and master all of the game's challenges. When you figure out how to advance Link's position in the world, you complete the loop of activity that keeps you fully engaged as a player, and fill out the last corner of the Triforce of Courage, making it complete. Your mind subsumes control of Link at an intuitive level, you begin to forget that there's any difference between you two.

The Triforce of Power

Ganondorf was a thief who found the Triforce and used it to fulfill his wildest power fantasies; he became Ganon, a beastly demonic swine. The piece of the Triforce he retained was that of Power. Ganon occupies the role of "Final Boss," a character who represents the last obstacle as the utmost challenge to Link and the player. He epitomizes the game system as obstacle, death, and greed. Really though, he's a Macguffin, a rube, a cardboard cut-out designed to make you forget that you're actually the one pursuing power, only finally achieving it with his death.

The world of Hyrule is a dynamic system, and it can be influenced by a few powers at your disposal once you've linked up via controller. The items making up the primary trinity of these powers are the sword, the bomb, and the arrow.

In *A Link to the Past* the first thing you get is the sword. The sword is a partially circumferential, limited radius vector collision test put out over a short duration and limited only by a brief pause between these tests—in other words, you can swing it all you want but not constantly. You can also add to this pause in order to make the circumference full and add to the power of the swing—that's the spin move you execute after holding down the attack button.

Secondly, you find the bombs. Bombs are a renewable resource generally gained by vandalizing the homes of innocent people, or by purchase, or by discovering them in treasure chests. Bombs consist of a delayed vector test against a fully circumferential radius equal to the radius of the sword swing but dealing more damage—

in other words they blow up real good. Bombs are also key to discovering non-essential secrets, such as caches of (stolen) wealth or power-enhancing items.

Thirdly, you find the arrows. Arrows are a renewable resource like bombs that operate along a straight vector, dealing damage between the amount of a sword swing and a bomb blast. Arrows are required in solving essential puzzles, such as shooting out the eye of a statue in order to open a door.

Many of the supplementary items found in dungeons and required for progress are fractal variations on these three fundamentally distinct but inter-tangled tools of power. The hook shot is the arrow's bastard child with the sword, the fire wand is the progeny of the arrow and the bomb, the hammer is a combination of the bomb and the sword.

The final battle against Ganon, in *A Link to the Past*, involves using the fire wand, the sword, and silver arrows in tandem, in that order, in a loop. Once you've gotten it, you're linked ego (Link) has consummated the pleasant Dyad of gameplay, and the Triforce is yours. But what do you do with absolute power?

The Triforce of Wisdom

Zelda is the holder of the Triforce of Wisdom. You get the vibe in all the games that even though Hyrule is not a democracy it might as well be, such a benign and wise leader being its female ruler. At least, the people believe in this wisdom, and religion has a lot to do with it.

In the mythology of Hyrule, the world was created by three goddesses, each with a complementary nature, as if the primal forces of the universe. These three left the Triforce as their legacy, their symbolic gift to the universe they made. The mythology of Hyrule is not the only one to bear such a symbol, or such a divine relationship structure.

Catholic Christianity claims that God is made up of three persons: Father, Son, and Holy Spirit, which co-operate as one inextricable being. While Hinduism describes three primal deities: Brahma the creator, Vishnu the preserver, and Shiva the destroyer. Many other games use such a structure in their backstories as well, such as the three Prime Evils of the *Diablo* series, Mephisto, Baal, and Diablo. Literature too—in *The Wizard of Oz* (the book), Truth, Courage, and Love comprised the three basic powers, and they carried over to the film in the form of the three gifts sought by the Scarecrow, the Cowardly Lion, and the Tin Man, respectively.

Religion has historically done a great job of giving context to governmental politics, and in the US, this triune structure plays itself out in the three branches of government: Executive, Legislative, and Judiciary. Likewise, the order of Maidens, Wise Men, and Knights that preserve Hyrule provide an implied function of balance and cross-checking.

Trinities, Triforces, triangles, intransitive triunes, whatever you want to call them, they simplify the complexity of a dynamic system into symbolism which can be readily understood and appreciated by the lowest common denominator. The drive to participate as a Knight, in order to gain information from Wise Men and then save the Maidens, may derive from the packaging that Hyrule's triangular mythos provides.

Perhaps wisdom, then, is the realization that these tidy little packages of the social symbolic may be distractions, and it is this enlightenment that holds Zelda hostage, both figuratively in her self-imposed role as ruler, and literally, as she is often captured or imprisoned by the powers that would distort the balance of the system.

The Golden Power

Let's take a step back, to the real world we live in, and the possible game-design philosophy of Shigeru Miyamoto, a man who lives in this real world with us. I would summarize his philosophy like this: the world is complex and changing, a dynamic system, but it can be made sense of, sometimes even poetically, by designing symbolic trinities of elemental factors which inter-relate in a non-hierarchical manner.

The golden power of the Triforce, then, is the ability to understand the world's complexities, to break it down into something manageable. However, the flip-side to this is propaganda, the propaganda of game design, the game we all are invited to play in this society. Zelda can use the golden power of the Triforce to impart wisdom, but by contrast, Ganon can use it to create a world filled with deceptions. The Triforce structure gives a very compelling sense of choice, of freedom, but very often the reality is that the choices are pre-designed for us, and therefore illusory. It all depends on the game, but always is the void in the center of the

Triforce—no system is a complete reality, they are always representations posing as totality. With the golden power however, you
can see that there is indeed a game being played, and then you can
infer who designed these games you're in. Sometimes it's the game
of society, often the games of other people, but most often, it's a
game of your own creation. Take a good long look in the Magic
Mirror, because that's the only way to escape the Dark World.

17

The Triforce and the Doctrine of the Mean

CHARLES JOSHUA HORN

> After the gods had finished their work, they left the world, but not before creating a symbol of their strength, a golden triangle known as the Triforce. A small but powerful portion of the essence of the gods was held in this mighty artifact, which was to guide intelligent life on the world of Hyrule.
>
> —*The Legend of Zelda: A Link to the Past*

At the heart of *Zelda* games are action, puzzles, and a well written story that usually focuses on the Hero of Time rescuing a princess and battling against dark forces. The games involve magic swords, interesting people, and faraway lands. Taking center stage, however, is a magical relic called the Triforce.

The Triforce was left behind after the three goddesses, Din, Nayru, and Farore created Hyrule. It's the manifestation of power, wisdom, and courage and, when combined, can grant the possessor her innermost desires. In most of the games, the Triforce is split into three parts and is instead possessed by Link, Zelda, and Ganondorf. Link possesses the Triforce of Courage, Zelda the Triforce of Wisdom, and Ganondorf the Triforce of Power.

But what *is* the Triforce really? Is it merely a byproduct of the creation of an ancient world? Or was it left behind with a purpose—namely that of ensuring the world of the three goddesses remains unchanged. Maybe the Triforce is not only a relic that has both led to the destruction and saving of Hyrule, but is also a guide to our lives, a means of showing us what's really important. More specifically, maybe the Triforce is a symbol for what virtues the goddesses wanted to show were the most important in their absence; courage, wisdom, and power weren't accidental. They were specifically chosen and there was certainly a reason for it. What that reason is, however, has yet to be uncovered. Although the information in the games is limited, we can still analyze what *is* known to learn more about the true nature and intent of the Triforce.

Are courage, wisdom, and power equal characteristics, as the Triforce places them? Did the goddesses make a mistake by placing power with courage and wisdom? And finally, how should one actually use the Triforce, both individually and as a whole? With Plato, Aristotle, and Kant guiding our way, the path seems as bright as the Triforce itself.

The Good Will and the Triforce of Power

Nothing in the world—indeed nothing even beyond the world—can possibly be conceived which could be called good without qualification except a *good will.*

—Immanuel Kant[1]

Given the history of Ganondorf and his devastating effects on Hyrule, it would be a good starting point to ask why power should be included in the Triforce at all. Why was it necessary to group something that could very easily be abused with other seemingly good virtues such as wisdom and courage? Surely, given the fact that Ganondorf has nearly destroyed Hyrule on several different occasions, the goddesses would have known the danger involved in implanting this particular attribute with the other two. Before arguing that power has a rightful place in the Triforce, I first want to explain why courage and wisdom shouldn't be given an automatic status as being better than power.

Courage and wisdom were entrusted to Link and Princess Zelda and they have utilized each effectively and accordingly. Let's try a thought experiment. What would have happened if these two pieces fell to someone else? Because they are courage and wisdom, would they instinctively be used in the same way that Link and Zelda use them?

---

[1] *Groundwork for the Metaphysics of Morals* (Cambridge, 1997), p. 7.

Or, could these two pieces of the Triforce be just as susceptible to evil as power, and through luck or fate or some reason unknown to us, the three pieces just happen to always fall into these three particular character's hands. I would like to think the latter and maintain that the Triforce pieces are just as neutral as the Triforce as a whole. There is something pure about Link and Zelda, in the same way that there is something impure about Ganondorf.

The Triforce as a whole will grant its possessor their innermost desires. If held by someone corrupt, then Hyrule will be filled with darkness. If held by someone pure and balanced in courage, wisdom, and power, then Hyrule will become a paradise. Each piece could be used for good *or* evil, in the same way that the individual pieces can.

Immanuel Kant tells us that the only thing good without exception is a good will. In other words, everything except a good will could be used in a bad way. When we act only from a sense of duty and never treat someone merely as a stepping stone, we would be fulfilling his concept of the good will. In essence, we can deduce from this that everything else *could* be used for evil acts. Take something like charity that is always a seemingly good thing. If you were to give the beggar in the town square of *Twilight Princess* one hundred rupees, this could be construed in a negative way. What were your true intentions? Did you want to impress someone? Or build a résumé? Did you want recognition in some way? Kant words it like this:

> Intelligence, wit, judgment, and the other talents of the mind, however they be named, or courage, resoluteness, and perseverance as qualities of temperament, are doubtless in many respects good and desirable. But they can become extremely bad and harmful if the will, which is to make use of these gifts of nature and which in its special constitution is called character, is not good. (p. 7)

An outsider wouldn't know your true intentions and could therefore assume that you may not be acting with a good will, because you aren't acting from a sense of duty. Instead, you're acting from self interest. For Kant, a good will can *never* be construed as a bad thing. This means that although we haven't seen it yet in the hands of Link and Zelda, they could use the Triforce of Courage and Wisdom just as negatively as Ganondorf used the Triforce of Power.

Because courage, wisdom, and power could all be used for good or bad purposes, they are neutral.

We shouldn't take this idea lightly. I by no means want to give the impression that this concept is simple. On the contrary, this is sometimes considered the beginning point of thought for the ethics of a brilliant philosopher. What exactly does it mean to have a good will anyway? For Kant, it means that we act from a sense of duty. We should act from a sense of duty so that we are sure that we are being moral. We should do it for its own sake, not for anything else. Link never rescues Zelda because he wants a reward. Zelda doesn't lead Hyrule with grace and wisdom because she wants recognition. Instead, they act from a sense of duty and are following their good will. As a result, Kant's concept of the good will gives us conclusive evidence that all three pieces of the Triforce are neutral and as a result, equal.

The Ring of Gyges

Now that we've established that power is equal and neutral with respect to courage and wisdom, it would be a rewarding venture to ask whether or not power should have been replaced with another quality. After all, Ganondorf has effectively turned Hyrule into a dark civilization on more than one occasion and even led to its flooding under the Great Sea. So, why did Din not choose to leave behind something else to nurture Hyrule? Why not love, patience, faith, ambition, or any number of other qualities? Perhaps with a look at a part of ancient philosophy, we may be able to see that power isn't nearly as bad as Ganondorf makes it seem.

In Book II of Plato's *Republic*, we find the legend of the "Ring of Gyges." The ring in this myth is very similar to the one ring from Tolkien's *Lord of the Rings* books. The ring makes its wearer invisible and the effect is corruption of the soul. The story begins with Gyges finding the ring in a cave and realizing that while he wears the ring and becomes invisible, he can do anything and get away with it. He takes this opportunity to seduce the queen, kill the king, and rule the kingdom of Lydia.

With this story, Plato makes us question whether power will eventually corrupt any soul. More importantly, why should we be just? There are two fundamental responses for why people should be just. First, people should be just only because they are afraid of punishment and second, people should be just because it is good for its own sake. So, does power corrupt and absolute power corrupt absolutely, as the saying goes? If the answer is yes, then power *does* have a separate place from courage and wisdom in the Triforce. If it corrupts any heart, then Ganondorf never had a chance against resisting the Triforce of Power and we shouldn't hate him, but pity him for not having a choice in the matter.

The truth, though, is that Ganondorf did have a choice. He chose to steal the Triforce to rid the desert of the harsh winds hurting his people, the Gerudo. It was this choice to lust after power that affected the Triforce in the way that it did, not the idea that power was somehow different than courage and wisdom. The goddesses created the parts equal and, as such, have a neutral status.

The story of Gyges can also tell us more about Ganondorf—namely, what happened to him as a result of taking the Triforce of Power. In this part of the dialogue, Plato uses Glaucon and Adiemantus to argue that it is more beneficial to be unjust. The unjust are usually wealthier and honored, whereas the just man is miserable. Socrates, who is a character in most of the dialogues written by Plato, rejects this outright and maintains that just people are moral because justice is good for its own sake, not because one would get wealthy or honored.

When we apply these cogent arguments to Ganondorf, we quickly realize that Glaucon's and Socrates's arguments both seem to apply to the Gerudo King. Ganondorf has wealth and honor while he is King of Hyrule. However, as Socrates points out, an unjust man is usually alone and morally bankrupt. Ganondorf fits these criteria too. So who is right about justice and consequently, the nature of Ganondorf? Is justice merely a social custom that wouldn't exist if people didn't have to worry about punishment? Or would justice persist regardless of society?

When we look at Ganondorf, we can see that Socrates's argument has more merit than those of Glaucon and Adiemantus. Ganondorf has wealth, but only as a result of his lust for power and possession of the Triforce of Power. He has status, but only through taking Hyrule. He has honor, but only through fear. None of his seemingly advantageous qualities are true and of his own merit, but rather only through possession of the golden triangle.

Socrates would argue that Ganondorf is morally empty because justice isn't a matter of societal influence, but rather from our soul being in balance. Ganondorf wasn't in balance in the soul or the heart. This is apparent in the splitting of the Triforce when he touched it midway through *Ocarina of Time*. He only maintained that part of the Triforce which he truly desired, that of power. Link received the Triforce of Courage and Zelda received the Triforce of Wisdom. Now the question becomes, how *should* the Triforce be used?

The Doctrine of the Mean

Although it was an inanimate object, the Triforce had the power to bestow three titles which gave the person who received them great powers: "The Forger of Strength," "The Keeper of Knowledge," and "The Juror of Courage."

—*The Legend of Zelda: A Link to the Past*

So it seems that power is not only necessary to the Triforce, but equal to its counterparts—how should one use each of the pieces? Clearly, Link's and Zelda's actions seem to set an example. But, how do they use them in a way that is not only productive, but also good? In fact, do we ever really see Link or Zelda use their respective pieces? We only know that they have them from the symbols on their left hands that only appear when close to another piece.

We can take Ganondorf's use of the Triforce of Power as an example of how *not* to use a piece of the Triforce. Ganondorf uses the Triforce of Power several times throughout the series and, as you'll notice, this use is drastically different from Link's and Zelda's. Did the goddesses want the pieces of the Triforce to be used at all? Surely the answer is yes, or why leave them to begin with? We know from the first quote of the chapter that the Triforce was meant to "guide intelligent life on the world of Hyrule." The goddesses wanted the Triforce pieces to be used and they obviously didn't like the way that Ganondorf was using his part, because they take it from him at the end of *Twilight Princess*. The intention of the goddesses was for the Triforce to be used in moderation, as Link and Zelda do.

When philosophers study ethics, they ask how one ought to live. What moral guidelines should we follow, if any, in our day to day lives? Some have responded that we should always act in a way that will benefit the highest number of people. Others have responded that we shouldn't treat people as objects. Some have even argued that there's no such thing as morality. Aristotle asks us how we can build our character in the best way. Why is Link a good character? Why is Ganondorf such a bad one? It's by understanding Aristotle that we can determine the true intentions of Din, Nayru, and Farore when leaving behind the Triforce.

Aristotle's doctrine of the mean gives us a rough guideline of how to act. A virtue or vice is a disposition to think and act in a certain way. A virtue is when that disposition falls between two extremes of excess and deficiency. Aristotle identifies particular virtues and argues that the corresponding vices are using those qualities too much or too little. For instance, pride is a virtue according to Aristotle because it falls between two extremes. The extreme deficiency of pride is humility and the extreme excess of pride is vanity.[2] Humility and vanity would both be vices. Another virtue that Aristotle defines is courage.

How does Link use the Triforce of Courage? Does he use it like a coward and therefore exhibit the extreme deficiency of courage? Anybody that can face creatures such as Gohma and Volvagia and live to tell the tale is certainly no coward! Does he use it in excess? I don't think that we ever saw Link run straight to Ganon's castle as soon as Zelda is captured to rescue her. This would be rash. Instead, Link gains the weapons and skills he needs before rescuing Zelda. In fact, when Link first walks into a dungeon, he doesn't run to the boss room. He gets the necessary map, compass, and weapon before tackling the boss. This is the truest example of courage for Aristotle. Link isn't a coward and he isn't rash. He acts between the extremes and, as such, always triumphs over evil.

What about Zelda though? What would Aristotle say about this case? Isn't wisdom inherently good? Surely we wouldn't want to conclude that too much wisdom would be a bad thing. Actually, let us try a thought experiment. Imagine that Ganondorf has Zelda trapped and he is asking for the location of the Ocarina of Time to open the Sacred Realm and obtain the Triforce itself. Would it be better for Zelda to have the knowledge of the two possible outcomes and choose not to tell Ganondorf, or to be so wise and virtuous that the thought never even occurs to her to tell him where the Ocarina is?

Aristotle would argue that the truly virtuous person is one who will act because the virtuous act is purely internalized, not one who debates between right and wrong. He tells us that people are crea-

---

[2] Aristotle, *Nicomachean Ethics* (Penguin), p. 89.

tures of habit. People will *be* what they constantly *do*. In other words, if we are constantly virtuous to the point where committing immoral actions would never occur to us, then this is a case of a much better character than somebody who still has to debate between right and wrong. However, this advanced character development comes at the price of wisdom in regard to this particular virtue. If one were to be truly virtuous with her wisdom, then the evil act would never occur to her.[3]

Lastly, we have Ganondorf and his abuse of the Triforce of Power. The goddesses would have wanted this piece of the Triforce to be used in very much the same way as the other two pieces because they are equal. We should use it in moderation between two extremes. The deficient side of power would be complete inaction and on the excess side is an insatiable lust for power. Who does that sound like? Ganondorf uses the Triforce of Power in excess and he uses it often. A vice would be watching injustice take place without doing anything about it. If Midna were to allow the Twilight Realm to merge with Hyrule and turn both into a dark place, she would commit the vice of power, inaction. On the other hand, if we did nothing but lust after power above and beyond anything else, then we would have the excess.

Courage, wisdom, and power could all be used for good or bad actions. One may think at first that something is intrinsically good about courage and wisdom and if we listen to Glaucon, intrinsically bad about power. However, we must reject these claims after closer examination. Someone could be courageous in stealing, for instance. In much the same way, somebody could be wise in knowing how not to be caught when stealing; but, we wouldn't want to say that these two qualities are good here would we?

The Lesson and Legacy of Din, Nayru, and Farore

If we've learned anything by watching Link, Princess Zelda, and Ganondorf over the years, it's that our actions, however small, may

---

[3] Aristotle distinguishes between different types of wisdom, and each kind falls under the heading of intellectual virtues—not moral virtues. Only the moral virtues fit into the Doctrine of the Mean. What I mean by Zelda's wisdom is more of what Aristotle would regard as prudence, which is a moral virtue, and is the knowledge to choose the correct actions in particular practical circumstances.

have a profound impact on all those around us. We're all susceptible to bad choices at some point or another in our lives, and the first step in the right direction is accepting this fact. The important thing is to try to be powerful, wise, and courageous when the necessary occasion calls for it. If we do this, then the Triforce may not be a fictional entity at all, but instead, a bright guiding force in our sometimes dark world. The overarching lesson involved in the *Zelda* games is that courage, wisdom, and power are formidable forces in both Link's world and our own, and how we choose to act on these forces can make all the difference in the world.[4]

---

[4] I would like to thank Luke Cuddy, Scott Davison, and the University of Kentucky Writing Center for their helpful comments on earlier drafts of this chapter. This chapter is written in memory of my grandfather, Bob Calloway, a man of immense wisdom.

Level 9

Don't Patra-nize Me!

18

How Can There Be Evil in Hyrule?

DWAYNE COLLINS

There exists in philosophical circles something innocently referred to as the "problem of evil." This problem (conundrum, paradox, or whatever you want to call it) arises when somebody tries to reconcile the idea that God exists and that there is evil in the world— we'll get into the specifics soon enough. On Earth, solving the problem of evil turns out to be a very tricky process. Often it lies unsolved to anyone's ultimate satisfaction. For the people of Hyrule, however, a satisfactory answer is much more forthcoming. After all, things on Hyrule are governed by a different set of rules than things on Earth.

The Adventure Begins . . .

In order to think about solutions to the problem of evil, we should know what that problem is. Before we get to that, though, there are a few assumptions that are working their way through this chapter. The first is that evil exists, plain and simple, whether it's the younger sibling that saves over your game, Ganondorf, or the homicidal guy down the street. It's there and it's not nice and everyone can pretty much agree on that.

The second assumption is that when I refer to God, I'm referring to a monotheistic one of the Judeo-Christian variety—you know the type: all-powerful, all-good, and all-knowing all the time. While the problem of evil can (and does!) exist in many different religious traditions, attempting to write about *all* of them would be a book all on its own (and I'm sure it's out there somewhere if that's your thing). Any other style of God is outside our consideration here with the notable exception of three female varieties, as we'll see.

Introductions aside, let's get to the problem. Generally speaking, there are two types of problems when it comes to evil: the logical and the evidential. The logical problem deals with evil and God as two things that are inconsistent with one another and therefore it's impossible for the two to coexist. The evidential problem takes the approach that the existence of evil doesn't make it impossible for God to exist, just that it's pretty good support for her nonexistence.

The Logical Problem of Evil

The logical problem of evil was best put forward by J.L. Mackie. It works to disprove the existence of God by showing that the two ideas are logically inconsistent with one another.[1] When presented with a logical problem such as this, one normally has a number of related statements (in this case, two) that are not all obviously true or false in and of themselves. The goal is to somehow reconcile these statements to prove them either consistent or inconsistent with one another. If all of the statements can be proven true they are logically consistent and can be considered logically plausible, if they cannot all be true, they are inconsistent and impossible.

So how do we solve this type of problem? The best way is to find a third idea that is necessarily true to pair with one of the original duo that will either prove the other is false or that both are true. In our case, we're trying to prove conclusively that one of the two statements is logically possible while the other is not, thus showing our statements to be incompatible with each other. Before getting to the more complicated matter of the divine, let's go with an easier example. Say we have the following two statements:

1. **Metallic arrows are highly effective against Ganon.**

2. **Metallic arrows are useless against Ganon.**

Now we know that both of these statements can't possibly be true since they contradict one another. For these two statements it's

---

[1] For the original text of Mackie's argument, see "Evil and Omnipotence," *Mind* 64 (1955), pp. 200–212.

pretty much obvious to those who have played *Link to the Past* which is correct, but for the sake of example let's say we need to come up with the third *true* statement that will help prove one of them to be wrong (forgetting, for the moment, that we could use trial-and-error to find out the answer):

3. In *A Link to the Past*, silver arrows are needed to defeat Ganon.

From this we easily reason that since silver arrows are metallic arrows and are necessary to defeat Ganon, the second statement is logically inconsistent with the first and can't be true if the first is true. The third statement tells us which of the first two statements is the correct one.

When one attempts to do this with a more abstract problem such as the co-existence of God and evil the process becomes a little more complicated. What, then, are the two original statements for the logical problem of evil? As we've already stated, we're going to assume that evil exists—this is Mackie's first premise of the logical problem of evil. On Earth there are numerous examples around us of evil and suffering. In Hyrule, it's pretty much a given that evil exists in the form of Ganondorf and his ilk.

The second premise in the logical problem of evil is also one of the assumptions outlined earlier—that God exists and is all good, all powerful, and all knowing, all the time. This one is a little more difficult to prove—on Earth it's considered to be something taken on faith. When it comes to Hyrule, there's not much that we know for certain about the Goddesses who created Hyrule. We know that the three Goddesses were definitely powerful if they were able to create an entire world, but we do not know if they were *all*-powerful. This is a very important distinction that should be kept in mind when attempting to solve the logical version of this problem for the Hylian people.

So this leaves us with our two statements for the logical problem of evil:

On Earth:

> **(e1) God exists and is all-powerful, all-knowing, and all-good;**
>
> **(e2) Evil exists**

In Hyrule:

(h1) The Goddesses exist;

(h2) Ganondorf (evil) exists

Now we can start to see the problem. For Earth, consider the two points above: God is all-powerful, all-good, and all-knowing yet evil exists. There is a fundamental conflict between those two premises—if God is all-good, then why would that God allow evil to exist? Perhaps, you may suggest, God cannot simply will evil out of existence? Ah, but God is supposedly all-powerful and all-knowing—nothing would be able to be beyond God's power in this case.

This leads us to the third statement which the logical problem of evil makes use of to disprove the existence of God (Mackie does not attempt to disprove the existence of evil because there is empirical evidence that evil exists, while in the case of God the evidence is much less concrete which makes it an easy target):

(e3) An all-good being would try to eliminate evil as much as possible.

This statement is reasonably true to the effect that it implies the following: any all-good being could not sit by and let evil exist if they were capable of eliminating it. This would mean that evil and the existence of the type of God we've described cannot co-exist because that God could and would destroy all evil in the world, if that God were truly all-good and all-powerful.

In Hyrule, however, applying the same argument *does not matter*. On Hyrule, there is no evidence or claim that the Goddesses were either all-good, all-powerful, or all-knowing. In this case their existence alongside Ganondorf's is not inconsistent since it could be claimed that they have neither the power nor the inclination to eliminate him through divine action. For the sake of argument, though, if there was a claim that the Goddesses were just as good and powerful as the Earth's God we'd be left in the same position. After all, the same inconsistencies plague both sets of statements. To keep things interesting, we're going to continue to assume that the Goddesses of Hyrule are considered to be wholly good and powerful along the same lines as God is on Earth.

There are some responses to be made against this argument, however. One is to qualify our third statement and try to give God and the Goddesses of Hyrule the benefit of the doubt. Our revised third statement would be that a wholly good being would eliminate evil *unless there was a superior moral reason not to*. Or, in other words, unless a greater good would come of the evil being allowed to exist. On the surface, this qualified statement would attempt to reconcile our original two ideas so that the coexistence of God and evil would be logically consistent. The traditional argument to counter this modified statement, however, is that if God was as all-powerful as is claimed then God could accomplish that greater good without the need to employ evil whatsoever. This brings us back to the two ideas of evil and God, Ganondorf and the Goddesses, as being logically inconsistent with one another.

Alvin Plantinga, rather than attempt to prove that God and evil can coexist, gives us the response that mostly solves the logical problem of evil by showing that the existence of evil does not necessarily exclude the possibility of God.[2] In other words, Alvin shows that God and evil are not logically inconsistent, although not necessarily consistent either.

Essentially, the argument goes along these lines. Out of all the possible worlds that God could create, it stands to reason that God would create the best possible one rather than creating a shoddy one (and, being all-knowing, God would be capable of knowing which would be the best possible). Thus, in creating this world God created the best possible world and, likewise, in creating Hyrule, the Goddesses would have created the best possible world. Since evil exists in both worlds and God and the Goddesses are in both cases considered all-good, it seems there *must* be a reason why that evil exists, since they created the best of all possible worlds with evil in them.

The reason given is known as the free will defense: the best of all possible worlds includes the existence of human beings with the free will to choose between good and evil. Once given complete free will by God, evil must be allowed to exist as human beings must be allowed to choose it—otherwise complete free will could not exist.[3] For Hyrule we know that the Triforce was placed into

---

[2] For the original text of Plantinga's argument see *The Nature of Necessity* (Oxford University Press, 1971), pp. 164–193.

[3] Plantinga uses an argument based on something known as "transworld depravity" to support the free-will defense. I have not gotten into the concept here for simplicity's sake but the interested reader can go to Plantinga's original work.

the best possible world created by the Goddesses in addition to the creation of free will. Much like free will, if the Triforce was designed to grant any possible wish, no matter how good or bad, then evil must be allowed to exist, or else the power of the Triforce would be limited.

In the end, evil and God are no longer shown as inconsistent with one another because true free will cannot occur in a world where God or the Goddesses would limit the choices available to that world's occupants. Plantinga's free will defense has succeeded in showing that, from a logical perspective, evil and God are no longer inconsistent but could almost be said to be consistent. Logically, the problem has been addressed—but logic is only one part of the problem.

The Evidential Problem of Evil

The evidential problem of evil picks up where the logical ended. We know that God and evil, and the Goddesses and Ganondorf are not logically inconsistent with each other. However, doesn't the existence of evil and Ganondorf give us a pretty good reason to doubt the existence of God or the Goddesses, or at the very least to doubt that they are entities we would consider 'good'? The evidential problem of evil is aptly named because it puts forward that the existence of evil is evidence that we can reasonably doubt the existence of God and that we are perfectly rational in doing so (which is very different than logically denying the existence of God).

Remember that in the logical problem of evil, it was put forward that God or the Goddesses would only permit evil to occur in the case that it allows a greater good to exist. Remembering that, we presume God and the Goddesses of Hyrule to be all-powerful and all-knowing. The evidential approach to the problem takes the stance that if that were truly the case God would easily have been capable of achieving whatever those greater goods were without the need for evil, as nothing is beyond the power of God or the Goddesses.

In addition to the idea that nothing is beyond the power of God or the Goddesses of Hyrule is the idea that there is no good that can justify the existence of evil. Given the amount of evil and the horrendous atrocities that can occur in the world, the evidential approach takes the stance that there is no good that could be worth the suffering we have seen in the world (such as the death of millions, for example). For these reasons, people can feel rationally justified in thinking that God probably doesn't exist.

But wait! Surely someone has made a counter point? Don't worry—they have. Essentially, for the counter point to the "no good justifies evil" approach, theists (as opposed to atheists) point out that we can only be justified in saying that no greater good can come from evil *if* all the goods that we know as human beings are all the goods that there are. In short, theists would argue that humans and the people of Hyrule would need to be all-knowing to know that evil cannot lead to a greater good. You can assume who is all-knowing in this situation.

For the evidential argument, the limits of human knowledge prevent an adequate refusal of the arguments. The theists will put forth that since God and the Goddesses of Hyrule are completely good and all-knowing that a greater good *must* come from evil; we simply aren't smart enough to figure it out. Their opponents would likely respond that people, based on the knowledge that they have available, would still be rationally justified in their doubt of the divine. As you have no doubt noticed, solving the evidential problem is not so easy as solving the logical.

Theodicy on Death Mountain

In the evidential problem of evil above, the attempt to explain the actions of God or the Goddesses is an example of creating what's called a *theodicy*. The ultimate goal of a theodicy is to come up with some irrefutable goods that could justify the existence of evil. An important point to consider is that those goods don't *actually* need to occur; a theodicy only attempts to make the case that they *could* occur and provide reasonable support for why God (or the Goddesses) would allow the existence of evil.

So far, in the attempts to compare the problem of evil as it exists in this world and as it exists in Hyrule, there have been the beginnings of a theodicy for *The Legend of Zelda*. Let us embark upon the *Theodicy of Zelda* as someone such as Sahasrala might endorse, or that we could imagine being supported by the pages of the Book of Mudora.

We are tasked with devising a reason for why the Goddesses of Hyrule allowed evil to exist as part of the world that they created. As stated earlier, we're going to assume that the Goddesses are wholly good entities with limitless knowledge and power. Taking all the criteria put forward about the problem of evil above, we know that the existence of evil in Hyrule *must* be of such a nature that a greater good is the result of its existence—our job is to explain this.

We could take a page from John Hick and follow the lines of his soul-making theodicy.[4] Hick argues that evil is necessary for people to be able to grow spiritually. Clearly we can reason that if people on Earth need the ability to grow spiritually, then the same can apply to people in Hyrule. However, if we were to be true to Hick's approach then we would need to argue something along the following lines: surely the amount of evil in Hyrule is more than what people need to experience in order to grow spiritually? We're talking about things like flying eyeballs that spin around pieces of what looks like brains, here (even if that was in the Dark World and not Hyrule proper). Also, isn't the distribution of evil a little random? What did the people of Kakariko village ever do to deserve the amount of evil that ends up in their lives on a fairly regular basis (after all, as of writing this there have been a total of fifteen titles in the *Zelda* series)?

The soul-making theodicy would argue that in both cases above it's necessary for evil to be excessive and random. If people knew that evil only occurred as much as was necessary, and no more than that, people would be far less inclined to attempt to overcome evil. Similarly, if evil was not randomly distributed, people would be less inclined to try to overcome it as they would know that evil, really, only happened to people that deserved it. In the end, people would never make an attempt to grow as spiritual and moral beings.

To better understand the soul-making theodicy, we could create a game-making theodicy. If a game was too easy, we'd likely get bored playing it rather quickly and give up, heading to the store for the latest release of *Final Fantasy*. Not only that, we'd be less inclined to play it several times and improve our playing skills (or buy the next title in the series). Likewise, if a game was too predictable the same thing would probably occur—we'd stop playing

---

[4] For the text of Hick's soul-making theodicy see Stephen T. Davis, ed., *Encountering Evil: Live Options in Theodicy* (Westminster/John Knox, 1981), pp. 39–52.

and move on to the next title. With the game-making theodicy players need evil to exist in order to continue to grow as players, just as with the soul-making theodicy. Under our game-making theodicy, we could also argue that there is another greater good provided by evil in Hyrule: that a great game series was brought into being (although this would complicate our efforts here since we would need to include ourselves as some sort of intermediary between God, the Goddesses, and Link).

Returning to the soul-making approach, some have put forth the idea that even if excessive amounts of evil are necessary to convince people to undertake moral betterment, isn't it *excessively* excessive? In the grand scheme of soul-building, is there a difference between the death of four million people versus ten million? Isn't Ganon sufficiently evil on his own to convince the people of Hyrule to improve themselves spiritually rather than adding a myriad of level bosses to the world?

While I can't give an answer to this for the case on Earth, it's possible to come up with a suitable response for Hyrule. One could argue that the Goddesses actually do consider the amount of evil represented by Ganon and his ilk to be excessive, even for the purposes of soul-making. Why else would they have a *chosen* hero in the form of Link? As we saw with the free will defense, once free will was created, the Goddesses would not have been able to limit the choices available to people; thus Ganon was free to choose to become evil. Similarly, with the creation of the Triforce to respond to anyone's desire regardless of how moral or immoral that desire was, they could not limit what the Triforce would do without undoing what they had set out to create in the first place.

If the level of evil in Hyrule was so pronounced that the Goddesses felt it excessive for their purposes, the only way that the Goddesses would be able to deal with it would be under the terms they set out when creating Hyrule in the first place—unless, of course, they wanted to destroy free will. Thus, the Goddesses would have made it possible for a hero to be chosen who was capable of defeating evil and reclaiming the Triforce. Yet the Goddesses also would have ensured that their Hero had sufficient free will so as to be left to choose their own destiny.[5] Hence, Link

---

[5] Whether or not Link has free will is a different discussion, and is addressed in Chapter 14 of this volume.

acts as a solution to the problem of evil in Hyrule as an entity enabled by the Goddesses to counteract any excessive amount of evil in the world and return Hyrule to what could be considered a "normal" amount of evil.

Rescuing Princess Zelda

For Earth it's hard to solve the problem of evil outside of the logical setting presented in the beginning of this chapter. Hyrule has Link, who is clearly marked as a divinely-selected hero throughout the game and was chosen to stop Ganon, reclaim the Triforce, and return peace to Hyrule. Earth lacks such people as clearly and absolutely devoted to the eradication of evil as Link is—not to mention that defeating evil is not as easy as simply reclaiming the Triforce and making our deepest desire come true. The case that God has put people such as Link on Earth could be made, but without the clear indicators of divine selection that are connected to Link, the case would be relatively weak.

The Triforce acts as a representation of free will in Hyrule and shows how the existence of evil in the world can be reconciled with the existence of the divine. Link acts as a solution for the problem of evil in Hyrule in that he proves the existence of divine intervention when evil becomes excessive. Not only that, but we can have a damn good time helping him in the process.

19

The Legend of Feminism

JOYCE C. HAVSTAD and IRIS M. JAHNG

It would be easy to direct many of the usual feminist criticisms at the series of videogames that form the *Zelda* franchise. For instance, most of the series relegates the character of Zelda to a bleak and boring existence as basically a plot object. And, very little is done to develop the character of Zelda, despite the fact that she is frequently the chief motivating force for the adventures of the main character, Link. Then, of course, there are the circumstances of her existence as a motivator for Link's adventures. Predictably, she is a princess. Even more predictably, she usually needs to be rescued. And to compound all the insults and injuries, the series features what might be interpreted as one of the earliest forms of videogame prostitution: Link's ability to "replenish his life" by vanishing into cottages with frocked characters who seem to exist solely to lure him into their, uh, homes. (This was a feature of *The Adventure of Link*.)

But this picture paints only one side of Zelda's story. Throughout the series of games, Zelda exhibits real strength of character. In particular, she is often associated with the Triforce of Wisdom, and usually acts as a sort of moral compass to guide Link, motivating but also directing his adventures to the appropriate targets. If Link's perpetual enemy, Ganon(dorf), represents evil, then it is certainly fair to say that Zelda represents good. All this makes Zelda a very consistent character, and one with a lot of integrity. And besides, there are other female characters whose roles, although more peripheral than Zelda's, still go beyond those of simple villagers or idealized prostitutes. There are the occasional disguised versions of Zelda, as well as other, more distinct female characters. As is the case in many actual mythologies, the creators of Hyrule are usually depicted as three Goddesses: Din, Nayru, and Farore.[1] And the Twinrova sisters, who appear in several games in the series, demonstrate a sort of malicious intent as well as some arcane spell casting that is often associated with witches in traditional story forms. But all of these portrayals are very typological.

There is a long tradition, one that began with oral histories, proceeds through literature, and now continues on in videogames and other modern digital media, of placing women in certain stereotypical roles: as maidens, mothers, or crones. This phenomenon of portraying women as iconic characters in certain roles is worth noticing, as well as exploring a little further. What unites these depictions is that they are all figures with spectral but rather passive roles in their society. The chief example of this in the Zelda games is Zelda herself. There are also examples of the other typologies in characters from *The Legend of Zelda* series, the mothers (like the goddesses of Hyrule) and the crones (like the Twinrova sisters). Why are women so consistently portrayed according to these types, in this series of videogames but also in other story forms? Examining the work of one very famous and influential feminist philosopher, Simon de Beauvoir, will help provide an answer to such questions. Furthermore, since the mythology of *Zelda* is the product of male imaginations, examining the world they have created may say something about the way these men imagine women in the world that is not merely played in, but actually inhabited.

The Women of *Zelda*

Examining *Zelda* requires quite a bit of work, for three main reasons. The first is that there are so many games in the series. The second is that the character of Zelda is, like Link, not necessarily the same person in each game. But in every one there is at least

---

[1] This mythology is first revealed in *Ocarina of Time*. However, that version of the creation story does contradict another legend described in the earlier game *A Link to the Past*. According to the English manual of that game, Hyrule was created by three gods, not goddesses. But given the adoption of the goddess mythology and the continuing role of the goddesses, especially Nayru, throughout further installments in the Zelda franchise, it seems fair to characterize the feminine version as the dominant mythology.

mention of a female character named Zelda, and she often has a particular set of characteristics that creates continuity among all of the versions of *Zelda*. Without getting into the inextricably complicated issue of the *Zelda* timelines, the reappearance of the name and personality of Zelda in different characters is not usually a result of her being the same actual person.

This phenomenon is somewhat explained in the English manual of *The Adventure of Link*, according to which it is a tradition of Hyrule's monarchy for each princess in the royal family to be named Zelda.[2] So each princess of Hyrule is a Zelda, and their similarities in role, personality, and name are explained by this pattern of common inheritance. Third, there are the occasional appearances of disguised Zeldas. The two chief examples of this phenomenon are Sheik, in *Ocarina of Time*, and Tetra, who appears in both *The Wind Waker* and *Phantom Hourglass*, as well as briefly in *Four Swords Adventures*. In these cases each character is actually another version of Zelda.

Together, these complications mean that there are many different persons named Zelda as well as several not named Zelda, all of whom in some way represent the general character of Zelda. That these Zeldas have common characteristics is significant, capturing a sort of essence of Zelda-ness, which is representative of the consistent and coherent personality of the most important woman in *The Legend of Zelda* series. Discussing Zelda's role throughout the games of the franchise illuminates the remarkable consistencies in the different characterizations, and helps to develop a consistent understanding of this Zelda-ness.

The first Zelda, from the original *Legend of Zelda*, displays few personality traits, since she is not actually seen until the end of the game. But she does play an important role in that her actions set the stage for Link's first adventure, and these actions can tell us something about her character. The plot of the first game revolves around Link's mission to collect the eight pieces of the Triforce of Wisdom that Princess Zelda hid from Ganon, an invading Prince of Darkness who has taken over Hyrule. Once Link has united all

---

[2] Once, an early prince of Hyrule wanted to inherit the Triforce. He and a corrupt magician questioned his sister, the Princess Zelda, about its whereabouts, but when she refused to disclose anything, the magician cast her into an impenetrable sleep. In despair, the prince decreed that all the princesses of Hyrule be called Zelda.

eight pieces, he must fight Ganon, who possesses the Triforce of Power, in order to defeat him and rescue Zelda, whom Ganon has imprisoned.

So at the start of the *Zelda* franchise, Zelda herself already displays several of what will become her key characteristics: royalty, wisdom, resolve, and foresight. Throughout the series, Zelda is associated with royalty, usually as a princess, a daughter of the king of Hyrule. Making Zelda the possessor of the Triforce of Wisdom implies that Zelda herself is very wise. And this wisdom is linked to a kind of foresight: Zelda knows that she must hide the Triforce of Wisdom from Ganon, and is able to do so before he captures her. She also sends her nursemaid Impa to find a hero to unite the Triforce and defeat Ganon. This hero turns out, of course, to be Link. Finally, Zelda exhibits characteristic resolve in her refusal to betray the location of the pieces of the Triforce to Ganon, as well as in her stoic acceptance of her role in the story: to be captured and imprisoned by Ganon, waiting in hope that someone else can complete the task of defeating him.

The next Zelda, from the second game *The Adventure of Link*, certainly displays the characteristics of royalty and resolve. It turns out that, according to legend at least, this Zelda is actually the first Zelda, who was put into an eternal sleep by a magician long ago. She too was a princess, and it's she after whom all the following Princess Zeldas are named. And it was her resolve, in the form of a similar refusal to betray the location of the Triforce, which resulted in her being cast forever into sleep. Similarly to the first game, the player does not directly interact with the character of Zelda until she is awoken by a victorious Link at the end of the game.

The next game in the series, *A Link to the Past*, presents a slightly different Zelda. In this game, Zelda is the princess of Hyrule as well as one of seven maidens, each descended from the Seven Wise Men. These sages long ago sealed the evil thief Ganon in the Golden Realm after he had stumbled upon it and obtained the Triforce of Power. The Golden Realm became the Dark World, and at the time Link's third adventure begins, Ganon's alter ego (Agahrim) in Hyrule strives to capture the seven maidens and imprison them in the Dark World in order to release Ganon. In this game, Zelda's foresight is more literal, in the sense that Zelda actually has telepathic powers. This is how she alerts Link to her plight, so once again she provides the motivation for Link's heroics by calling for help while otherwise awaiting rescue. This behavior exhibits her usual resolve, foresight, and wisdom.

However, Zelda is not always an important character in a *Zelda* game. In some, such as *Majora's Mask* and *Link's Awakening*, she is only mentioned in the set-up. But there is plenty of Zelda in *Ocarina of Time*, which tells the tale of Link's adventure as Zelda dreams of Ganondorf's evil and Link's arrival at Hyrule Castle, along with an account of how the Triforce was first obtained from the Golden or Sacred Realm. And Zelda, as usual, gets the Triforce of Wisdom. She also displays her trademark royalty, wisdom, and foresight (both literal and figurative). But she also has a different role than usual, one that is more active.

In *Ocarina of Time*, Link is led to temples throughout Hyrule by a guide named Sheik. Sheik, it turns out, is Zelda in disguise or transformed somehow.[3] Sheik is a much more masculine character than the usual Zelda, so as Sheik Zelda plays a much more active role in assisting Link. She accompanies him instead of merely directing his quest and then waiting for him to accomplish it. And as soon as she reveals herself as Zelda, a woman, she is captured by Ganondorf and must again wait for Link to rescue her. This has critical implications for Zelda's femininity and the resolve that is usually associated with it. When, as Sheik, she steps into a more masculine role, Zelda loses the passivity that so characteristically marks her with resolve or resignation. But as soon as she reveals herself as Zelda, and a woman, she gets captured as usual. This emphasizes the close association between Zelda's role as a woman and her resolve, typically associated with a sort of passive resignation with a fate that Link must rescue her from.

In *Oracle of Seasons* and *Oracle of Ages* Zelda is her typical self: royal, wise, and resolved. She also displays prophetic abilities, which inspire her to find Link. And she is, as usual, captured and in need of rescue, although this time from sacrifice by the Twinrova sisters. The Twinrova sisters, who were in *Ocarina of Time* and *Majora's Mask*, reappear here in much more focal and malicious roles. Another recurring character from several previous games, Impa the attendant or nursemaid, presents an interesting contrast

---

[3] Whether Zelda is merely disguised as Sheik or has actually transformed into a man is the subject of some debate. It may be that in the Japanese version of the game she has actually transformed, whereas in the game released in the US, the implication is that she is simply disguised.

as a character to the Twinrova sisters. She obeys and assists Zelda in all of the games in which she appears in her capacity as Zelda's guardian, whereas the Twinrova sisters are at the very least mischievous and in these games, frankly evil.

Finally, we meet two other female characters, the oracle of seasons Din and the oracle of ages Nayru. These two women are characters whose type resembles Zelda's usual type. They are young, beautiful maidens who occupy traditional female parts as, respectively, a dancer and a singer. The manuals describe Nayru as "wise and serene" and Din as very beautiful. It turns out that they are oracles, possessed of important powers, yet they rely on Link to help them. They are kidnapped, as Zelda so often is, and must be rescued by Link.

In *The Minish Cap, Four Swords,* and *Four Swords Adventures,* both Zelda and Link are very young characters described as friends. This results in a somewhat simplified portrayal of both, although it is also consistent with the later, more developed characters. In *The Minish Cap,* Zelda is the daughter of the King of Hyrule and a childhood friend of Link, grandson of the Master Smith. He, with the help of the Picori, must rescue Zelda after she is turned to stone by Vaati. In *Four Swords* and *Four Swords Adventures,* Zelda is, as usual, a princess and in both games her foresight initiates the adventure when she senses trouble with the seal imprisoning the evil Wind Mage, Vaati. She brings Link with her to check on the evil magician and in both games ends up needing to be rescued by him. In *Four Swords Adventures,* she travels and fights with Link, but Link is required to defend her in order to prevent her four-part heart meter from being depleted completely, which would kill her and all the versions of Link. So once again, even when she accompanies Link, she is particularly vulnerable and relies on Link to protect her.

Like *Ocarina of Time, The Wind Waker* features a disguised version of Zelda. In this game, Hyrule has long been under water, and Link is a young boy who rescues a girl named Tetra, leads a band of pirates. When Link's sister is kidnapped, Tetra sails with Link to rescue her from the Forsaken Fortress. Ganon is behind the mischief, and he eventually recognizes that Tetra is yet another Princess Zelda, when he notices a piece of the Triforce of Wisdom worn as a pendant around her neck. Once the Triforce becomes whole again, Tetra is transformed into the traditional Zelda, but she still participates more actively in this adventure than Zelda usually does by wielding the crucial Light Arrows. Like Sheik, Tetra is somewhat different from the usual Zeldas, but unlike Sheik, she is initially unaware that she is in fact Princess Zelda. She's associated with the Triforce of Wisdom, and as the leader of the pirate band displays some of Zelda's usual status as a leader. Her royal blood eventually cements this characteristic. And like Sheik, her character is somewhat freed from Zelda's usual passivity.

Finally, *Twilight Princess* presents a very intriguing version of Zelda. Once again, she is royal and wise. In this game she is more than just a princess of Hyrule, she is the leader. She also possesses the Triforce of Wisdom, and has as much resolve as ever. She must wait, imprisoned, as Ganon turns her land into the Dark World and its people into spirits. She gives up her body to aid Midna, another instantiation of female royalty, and once again assists Link with the Light Arrows. Perhaps this continual association of Zelda and archery emphasizes her metaphorical distance from combat. By limiting her contribution in battle to firing arrows, which is typically done slightly removed from the actual fight, Zelda is allowed to help while still retaining something of her feminine isolation. Midna herself is a critical part of *Twilight Princess*, and like the oracles, her character is incredibly reminiscent of Zelda's. She too is a princess, royal and resolute.

All told, this exploration of the maidens throughout *The Legend of Zelda* series, Zelda incarnations and otherwise, display a remarkable consistency. They are beautiful, wise, and remote. They are figurative leaders of their people but tend to plan for and assist with the inevitable struggle against evil rather than engage directly in the heroics of adventuring and fighting it. These maidens are consistently portrayed, as well as markedly distinct from the other kinds of female roles occasionally depicted in the *Zelda* games, but which also frequently match up with other typologies. So the question arises as to why it might be that the women of *Zelda* are so typological. What sort of conception of women underlies the formation and mythologizing of these sorts of icons: of maidens, mothers, and crones? One female philosopher in particular, Simone de Beauvoir, said some incredibly insightful things about the common conception of woman that help explain the standardization of these characterizations.

The Mythology of Woman

In *The Second Sex*, Simone de Beauvoir acknowledges that there are very real differences between the sexes, but this is not to say that one is necessarily better or worse than the other.[4] Beauvoir argues that differences in situational factors, which began with biological differences, account for the historical subordination of women that persists to this day. Women can get pregnant and are physiologically equipped to care for their young. Infants need much attention and care because they cannot survive independently. A woman who's tending to a newborn's needs is less likely to take care of her own, so this became the responsibility of the man in her life. This explains the origin of women's dependence on men. This dynamic has been reinforced through women's demotion to second-class citizen status and their institutional disadvantages in capitalist economies. Women are left with few means for adequately taking care of themselves and are therefore stuck in an unbreakable cycle of dependence upon men, which is subsequently taken as evidence of allegedly inherent inferiority.

Because women have been historically subordinated to men, this places men in a position of advantage and privilege over women. One consequence of this is that history is most often described from a male point of view, even though this represents only around half of the entire species. So, the definitions that have been established and accepted come from the male perspective, even those pertaining only to the female portion of the population. This may explain the discrepancy between the definitions for 'woman' and 'female'. Beauvoir points out that it is not enough to be a female to be a woman. Women are not born, but made, and they are both female and *feminine*. The notion of femininity is slippery and mysterious while at the same time pervasive and sought after: some men desire it, some women want to embody it, and other women reject it. This concept of femininity is integral to understanding what Beauvoir calls "the myth of woman."

Beauvoir's account of the myth of woman has three components: woman as Mother, woman as Wife, and woman as Idea. In referring to the myth of woman, Beauvoir is speaking of the view of woman as feminine, as voiced by man to serve his own interests and purposes. Describing femininity as a myth emphasizes the difficulty in comprehending what femininity is, since myths are ideas that transcend the mind and cannot be grasped in their entirety. The lack of ostensive description of femininity is attributed to the

---

[4] Simone de Beauvoir, *The Second Sex* (Vintage, 1989).

difficulties associated with comprehension of myths. And just as the typological female characters in the *Zelda* games correlate to different stereotypical female roles, the three parts of the myth of woman also represent different features of female life, isolating them so that they stand opposed to each other. This demarcation, both within the myth of woman and in the typologies, is not necessary, as the different parts of each are not mutually exclusive. But although it's plausible for one character to occupy space outside these characterizations, this possibility is seldom explored.

Stories and the female characters depicted in them are one channel through which ideas regarding femininity proliferate. The maiden, and Zelda as the paradigmatic maiden, appears to be what Beauvoir was describing with the third component of the mythology of woman, woman as Idea. There exist striking similarities between woman as Idea and the maiden typology. The phrase 'woman as Idea' is derived from the Platonic world in which Forms exist in their perfect state. Eternal and immutable, they are then instantiated in less-than-ideal versions in our world. Within this Platonic framework, different essences are possessed by man and by woman, and this explains the differences between the two. Beauvoir's account of woman as Idea refers to an ideal of femininity that individual women try to emulate. Though she personally rejected this view, this is why the myth of woman can be interpreted as the myth of femininity. While no permanent feminine ideal exists, many women and men act as if it does, and the ideal of femininity, or the Platonic woman, can be roughly sketched from Beauvoir's thoughts and comments on the Idea of woman that she disperses throughout her exploration of myths.

Cultural variations regarding standards of beauty are one source of difficulty in describing the feminine ideal. But even so, Beauvoir is committed to the necessity of the ideal's beauty, which can be determined by cultural norms. As well as being beautiful, she's also expected to be youthful and in good health. These traits appear in all known accounts of femininity. When virginity is added to the list, the result is that men find this combination constituting the feminine ideal erotically attractive. Zelda is young and beautiful, and she also seems healthy, or at least healthy enough to hold or hide the Triforce of Wisdom, defy Ganon, and survive imprisonment. While Zelda's virginity or lack thereof is never addressed, it seems reasonable to think of her as a virgin. Zelda is essentially virtuous, acting as the bodily representation of good throughout the

Zelda games. In legends, these are generally attributes of the characters that are pure and virtuous, and virginity has long been associated with the notion of the pure and virtuous female.

The final feature Beauvoir discusses is that of the feminine body's possession of qualities of inertness and passivity. In contrast, masculinity is marked by fitness, strength, and action. Masculinity and femininity share an oppositional relation with one another in that what one has, the other lacks. Hence, the man is active, and the woman is passive. Yet again, this is observable in Zelda. There are few ways to make a character more passive than by having her locked up in a distant castle, waiting for her hero to rescue her.

Given the dominance of the male perspective in historical and fictional accounts, it is unsurprising that stories from all epochs reflect this relation between man and woman. As the active figure, man is the hero of the story, and woman is the special prize that awaits him after he emerges as the victor. Her significance cannot be denied, since it is through her that the hero is allowed to succeed, and she serves as the driving force of his actions. But within the ideal of femininity, woman accepts man's dominance and submits to him. Consequently, victory involves woman's recognition of man as her destiny. This ideal is also reflected in Zelda, since she has been established as wise and with great foresight, yet passively and patiently waiting for Link to defeat Ganon and rescue her, and fulfilling her destiny.

So woman is essential to the hero's journey insofar as she provides him with the vehicle to project his transcendence. At the same time, her passivity likens her to an object and she is little more than a mere thing. A result of this is that she ceases to be regarded as a living being, and instead resembles an ideal or glorification. This objectification can be seen in the *Zelda* games, both literally and metaphorically. Without the tasks of rescuing Zelda and piecing the Triforce of Wisdom back together, there would be no journey for Link to embark upon. Because of Zelda, Link can become a hero; and without Zelda, there would be no games at all. In *The Minish Cap* Zelda is literally an object, since her body has been turned to stone. In *The Adventure of Link*, Zelda spends the entire game in a deep slumber until awoken by Link. This objectification can be observed in other games as well in that Zelda is hidden away in a remote location, and her lack of physical presence lends itself to not thinking of her character as a real living and breathing person. Link is motivated to rescue her from the passive captivity forced upon her by Ganon, which denies her the ability to act for herself. This essential yet distant role of Zelda allows her to be glorified and objectified, personifying woman as Idea.

According to Beauvoir, the problem with this objectification or glorification of the feminine ideal is that it does not necessarily reflect reality. But it still impacts the reality of women in terms of how they see themselves. And since there is not necessarily a strong link between the Idea and reality, there are many instances when a particular individual is deemed as not living up to the feminine ideal. Unfortunately, instead of questioning the ideal itself, the woman tends to be criticized for her lack of compliance. The result of this is that a woman must either accept her passivity and be regarded as a 'true woman,' or she can assert herself, act independently, and cease to be attractive to man. Fortunately, this seems to be a dated attitude, and there are reasons to be optimistic regarding changes in the ideals of femininity and woman in both stories and reality.

Zelda and Reality

There are several reasons why the way women are portrayed in *Zelda*, and in other story forms, has an impact of the role of actual women in the real world. For one, how the creators of these videogames portray women reveals something about how they view women. It also reveals something about what portrayals of women they think will be most persuasive and compelling to those who might buy and play their games. But most importantly, it reveals something about what feels realistic to the designers and to the players. This is because these videogames strive to mimic reality. The mimicry is not the sort that tries to make something look precisely realistic, but rather to make it feel real.

This phenomenon has been explained by a creator of several games in the *Zelda* series, Eiji Aonuma. He describes the philosophy of the inventor of *Zelda*, Shigeru Miyamoto, in the following passage: "*Zelda* is a game that values reality over realism. In the art world, realism is a movement which faithfully replicates the real world to whatever extent possible. Reality, though, is not mimicking the real world. The big difference is that even using more exaggerated expression can be an effective means of making things feel more real."⁵ So games in *The Legend of Zelda* series do not try to exactly replicate the real world. What they try and do is make a player feel like when they play a *Zelda* game, they are in a real world.

Although the characters in the *Zelda* games are not meant to look and act precisely like real people, they are meant to feel like real people. That presents an interesting question: What is it about these stereotypical accounts of women, particularly the maiden Princess Zelda, which feel so real? Is it just that they are familiar figures from literature and other portrayals? Or is it that they represent how women are actually perceived, and what their roles are really thought to be? Perhaps it is something of both. And although the women of *Zelda* are often stereotypically and ideally feminine, they are not always so.

The *Zelda* games often portray Zelda as the epitome of the ideal of femininity, but they also contain occasional digressions from it, particularly in the two characters that are revealed as disguised versions of Zelda herself. Sheik and Tetra are far less passive than the other Zelda instantiations, and participate in the action more than the other women in the *Zelda* games. It may be significant that Zelda is represented as different characters with different names when she behaves in a manner that is more masculine than feminine, but it is still promising that she is allowed the opportunity to take action. If this is due to the importance creators of the *Zelda* games place on making the experience feel real, then perhaps this indicates a shift in the dominant attitudes toward and perceptions of femininity. Beauvoir saw a link between the way man defines and portrays woman, and the objective reality both inhabit. Her analysis offers an interesting explanation for why there is an ideal of femininity and what it constitutes. This idea is often exhibited by the way women are portrayed in the *Zelda* games as well as many other sources, and changes in the portrayals may result from changes in the conceptions of woman and femininity.

Perhaps changes in the reality of Zelda reflect real changes, and if the definition of woman really changes, then perhaps changes in women's status, perceptions, and relationships will follow.

---

⁵ From an edited transcript of a speech made on March 24th by Eiji Aonuma at the 2004 Game Developers Conference in San Jose.

It's a Secret to Everybody

20
Getting to Know the World Next Door

ROGER NGIM

One of the casualties in this new age of video games is the instruction manual, those glossy booklets from the 8-bit era that came stuffed into the plastic cases and cardboard boxes with the game cartridges. In addition to their charmingly nonsensical back-stories badly translated from Japanese and the goofy illustrations that looked nothing like the pixilated characters on screen, the manuals offered players indispensible information, specifically how to use the controller to jump, duck, punch, kick, aim, fire, pick up, and drop. Without instructions, I could push buttons forever and never once perform a Hurricane Kick (down, down-back, back, then kick) in *Street Fighter*. But with the manual in my lap, propped open to the list of special moves, I could kick some serious butt. This required splitting my attention between the television screen and the booklet, alternating between being immersed in the world of the game and being jarringly aware of the real-world act of playing a game.

Today's video games still come with instruction manuals but more out of tradition than necessity, as most games do an adequate job of explaining themselves through built-in tutorials or intuitive game play. Technological advances have given designers the ability to create game worlds so close to our own that we can navigate and function in these spaces without cracking open the manual. Nowhere is the proximity of these worlds more evident than in the release of Nintendo's Wii, with its wireless controller that operates on naturalistic movements: To throw a bowling ball, step forward and swing your arm. The analog world we have put so much effort into digitizing is returning to the analog.

In a course I taught on games and culture at the University of California at San Diego, we spent quite a bit of time puzzling over the complex relationships between a player, his avatar, the game world he occupies, and the encompassing real world. Such discussions were inevitable given that these vast and vividly rendered new worlds are infiltrating, if not threatening to swallow up, our old one. Complicating matters is the fact that these alternate realities are now full of other people. Whereas a player's actions once were guided solely by the game's rules (its algorithms), today gamers are free to contaminate pristine virtual landscapes with the messiness and imprecision of their real-world social behaviors. Imagine Pac-Man scooting down the aisles making racist remarks and hitting on Ms. Pac-Man. As game worlds bestow on its players the freedom to be themselves, games veer sharply away from the utopic.

Actually, games have never been the safe havens we imagine them to be. They are gated communities, tidy and organized but ruled by fascistic neighborhood associations whose bylaws are printed inside the lid of the Monopoly box or written into the code of a computer program. Even when 2-D refugees Mario and Link graduated to three dimensions in the 1990s, the gates swung open only to reveal a new fence in the foggy distance—freedom abruptly ended at an impassable river or unscalable wall. Yet it is these very limitations that both define the game and attract players who, like crated dogs, enjoy the safety and comfort of entirely knowable surroundings. This is my world. I have my water dish, my blanket, and my chew toy—everything I need until the master comes home.

One of the lessons of my course is that all games, from backgammon to *Grand Theft Auto* and beyond, offer this contrived confinement. What would we gain if our virtual spaces required the same amount of time and effort to get to know as the real world, if the world of *Zelda* stretched endlessly in all directions or if a chessboard had an infinite number of squares? Our virtual spaces, whether we are talking about *World of Warcraft* or *The Settlers of Catan*, scale-down reality so we can admire it, study it, and shake it up like a snowglobe.

While games exist within delimited spaces—a crucial part of the definition of a game—their relationship to the real world has been broadening and growing increasingly ambiguous. Games and game structures (such as competition, point systems, and rewards) have found their way into our everyday activities, from grocery shopping, to online banking, to primetime television. Designers of "serious games" have been using game technologies to recruit, train, and manage workers in the corporate and military worlds. Phones, iPods, laptops, and the Internet are all portals to game worlds. Virtually every free moment we have presents an opportunity to play.

This situation demands a re-evaluation of what games are and how they work from the broadest possible perspective. This raises the question of where in academia the study of games belongs. Sociology? Cultural studies? Philosophy? Literature? Art? Performance studies? Computer science? The difficulty in comfortably situating game studies in any one discipline suggests that it could be its own department, with video games, board games, role-playing games, and collectible card games among the concentrations. Fanciful thinking, maybe, but we need only look to the existence of film departments to realize that we will never gain a full understanding of games if we continue to take a fragmented approach to studying them. Would we learn what movies are if one group studied the chemical processing of film, another looked at narrative in film, while still another examined the social behavior of moviegoers, and the groups never talked to each other?

Getting skeptics to take the study of games seriously can be a challenge, and I am not only speaking of colleagues and administrators. My course on games, which I called "Playing by the Rules: Games In and Out of the Ordinary World," fulfilled a general education requirement for first-year students. Not surprisingly, it proved a very popular class. What I didn't expect was that many students would resist the idea that the games they play could be objects of scholarly study. They could accept film, popular literature, high-tech gadgets, and television as topics for college courses, but games somehow were out of bounds in higher education. I found that they easily understood that *Mouse Trap*, *Magic: The Gathering*, and *World of Warcraft* are cultural artifacts, but had a much harder time looking beyond the fun and perceived frivolity to identify the games' embedded meanings. They belonged to a generation of gamers, yet they had difficulty recognizing the influence of games in their everyday world.

These students, like most of us, partitioned off games from the "serious" portions of their lives, yet could slip easily and unassisted into the game world. To them, the idea of an instruction manual for the self-explanatory realities of today's games probably makes as little sense as an instruction manual for the real world. Perhaps there no longer is such a thing as preparing to play a game—learning the game is the same as playing the game. That may be just one of the ways that the game world is renegotiating its boundaries, insinuating itself into the real world. This fascinating process of merging, transposing, and metamorphosing is creating virgin territory for game scholars to explore. Like geologists, we're watching with amazement as a new island rises from the sea.

Heroes of Hyrule

ROBERT ARP is a Research Associate through the National Center for Biomedical Ontology and works with the Ontology Research Group in Buffalo. Despite his love for the Zelda games, he still thinks Mario could kick Link's ass in a virtual back alley brawl.

PAUL BROWN teaches English and Media at a high school in North-East England. He recently completed an MA in Computer Game Studies and is continuing his work on player motivation through a PhD at the University of Manchester. He has been playing computer games since 1983, when his father brought home a Texas Instruments TI-99/4A. "Not only a great computer," he thought, "but also one whose name really trips off the tongue! It can't fail to conquer the market." His current ambition is to discover the rift in the space/time/reality/fantasy continuum that must inevitably lead to Hyrule. Once there, he intends to buy a nice cottage in Kokiriko village and gain reflected glory by telling everyone he is Link's best friend.

MICHAEL BRUCE has multiple degrees in philosophy and works as a residential treatment counselor for at-risk boys. He publishes in comparative philosophy and spends his free time juggling his own Triforce: life—philosophy—poverty!

DWAYNE COLLINS is a part-time master's student in the Faculty of Information Studies at the University of Toronto and received his BA (Hon.) from Peter Robinson College, Trent University, in Peterborough, Ontario. He balances school with full-time work as the Steward of Sadleir House, a cultural and educational facility also located in Peterborough. His primary area of research focuses on identity and video games and the intersection between the player and the game experience. Dwayne also has an irrational fear of falling through puddles into a parallel dimension and turning into a pink bunny and thusly keeps a mystical mirror in his pocket at all times.

DARIO S. COMPAGNO is a PhD student in Semiotics at the University of Siena (Italy). In the daytime he seeks answers to matters of the greatest importance, like what came first, the text or its author; at night he plays games like Wesnoth (for academic purposes only). The episode of *Zelda* he loves most is *Link's Awakening*. One night, he dreamt of an isle . . . and he has been dwelling in there ever since. Be quiet!

LUKE CUDDY teaches philosophy at Southwestern College and lives in San Diego. A longtime gamer, he has recently taken up writing which is so much easier than defeating Ganon! He has written for *Quentin Tarantino and Philosophy*, *Battlestar Galactica and Philosophy*, and *Dialogue*. When he isn't nerding out with a book or a video game he travels the mountain ranges, randomly bombing rocky cliff sides, babbling on about the entrance to Level 9.

PATRICK DUGAN is an independent game designer who lives and works in Buenos Aires, Argentina. His primary focus is on how games can work as propaganda and as tools for enlightenment. He shorted Ganon on the stock market during the upset of January 2008, and now has a tremendous bank account denominated in souls.

SEAN C. DUNCAN is a doctoral student in the Department of Curriculum and Instruction and member of the Games + Learning + Society Initiative at the University of Wisconsin, Madison. His research deals with digital media literacy, online gaming communities, and learning. He often dreams of sailing on a Great Sea in a talkative red boat.

KRISTINA DRZAIC is a videogame designer, a creator of movies and a master of secrets. She once spoke to a gossip stone and used the knowledge therein to earn a BA in Film from the University of Notre Dame and an MS from MIT's Comparative Media Studies Department. Due to fate she is now in Australia filming Re-dead and hoping to unite her Triforce.

TONI FELLELA is a doctoral candidate in English at the University of Connecticut. Her focus is on popular culture and twentieth century American novels. Living in Providence, Rhode Island, Toni just may be a testament to the adage "Rhode Island born, Rhode Island bred, Rhode Island dead." She's proud to announce that she has won several local dance contests, taking aback innocent onlookers with Darunia's dance.

JONATHAN FROME is an Assistant Professor of Film and Digital Media at the University of Texas at Dallas. His research focuses on how media generate emotions. Instead of driving to work, he often glides through the air with a Deku leaf.

JAMES PAUL GEE is the Mary Lou Fulton Presidential Professor of Literacy Studies at Arizona State University. He has published widely in the areas of sociolinguistics, discourse analysis, literacy studies, and, most recently, video games and learning. Unlike Link, he is right handed (most of the time) and talks, but he does check his left hand each morning for a Triforce mark.

JOYCE C. HAVSTAD is a PhD student in the Philosophy Department as well as the Science Studies Program at the University of California, San Diego. She usually remains in the Light Realm of philosophy of biology, bioethics, environmental ethics, and technology studies, but occasionally enjoys straying into the Dark Realm for some aesthetics, philosophy of film and television, cultural studies, and feminism.

CHARLES JOSHUA HORN is a graduate student in the doctoral program at the University of Kentucky. Joshua earned his BA in philosophy and government at Morehead State University. His interests range from ethical theory to political philosophy. Josh often wanders the local horse tracks in Kentucky, humming Epona's song. It hasn't worked yet, but he's hopeful.

IRIS M. JAHNG has an MA in philosophy from San Diego State University. Her research interests are ethics, political philosophy, and philosophy of science. She sometimes goes to small ponds with a whistle, hoping to find a stairway beneath the water.

ANNA B. JANNSEN can't help but think of the great mysteries of life and death when she plays video games, macabre as it may sound. Partially because she dies in them so often, but partially because that's the kind of gal she is. Drawing from her diverse interests and her post-graduate education in media, philosophy and publishing, Anna offers a map to these ancient, feuding philosophies, because it's dangerous to go alone.

CARL MATTHEW JOHNSON, a beach bum based primarily out of Waikiki, has cleverly deceived friends and acquaintances into believing his self-stylings as a philosophy MA candidate and raconteur at the University of Hawaii at Manoa. From 2004 to 2006, he posed as an English teacher in distant Toyama prefecture, an area best known for heavy snows, cheap electricity, and a crippling bone disease called itai-itai byÿ (literally, "ouch-ouch disease"). Asked about his dreams, Carl remarked, "Oceans as far as the eye can see."

DENNIS MILLARKER is a Graduate Teaching Assistant in the Department of Philosophy at Florida State University. He eagerly looks forward to attempting to write off his Wii as a business expense following the publication of this volume.

ROGER NGIM divides his time between the game world and the real world. A former writer, editor and arts critic, he earned an MFA from the San Francisco Art Institute and has exhibited work nationally and internationally. He's an avid board gamer and has lectured on games and culture at the University of California at San Diego.

PETER RAUCH is an itinerant writer trying to be less itinerant. When he was a child, he stumbled upon a magical sword, and woke up to find he'd earned an SM in Comparative Media Studies from MIT. He's particularly interested in how videogames embody ideologies in virtual worlds, and maintains a blog at undisciplinedtheory.blogspot.com.

RACHEL ROBISON is a graduate student in the philosophy department at UMass Amherst. She does research in metaphysics and epistemology, and has published papers in epistemology. When she goes clubbing in Hyrule her favorite dance is the ocarina (hey ocarina!).

LEE SHERLOCK is an MA student in Digital Rhetoric and Professional Writing at Michigan State University, with a Graduate Certificate in Serious Game Design. When he's not working on game studies projects or grading papers, he can be found looking for a Book of Mudora that will help him decode critical theory. He was so geeked for the release of *Twilight Princess* that he bought it months before he had the Nintendo Wii to play it on.

JOAQUÍN SIABRA-FRAILE is involved in various research projects at *Consejo Superior de Investigaciones Científicas*, Spain. He is the author of *Mimesis from Greek Tragedy to Videogames*, *Virtuality Genres* and even funnier papers about digital arts. He claims to be one of the happy few who have seen *Pac-man*'s last screen—but we don't believe him. Wakka wakka.

DOUGLAS WILSON is a game designer, writer, code monkey, and general misfit. He is currently working on a doctoral thesis in Game Studies and Digital Media. Doug spent the previous year designing games at IT University of Copenhagen on a Fulbright grant. Before escaping to

Denmark, he spent six years at Stanford University, where he graduated with a BA in Interdisciplinary Humanities and an MS in Computer Science. Doug is interested in political gameplay, and also the connection between memory, nostalgia, and spatiality in videogame worlds. He longs to return westward to California some day, but for now, eastmost peninsula is the secret.

Index